W9-CCL-110

Middleton Public Library
7425 Hubbard Ave
Middleton, WI 53562

RECKONING

RECKONING

The Epic
Battle Against
Sexual Abuse
and Harassment

LINDA HIRSHMAN

Houghton Mifflin Harcourt
Boston   New York
2019

Copyright © 2019 by Linda Hirshman

All rights reserved

For information about permission to reproduce selections
from this book, write to trade.permissions@hmhco.com or to
Permissions, Houghton Mifflin Harcourt Publishing Company,
3 Park Avenue, 19th Floor, New York, New York 10016.

hmhco.com

Library of Congress Cataloging-in-Publication Data
Names: Hirshman, Linda R., author.
Title: Reckoning : the epic battle against sexual abuse and harassment /
Linda Hirshman.
Description: Boston : Houghton Mifflin Harcourt, 2019. |
Includes bibliographical references and index.
Identifiers: LCCN 2018051341 (print) | LCCN 2018060829 (ebook) |
ISBN 9781328566751 (ebook) | ISBN 9781328566447 (hardcover)
Subjects: LCSH: Sexual harassment of women — United States —
History — 20th century. | Sexual harassment of women — United
States — History — 21st century. | Sex crimes — United States —
History — 20th century. | Sex crimes — United States — History —
21st century. | Sexual harassment of women — Law and legislation — United
States. | Trials (Sex crimes) — United States.
Classification: LCC HQ1237.5.U6 (ebook) |
LCC HQ1237.5.U6 H57 2019 (print) |
DDC 305.420973 — DC23

LC record available at https://lccn.loc.gov/2018051341

Book design by Chrissy Kurpeski
Typeset in Minion Pro

Printed in the United States of America
DOC 10 9 8 7 6 5 4 3 2 1

This book is dedicated to a virtuous circle of women who are at once activists, writers, lawyers, and teachers: Catharine A. MacKinnon, who taught my dear departed Jane E. Larson, and Jane, who taught Michele L. Dauber, who came full circle back to MacKinnon, as do we all.

Contents

Preface

Tanya Harrell was just doing her job at a New Orleans McDonald's in 2017 when a guy she worked with shoved her into the bathroom, locked the door, and tried to rape her. The only thing the twenty-year-old could do was cry and cry — "until he heard the manager calling where were we," she says, "and he finally let me go."[1]

Harrell wasn't going to get any help, she knew, because the last time she'd complained that a coworker had harassed her, her shift manager at McDonald's suggested the touching was consensual. Sure enough, when she told the new manager about the attempted rape, the boss treated her story like it was nothing. Harrell, who had left high school so she could work to pay for the medicine her grandmother needed, could not leave her low-wage job.

One year later, on May 22, 2018, Time's Up Legal Defense Fund, an initiative founded by prominent women in the entertainment industry, announced that it would be paying for Tanya Harrell — and a dozen other low-wage workers around the country — to sue McDonald's and its franchisees for harassment. After all, sexual harassment had been recognized as a violation of the 1964 Civil Rights Act for more than thirty years.

What a difference a year makes.

In some respects the movement against sexual harassment, now known as #MeToo, has felt like a tsunami, a sudden eruption no one could have anticipated. In this version, the waters rose on October 2017, seven months before Tanya Harrell's moment of empowerment, when the *New York Times* announced that Hollywood producer Harvey Weinstein had paid off sexual harassment accusers for decades.[2] Mere days after the *Times* story appeared, a tweet by the actress Alyssa Milano gave new life to a slogan that had originated in 2006 with an established black activist, Tarana Burke.[3] If all the women who have been sexually harassed or assaulted wrote "Me Too" as a reply, Milano thought, people might get a sense of the magnitude of the problem. Overnight, her tweet received fifty-five thousand responses, and #MeToo was the number one trending hashtag on Twitter; in the days and weeks that followed, the hashtag caught fire globally. By the year anniversary, the tag had appeared in almost fourteen million public tweets.[4] Within that year, more than two hundred powerful men in entertainment, media, politics, education, tech, and more had been brought down by the charges.[5]

But no social movement arises in an instant. All successful social movements rest on a long history of organization and activism. The racial civil rights movement did not start with Rosa Parks being too tired to stand up on a Montgomery, Alabama, bus. At the time Parks refused to give up her seat, in December 1955, she was already the secretary of the Montgomery chapter of the NAACP, which had been organizing against segregation for years. The same week in June 1969 that the first person threw the first rock at the police outside the Greenwich Village gay bar Stonewall, gay members of the Students for a Democratic Society were already planning an organizing meeting to bring what they had learned from their activism in the civil rights and antiwar movements to New York's simmering gay community.[6] Similarly, the women's movement against sexual abuse and harassment did not spring up overnight in response to a scoop or a tweet.

In *Reckoning*, I tell the story of women's fifty-year battle against sexual abuse and harassment. From the schoolyard to the steelyard, using the law and an evolving culture, against setbacks and self-inflicted wounds, against enemies and frenemies, by 2017 the movement finally gathered enough power to stand up and shout "Me Too." Or, more importantly, "Time's Up."

The battle against sexual harassment and abuse was unique. Women are a group that makes up the majority of the US population, a majority neither geographically marginalized, as were African Americans, into slave states and ghettos, nor concentrated, as were gays and lesbians, in specific neighborhoods, but integrated by ineluctable law of biology into every human institution. They are lovers of men, wives of husbands, and, whatever their sexual orientation, mothers, sisters, daughters, employees, and employers of men. Because women are a majority, they are intersected by every social dividing line.

The position of women—numerous, integrated—arguably makes their organization more fearsome and threatening to a predominantly male-dominated culture than any other movement. At the same time, it makes the pressure to ally with that male culture strong. From the beginning, as the first plaintiffs in the 1970s, to the election of 2018, women of color were the feminist vanguard. But a women's alliance is hard to pull off when white women in particular tend to vote with their more conservative husbands,[7] women sometimes instinctively defend their sons against claims of bad behavior,[8] and wives and lovers may value meeting traditional expectations of their roles vis-à-vis men above their political power.

This movement, both epic and sui generis, struggled for most of its history to apply the three basic rules for achieving successful social change in the American context: (1) claim the moral high ground, (2) hold regular meetings, and (3) prioritize your own interests. Women's situation made it challenging for them to make use of these three reliable techniques. Certainly they had a moral argument—the morality of equality. But they were invoking morality in a realm—sex—where moral talk is often regarded as puritanical and self-defeating. As for holding meetings, women were long reluctant to speak out, much less organize, against damaging and infringing, often covert, behavior by men, in a culture in which women themselves were likely to be blamed, demeaned, shamed, shunned, and fired for exposing that behavior. And finally, because women cross all other possible social divisions, their interests were always stretched in all directions—race, class, religion, region, sexual orientation. The feminist movement is not so much an intersection as a six-way roundabout.

Nevertheless, not only have women made, from this crooked timber, a movement, they have made a movement that confronts the critical place where oppressed and oppressors meet: in the relationship of sex. Resisting abuse and harassment in sex is uniquely problematic for a movement because sex is a source not only of danger and injury but of pleasure and fulfillment. Unlike the unambiguous oppression of whipping, shackling, criminal prohibition, forced psychotherapies, unequal pay, school segregation, and the like, sexual relations can be a good thing, and as a good thing, sex motivates people to defend access to it. It would be surprising to hear of African Americans who supported separate and unequal schools during the civil rights movement. But the women's movement includes more than one episode where women calling themselves feminists have gone to bat for powerful men over access to sex. Claiming the moral high ground when the subject is sex turns out to be harder than any other similar quest. And yet, it happened.

A decade after Betty Friedan's 1963 manifesto, *The Feminine Mystique,* gave a critical push to modern feminism (called the second wave, since the first wave of suffrage had ebbed), feminist law professor, activist, and scholar Catharine A. MacKinnon in the 1970s created the legal theory that sexual harassment of working women violated the Civil Rights Act of 1964.[9]

The mostly white intellectuals who started the movement found invaluable allies on the new front in black women, who had long been working in the public realm. Almost all the early plaintiffs challenging sexual harassment at work were African American. In 1986 Mechelle Vinson took her case all the way to the Supreme Court. And won.

Resistance to sexual abuse and harassment caught men by surprise. Although most African American women had never had the luxury of being stay-at-home moms, the rebirth of feminism in the 1960s had brought an unprecedented number of white women into the workplace. These new female workers were met with a massive campaign of harassment, which black women had always experienced. When newly empowered women started resisting the harassment as a violation of their civil rights, men weren't prepared: wasn't sex a "private" and "personal" matter, immune from the judgment of the market or the law? Women's activism triggered male (and female) resistance of massive scope. Male presidents of the United States, titans of industry, prize-winning artists, media moguls, and coworkers at McDonald's — all engaged in harassment and abuse and fiercely defended their rights when met with even the slightest pushback from the women in their worlds.

Indeed, as activists struggled to bring women's equality to reality, they encountered resistance on every front. Married women, especially married white women, did not want to trade the security of their marital bargain with high-earning husbands for some future equality in a job they might never want or need. Conservative activist Phyllis Schlafly mobilized a triumvirate of conservative Protestant evangelicals, Catholics, and Orthodox Jews to fight the ratification of the cherished feminist goal of an Equal Rights Amendment, and she stopped it in its tracks. Civil Rights–era liberals began to retire or were forced off the Supreme Court, and their seats taken by Republican-appointed conservative justices.

The conservative victories under the antifeminist Schlafly showed that when the movement turned to retail politics rather than elite judiciaries to achieve its goals, the going got very rough.

Yet ultimately the battle would have to be fought on that difficult terrain.

Uniquely, in the fight for sexual equality, the emerging conservative movement was not feminism's primary foe. In moving toward legal — and cultural — equality in the highly contested realm of human sexuality, feminists often encountered the most effective resistance from those claiming to be their allies: other liberals. In 1998 Equal Rights Amendment booster and feminist ally Bill Clinton, as president of the United States, started a sexual relationship with a twenty-two-year-old White House intern. Feminist icon Gloria Steinem took to the opinion pages that year to proclaim the feminist movement's support for Clinton.

The media, including the entertainment industry, liberal on other subjects, were at the same time enjoying an uninterrupted heyday as a 24/7 casting couch. This meant that the same men who expected ambitious and idolizing young women to service them sexually were the ones in charge of messaging regarding social change, or the lack thereof. *Newsweek* told women trying to pursue careers that they were as likely to be killed by a terrorist as find a husband after forty. *Time* proclaimed the Death of Feminism.[10] When colleges tried to tighten the rules about sexual assault on campus, liberals teaching criminal law avidly resisted the effort to shift the balance between victim and accused. Sometimes it seemed no one on either side of the political divide cared about women's sexual treatment. Beginning in the 1970s, conservatives mobilized against the new movement for women's rights in general, and liberals didn't recognize rights for women in sex. By 1991, feminism, on the rise since 1963, faced a terrible backlash from all sides.

A new generation of women, scarred by relentless media-driven attacks, began to look for a way out of the pitched battles they had seen their mothers wage and, too often, lose. Here again, the ambiguous relationship between heterosexual women and men was Kryptonite to the movement. This time, it wasn't conservative wives worried about the changes in alimony rules, should their breadwinners wander. The sexual revolution had taken much of the steam out of that position. This time, the backlash was internalized in the form of feminists' daughters not wanting to be cast as man-hating prudes by sexy liberal male writers and lawyers, potential mates after all. These "third" wave feminists would be the so-called "lipstick" feminists. High heels and you choose your choice. At the extreme, they would write books about how college girls should stop complaining about being raped in their dorms.[11] The pressures for conformity to a male heterosexual norm seemed nearly irresistible.

But by the oughts the waters were rising: a reenergized, millennial feminist movement was developing. Young women read MacKinnon in their women's studies classes. They groused online. The aging cohort of female senators elected in the 1992 Year of the Woman — a result of Clarence Thomas being confirmed to a seat on the Supreme Court in spite of Anita Hill's testimony on his workplace sexual harassment — was followed by a trickle of ever younger women, like New York senator Kirsten Gillibrand and California's Kamala Harris. Emerging from websites like *Angry Black Bitch* and *Jezebel*, a stream of female and feminist journalists penetrated the legacy media. One of them, a brave newbie, posted a spreadsheet online called "Shitty Media Men," which collected allegations of sexual misconduct; it immediately went viral.[12] And there was a watershed reckoning in the summer of 2016, when conservative Fox News host Gretchen Carlson sued the bullying, powerful head of the network, Roger Ailes, for sexual harassment and brought him down.

Undeterred by the reality of sexually misbehaving GOP House Speakers in the 1990s (Gingrich, adultery; Livingston, adultery; Hastert, pedophilia),[13] conservatives had long resisted women's claims to sexual equality on the grounds that virtue rested in the patriarchal home. When Republicans nominated and elected Donald Trump to the presidency of the United States, however, a critical shift began. The release of the *Access Hollywood* tape in October 2016 revealed the thrice-married Trump admitting to a long practice of abusing women: "Grab 'em by the pussy."[14] Rallying behind him, conservatives extended their bedrock support of oppressing women in the traditional religious marital order to embrace openly anything that kept women down, including acts of harassment and abuse in the public world for which they had previously vilified Democrats. A realignment was now fully on the table.

Like it or not, Bill Clinton's spouse did not present a clean choice where sexual misconduct was concerned. Many committed liberals resisted her candidacy by rallying around the white male insurgent Bernie Sanders. According to some exit polls, 52 percent of all white women voted for the abusive Trump. Even when fully empowered, the emerging movement against sexual abuse was never going to reach takeoff until the feminists recruited a critical minority of their white sisters and finally took on their liberal allies to create a united front, on the left.

The next development came from investigative journalists. In October 2017 two reporters published the story of big-time Democratic donor and Hillary Clinton supporter Harvey Weinstein abusing women in private while supporting women's rights in public. Women and their allies in journalism immediately began calling liberal men to account: along with Weinstein were MSNBC's Mark Halperin, coauthor of *Game Change*; Hamilton Fish, publisher of the liberal magazine the *New Republic*; NBC's *Today* host and political moderator Matt Lauer. These were the men who had covered the campaigns of Hillary Clinton, the first female candidate for president. How, women began to ask, can we trust what we learned from them?

The nascent alliance between feminists and liberals faced a crucial test when first one, and then a total of eight, women came forward with accusations of sexual harassment against Minnesota senator Al Franken, one of the few genuinely effective Democrats in the Senate. Democratic senators, led by the now meaningful number of women in their midst, organized Franken's resignation. Women were starting to show their teeth. Not all the old-school liberal allies liked the new order, but dismissing Franken gave the Democrats the sexual moral high ground against the party on the other side.

Now sorted out, the two camps met on the field of battle in July 2018, when the libertine conservative president Donald Trump nominated Judge Brett Kavanaugh to fill the crucial swing seat on the Supreme Court of the United States. Six weeks later, a psychology professor, Christine Blasey Ford, came forward to accuse Kavanaugh of committing sexual assault when they were both teens. A credible second accusation from Kavanaugh's years at Yale surfaced. The Republican-dominated Senate called both parties to a televised version of she said/he said. After the courteous, deferential, and soft-spoken Ford presented her testimony, Judge Kavanaugh performed a full-on aria of male rage. How dare they question him about his sexual behavior? President Trump delivered a mocking attack on Dr. Ford at a rally. Kavanaugh was confirmed with the support of every single Republican in the Senate. (Lisa Murkowski, one of five female Republican senators, voted "present" rather than yes or no.) As fit the pattern since the publication of *The Feminine Mystique* in 1963 and far earlier, crucial support for Kavanaugh's nomination came, this time in the form of a swing vote, from a married conservative white female (Republican senator Susan Collins) allying with the white men in her party.

All eyes turned to the midterm elections, a story that appears in the final chapter of *Reckoning*. Because of its constitutional structure, the United States Senate does not represent the majority of US citizens; each state, whatever its population, gets two senators. But the elections to the House of Representatives are the closest thing Americans have to a referendum on where American voters stand. Second-wave feminism, the brainchild of a Smith-educated Jewish intellectual from Westchester County, had never won a referendum. Has more than a half century of epic battle finally changed the playing field?

No less an authority than the avatar of second-wave feminism, Justice Ruth Bader Ginsburg, prophesied that this time the movement would prevail. "When I see women appearing every place in numbers, I'm less worried about a backlash than I might have been twenty years ago."[15] After fifty years of building and one year of volcanic protest, the supporters of the movement against sexual abuse and harassment were too numerous to push back. On November 26, 2018, the *New York Times* summed up the results of the great referendum of 2018: "'Kavanaugh's Revenge' Fell Short Against the Democrats in the Midterms." "Nationally," the *Times* reported, "exit polls showed that more voters opposed Judge Kavanaugh's nomination than supported it, and that women were far more likely than men to be against his confirmation."[16] Fifty-nine percent of women voters in 2018 backed the Democrats.[17] The best polls even showed white women breaking the Democrats' way.[18]

The movement we call #MeToo has, to a greater or lesser extent, aligned at last with the three basic rules for successful social change. First, women are claiming the moral high ground: massive numbers of women are now unabashedly sharing stories of abuse and naming harassing conduct as wrong. Second, the internet and the invention of hashtags have gone a long way in helping women organize and achieve solidarity. And many #MeToo institutions, like the Time's Up organization in Hollywood, are holding organizational meetings in real life. Finally, women — so far especially Democratic women — are no longer maintaining alliances with male politicians whose public commitment to feminism is shown to conflict with their private behavior. But with women a majority scattered among men everywhere, the movement must continue to claim some minimum of support from white women to win elections. In the aftermath of the triumphal midterms, the question is, was 2018 a rogue event or will the fifty-year battle against sexual abuse and harassment lead inevitably to a reckoning, now?

Tanya Harrell has gone back to school. She is strengthened, she says, by knowing about all the other women who went through what she did. And that so many of them have her back.

RECKONING

1

Naming It, Claiming It
1969–80

Chappaquiddick

She died slowly, gasping for the last pocket of air in the automobile sinking into the waters off Chappaquiddick Island. Mary Jo Kopechne, veteran of Robert Kennedy's 1968 presidential campaign, twenty-eight years old and devoted to the Kennedy family, had left her purse behind and simply climbed into the car with Senator Ted Kennedy. Now she was drowning in tidal Poucha Pond, and he was nowhere to be seen.

Ten hours after the accident, dry and fully dressed, Kennedy walked into the police station in nearby Edgartown, Massachusetts. Kennedy, the only surviving brother in the legendary political clan, after Bobby Kennedy was killed in 1968 and President Jack Kennedy assassinated in 1963, was widely rumored as a contender for his party's nomination in the 1972 presidential election. He told the police chief that he had been driving the car when it went off the bridge. Somehow, Kennedy's story goes, after he drove into the pond, he got out of the sinking car and surfaced above the rushing water.

He was next seen at the nearby rental cottage where his group of five married men and six women had been partying. After emerging from the pond, he said, he walked back to the party to get his pals there to help. Along the way, he passed several houses, indicating the presence of people who could have helped. But he did not stop.

It was July 1969. Years later, the screenwriters of a documentary about the incident have Kennedy say, "I'm never going to be President."[1] In his end-of-life memoir, he acknowledged that reality.[2]

But ten years later, Ted Kennedy thought he had finally been cleansed of Chappaquiddick. After he'd pled guilty to leaving the scene, an inquest had concluded with no new charges. Twice re-elected by his adoring Massachusetts constituents, surrounded by supportive Senate colleagues, Kennedy decided that the 1980 election was now or never: the Democrat in the White House, Jimmy Carter, was at an unprecedented low approval rating. Polls showed Kennedy could take him in a primary and likely beat Republican front-runner Ronald Reagan in the general. Carter's self-righteous demeanor in the face of inflation and a stagnating economy had rendered him virtually unelectable against the Republicans. Once again, a Kennedy would save the party. Chappaquiddick? The tenth anniversary passed in July of 1979 with nary a murmur.

So television anchorman Roger Mudd seemingly caught the candidate by surprise with his question in the first interview of the 1979 campaign.[3] The judge who presided over the hearing said he believed you lied about Chappaquiddick, Mudd began. Will anyone ever fully believe your explanation? Kennedy responded with a long string of utterly incoherent verbiage: "The problem is, from that night, I, I found the conduct, the behavior almost beyond belief myself. I mean that's why it's been, but I think that's the way it was," he rambled. "But that happens to be the way it was," he finally concluded. And then, interview over, he waited. After all, the media had blithely ignored Kennedy's brother, the martyred President John F. Kennedy, sneaking himself and his various bedmates in and out of the White House, and his other brother, the martyred presidential candidate Robert F. Kennedy, stirring the sex pots with Marilyn Monroe before she died in scandalous circumstances, in that case a notorious suicide.

Not this time.[4] From the moment Ted Kennedy set foot in the state of Iowa in 1979, it was clear that Iowa women — schoolteachers, plant workers — had not forgotten Chappaquiddick. Had voters been so inclined, reporters, from Tom Wicker of the *New York Times* to Jimmy Breslin of the *New York Daily News*, were ready to remind them of Kennedy's inadequate repentance. How about "Bless me, Father, for I have sinned"? Breslin suggested, for starters. Unlike Jimmy Carter, liberal Ted Kennedy was publicly feminist. He supported Medicaid payments for abortions and the feminists' dream, a constitutional Equal Rights Amendment, still awaiting ratification by a few more states. But in the private world, there were no women in any serious positions on his staff.[5] His reputation as a "known womanizer" gave the head of the National Women's Political Caucus, Iris Mitgang, "reason for pause,"[6] and female political reporter Suzannah Lessard "the creeps."[7] Kennedy lost Iowa 59 percent to 31 percent; a few months later support for his candidacy collapsed in the Catholic precincts of Chicago. With all the pausing and the remembering, the Chappaquiddick survivor and philandering women's-policy ally Ted Kennedy lost the primary to the upright Jimmy Carter. You might call it a #MeToo moment.

Coda

But it was a #MeToo moment with a big cost to women's other interests. In November the sexually virtuous Carter lost in a landslide to conservative Republican Ronald Reagan. In its nominating convention, the Republican Party had officially repudiated abortion rights and the Equal Rights Amendment. In Reagan's reelection four years later, pollsters noticed the first signs of an electoral gender gap. Women were migrating to the Democrats and men to the Republicans. Had he been the nominee in 1984, Teddy might have beaten Reagan. Women seemed stuck between womanizing

Democrats and antiwoman Republicans, and in political precincts, voters took note.

Naming It: Sexual Harassment

After Chappaquiddick, the Washington media began to take off their well-worn kid gloves where sexually misbehaving politicians were concerned. Kennedy's marriage, which had apparently been unraveling for years, suddenly became fair game. *Washingtonian Magazine* cited the senator's "roving eye" in a 1972 article entitled "Washington's Biggest Male Chauvinist Pigs."[8] The *Washington Post's* Watergate scoop that brought down President Nixon transformed Bob Woodward and Carl Bernstein's journalism colleagues into lean and hungry men. The journalists were hardly rabid advocates of women's equality. In the era of "family values," they were mostly in it for the scandal. But the groundwork was laid. In the mid-1970s, revelations about Democratic Congressional Campaign Committee chair Wayne Hays keeping his mistress on the payroll, and the even more powerful Ways and Means chairman Wilbur Mills cavorting with a well-known DC stripper, led to ejection of the two male leaders from the corridors of power. The errant politicos might be forgiven for some bewilderment over their harsh treatment after the halcyon years of untouchable Kennedy womanizers, but things were about to get a lot worse.

In 1972 Cornell University physics professor Boyce McDaniel was spending his days visiting his newly promoted administrative assistant Carmita Wood. The amorous physicist was about to set off a sustained chain reaction:[9] Wood was not glad to see him. He had been pestering her for years while she was a lowly clerical worker. But she had always been able to stay out of range. Now, in her new, better job as his assistant, he had her in his sights. He'd pin her against a desk or the wall, scrutinize her, and simulate masturbation in front of her with his hands in his pants pockets. Complaints to her supervisor brought her no relief. Finally, when her tormentor used the office Christmas party to pull her into a dance and put his hands under her sweater, she quit. When she applied for unemployment compensation in 1974, the New York State Unemployment Commission turned her down. Not wanting to work with Boyce McDaniel was her personal decision, the commission said.

Far above Cayuga's waters at the same moment, a young feminist, Lin Farley, was preparing to teach a field-study course at Cornell called Women and Work. Since there was no published material on the topic, she did what any self-respecting feminist would do in the mid-1970s: she convened a consciousness-raising group. In these sessions women shared their stories of something she had never seen described or reported. Every one of the women in her group had quit or been fired at least once because some man had targeted her for sex. As Farley put it, the women quit their jobs because "they had been made too uncomfortable by men." Farley and two colleagues, Susan Meyer and Karen Sauvigné, mobilized the Women's Section of the Human Affairs Program at Cornell to study, among other things, women and work. Hearing about the new academic program, Carmita Wood went to the Women's Section for help. Farley and her associates got her a lawyer.

The feminist activists distributed a questionnaire on sexual harassment to women attending a speak-out on the subject, and to women members of the Civil Service Employees Association in Binghamton, New York. They soon had their answer: over 70 percent of the 155 respondents reported some kind of experience with sexual mistreatment.[10] The group brainstormed about what to call it. What term applied to behavior ranging from repeated ogling to unwanted touching to forced sexual relations? They gave it a name:[11]"sexual harassment." In social change, naming is almost always a watershed. The abolitionists called slavery "man stealing," with all its implications of biblical sinfulness. More recently, concepts like "white privilege" and "unconscious bias" have enabled people to see how certain normalized behaviors and thought patterns fit into harmful race and gender categories.

In 1975 Lin Farley went to New York City to testify about the problem before the city's Commission on Human Rights.[12] She attracted the attention of Enid Nemy, a longtime reporter at the *New York Times,* whose story appeared under the headline "Women Begin to Speak Out Against Sexual Harassment at Work." Being about women, the article appeared in the women's pages, at this point Family/Living at the Gray Lady. Still, Nemy's reporting was impeccable. The article, describing the issue as "shrouded in silence because its occurrence is seen as both humiliating and trivial" and including harrowing stories of relentless harassment and desperate employees, is one of those iconic *Times* pieces that, looking back, sounded the alarm early.[13] Although the women didn't identify their abusers by name, as in today's movement, many of the women in the Cornell group identified themselves and described their abuse. A resourceful journalist could easily have outed the offenders. Nemy was hardly some radical feminist. She neither had nor wanted any part in the pending sex discrimination lawsuit the female *Times* reporters had filed against the paper the year before, and claims "she was never discriminated against at the *Times.*"[14] On the subject of the story's placement in the Family/Living section, Nemy said, "We were able to give more attention to feminism than if the stories had had to compete in the general stream of the newspaper."[15] The Cornell area women's movement was now a matter of record.

Now that they had named it, Lin Farley began writing a book, *Sexual Shakedown,* cataloging the offenses in detail. And they were legion: staring, requests for intimacy and dates, demands for intercourse, rape. Because women are in such a vulnerable place in the workforce, they experience disproportionately high turnover, low wages, and job segregation, which makes them more economically insecure than men. Since they are statistically poorer, they are subject to domestic inequality. Within three years of the DC Police Department opening its doors to women, Farley reports, women were being coerced into having sexual intercourse in exchange for better assignments. Want ads for office work explicitly sought an "attractive girl," waitresses were asked to "lie down and do it," female secretaries became rapidly less employable as they aged.[16] In the last chapter of Farley's book, "The Casting Couch," Herb Belkin, then president of ABC Records, opined that sexual practice in the entertainment industry was a great example of the free market. "The availability of people with mutual interests means no one gets forced . . . a chick comes in with a guitar and may go down on the producer before, during or after."[17] Or as #MeToo's Alyssa Milano put it thirty years later, "You can look at a lot of aspects of the underrepresented people in that industry being sex workers."[18]

Farley's solutions sound horribly familiar forty years later: integrate the workforce, enforce the rape laws, make harassment a violation of the Civil Rights Act, which already prohibited sex discrimination in employment. By the time of the book's publication, a handful of women, almost all of them black, had started making legal claims for harassment under the Civil Rights Act. Women will be 40 percent of the workforce soon, Farley inveighed. All they need to do is organize. She made a prediction: "Women's stamina, energy, and courage in the battles on rape and abortion have made recent history; because of sexual harassment they will change the face of modern work as well. The sexual harassment men have used to keep women subordinate will ultimately prove the issue by which working women will unite."[19]

Farley titled her solutions chapter "The Future." She was right. She just probably didn't think it would take four decades to happen.

9 to 5

The early activists can be forgiven for their hopefulness. It did seem, at the beginning, that the stars had converged. In 1973 Karen Nussbaum was working as a clerk typist at Harvard. Once she got a look at the conditions women were working under in the office, she decided to start a union for clerical workers — she called it 9to5.

She told a friend of hers from the 1960s antiwar movement, the actress Jane Fonda, about it.[20] Nussbaum and her union members' reports of the harassment they'd endured as secretaries inspired Fonda to conceive of a movie. She hired a young comedy writer, Patricia Resnick, to write it.[21] Fonda insisted that the movie be a comedy, because, ever the showbiz professional, she thought the 9to5 message would reach more people if it was presented in a likable way. No problem, Resnick thought, hadn't Hollywood icon Charlie Chaplin made a hilarious comedy in which several oppressed characters kill their boss? A few years earlier, when Resnick had been working as an assistant to the director Robert Altman, she'd met Lily Tomlin, who had asked her to write a few sketches. From day one, Fonda and Resnick had Tomlin in mind to play the film's brainy undervalued office supervisor Violet Newstead, and the country music star and novice actress Dolly Parton for the role of the gorgeous Doralee Rhodes.

When the movie came out in 1980, the picture of bad boss Franklin Hart Jr. (Dabney Coleman) in a restraint harness, chained to a garage door opener in his own bedroom, at the mercy of his female employees, was actually the watered-down revenge scenario. Originally, Resnick planned to have each of the three women workers try her hand at killing their obnoxious boss: the new girl (Jane Fonda) would shoot him, his personal secretary (Dolly Parton) would tie him up and hang him from a barbecue spit, and second in command (Lily Tomlin) would put poison in the coffee he always made her fetch. But after the studio gave the project to Colin Higgins to direct, he summarily booted Resnick ("one captain on the set and that's the director")[22] and sweetened up the feminist content.

Beneath its digestible exterior, the *9 to 5* workplace is a pitch-perfect representation of what women face, now, thirty-eight years later: discrimination as workers and harassment as sexual objects. The heroines are especially powerless and dependent women: Tomlin's Violet, a widowed mother of four, ambitious to rise; Parton's Doralee, the boss's sexually irresistible secretary; and Fonda, uncharacteristically mousy as Judy, the new hire, whose husband recently left her for his own secretary. Hart, the boss, takes Violet's ideas as his own and gives the promotion she deserves to a guy the clients will like better. He chases the resistant Doralee around the desk, dropping pencils to make her bend over, and terrorizes the newbie, Judy, about her incompetence in dealing with a sorcerer's apprentice of a Xerox machine. In a touch anticipating the 2017 headlines about *New York Times* reporter Glenn Thrush, accused of bragging about sexual conquests he never made,[23] Hart boasts that the virtuous Doralee is sleeping with him, and she finds herself not only besieged by the boss but isolated from her female coworkers because of his lies.

Fonda and the team traveled to 9to5 chapters around the country in the 1970s to gather material for the film. Resnick visited a major insurance firm in LA and got to know the women who worked there. The idea about a boss slandering his unwilling secretary came directly from a senior secretary there. In the film, while the three female protagonists have the boss restrained in his bedroom, they issue a series of memos, detailing an astonishingly modern series of reforms: part-time work, job sharing, personal decorations on work spaces, and an on-site day care center. Karen Nussbaum says it was simply the 9to5 Bill of Rights on celluloid.[24]

It's a Hollywood comedy, after all, so the women don't get together at the end to form a union, as early dialogue hints they might. Instead, replacement male screenwriter and director Higgins manipulates the story with a series of silly coincidences, and the movie ends with the deus ex machina of a formerly unseen male board chair coming to the women's rescue. But, for 1980, *9 to 5* had it all: an irresistible tune sung by the irresistible Dolly Parton; Fonda, a feminist movie star with her own production company; and a young, energetic screenwriter who scoured the pink ghetto for the facts.

After the #MeToo movement had brought down one of Hollywood's biggest producers and scores of smaller fry, the three stars of *9 to 5* reunited onstage at the 2017 Emmy Awards. Clustered at the podium, they reminded the award show's audience that they had in the 1980 movie refused to knuckle under to a "sexist, egotistical, lying, hypocritical bigot."[25] The *9 to 5* bit at the Emmys was supposed to be funny. But the ironic reference to Hollywood actresses who had continued to live the *9 to 5* story for thirty-seven years after the making of that film was really a reminder of just how hard the work of change can be.

2

Making the Legal Case for Women
1975–76

Catharine MacKinnon's Mind Speaks to Her

Still, starting in the 1970s, the ground was shifting. One day in 1975, a Yale law and graduate student, Catharine MacKinnon, came to Ithaca, New York, home of Cornell University, to perform. She was trying to pay the rent by singing and playing the guitar in gigs around the Northeast.[1]

In a familiar story for brainy women, Catharine had spent much time in the school library, in her case near Lake Minnetonka, Minnesota. On Saturdays, she would go with her father to the Minneapolis public library, which was much bigger. Her earliest memory of her "mind speaking to her" was when, at age six or seven, she saw the famous *Life* magazine picture of murdered Jews in a trench. *What were they thinking?* she remembers asking herself. Her mother, whom MacKinnon recalls as the smartest, most gifted person in the world, was, she also remembers, living up to none of her enormous gifts and "clinically depressed for half her life"; MacKinnon would never forget her mother's fate. In 1969 MacKinnon's father, a lawyer, was named to the federal bench by President Nixon and the family moved to Washington, DC. At the time, MacKinnon was finishing up her undergraduate career at Smith College.

To the casual observer in 1975, MacKinnon, with blue eyes, a chiseled profile, and a waist-length mane of chestnut hair often worn in a Gibson girl updo, looked like a prime candidate to step into the shoes of Gloria Steinem, the glamorous New York activist the '70s media had anointed as feminist in chief. But instead of living the good life in Manhattan media land like Steinem, MacKinnon was spending the 1970s in gritty New Haven, Connecticut, working toward her doctorate and then going to law school. Wherever she went, including Ithaca, New York, MacKinnon signed up to receive newsletters from local feminist organizations. She was gathering evidence of women's consciousness for her dissertation, which would ultimately become the book *Toward a Feminist Theory of the State*. From 1969 to 1974 MacKinnon could not get into Yale Law. An admissions committee chair, she later learned, kept pulling her file from the application pile because he did not like her feminist pronouncements.[2] It would certainly not be the last time a powerful man tried to shut Catharine MacKinnon out.

Meanwhile, MacKinnon sat in on a Yale Law course on sex discrimination. The course, like all of the early courses and law books on the subject, focused on strategies for achieving women's equality under the law. Consistent with this strategy, by 1975 Justice Ruth Bader Ginsburg, then a litigator and head of the ACLU Women's Rights Project (and author of one of the Yale Law textbooks), had embarked on her life's work of getting the Supreme Court to treat women equally to men in similar circumstances. And she was having a lot of success. Starting in 1971 Ginsburg had methodically set about coaxing the rather conservative Burger court to look hard at legal distinctions based on sex. The early cases focused on rules that gave preference to one sex over the other ("women get this, men get that"), leading to courts making "arbitrary legislative choice(s)," in violation of the equal protection clause of the Fourteenth Amendment. The first case Ginsburg brought took down an Idaho law that presumed men were more suited than women to be administrators of estates.[3] Obviously, nothing about women made them automatically different from men in the context of managing an estate. Ginsburg's success with the conservative justices reflects the relatively unthreatening image of feminism in those years. At the time, even Republican national committeewomen were pushing for the Equal Rights Amendment, which had sailed through Congress in 1972 and was pending ratification in the states.

But sitting in Yale's class on sex discrimination, MacKinnon wasn't satisfied with that way of thinking. Women are unequal to men in society, MacKinnon thought, because society stigmatizes their physical characteristics and constructs and then denigrates their social characteristics. Pregnancy is one obvious example of MacKinnon's insight. In the 1974 term the Supreme Court had held that denying health benefits for pregnancy-related disabilities did not violate the Fourteenth Amendment—in other words, treating people who could get pregnant worse than people who couldn't was A-OK;[4] after all, the policy distinction didn't apply to all women, only to those who were pregnant—all of whom were women! Instantly, MacKinnon saw that treating women equally to men doesn't do all the work to make them equal. Benefits were not being denied based on sex; pregnancy was being excluded from a list of compensable disabilities, thus ranking one group above the other on a scale of human worth and resource allocation. The point is not sameness or difference, but domination and subordination.

MacKinnon's approach also reveals much about race and class, because the standard sameness approach works best for the most privileged women. After all, they're the ones who most resemble men.

Ginsburg's analysis fell short. MacKinnon saw the gap.

Feminism and Harassment

In March 1975 Cornell's Women's Section sent a letter out to subscribers to its new feminist newsletter. "Dear Sisters," the letter began, does anyone have any ideas about how Carmita Wood might get some legal traction with her unemployment case? Hearing Wood's story, MacKinnon, who had been asking herself since she was six about oppressors' thinking, felt her head "explode." Wood's boss, a man, had wanted sexual access to Wood, a woman. The unemployment bureau was treating Wood as one particular woman who happened to attract her boss's attention. MacKinnon saw that Wood's boss did this to her because sexuality was what being a woman means socially. And that fate applies not just to Carmita Wood but to all women. And what he did hurt her, drove her out of her job. It subordinated and disparaged her.

Finally, in 1975 MacKinnon was also admitted to the JD program at Yale Law. Around 1976 MacKinnon, under the guidance of Yale professor Thomas Emerson, began writing about her ideas on workplace harassment. Under her standard — does it subordinate women as women? — sexual harassment was discrimination, she proposed. Which meant it was prohibited by the Civil Rights Act.[5]

The Civil Rights Act had been lying there, an unexploded grenade in the world of sexual harassment, for more than ten years. Since 1964, under the act's Title VII, it had been "an unlawful employment practice for an employer . . . to discriminate against any individual with respect to his compensation, terms, conditions, or privileges of employment, because of such individual's race, color, religion, sex, or national origin."

In 1974 payroll clerk Paulette Barnes, a black woman, knowing nothing of the theoretical debate swirling around workplace harassment, brought what is considered the first sexual harassment case in the United States against the federal Environmental Protection Agency in DC. Her supervisor demanded she have sex with him, and when she refused he fired her. The Lawyers' Committee for Civil Rights Under Law, originally a racial civil rights group, had begun to pursue sex discrimination cases against the federal government after Congress applied the Civil Rights Act to the government in 1972, by virtue of the Equal Employment Opportunity Act. Without the benefit of MacKinnon's deep explanatory work,

Lawyers' Committee lawyer Rodd Boggs and Judy Lichtman of the Women's Defense Fund had figured out that the harassment experienced by Barnes was some kind of sex discrimination.[6]

Unsurprisingly, the trial court ruled that Barnes's discharge did not violate the law's ban on sex discrimination. The judge found that Barnes's supervisor had fired her because she refused to have sex with him, not because she was female. The supervisor's treatment didn't extend to all women, he held. Barnes lost her suit and began the process of appeal.

If the first *Barnes* decision sounds like nonsense now, the trial court was simply following the logic of other Supreme Court decisions of the early 1970s, when the court could not seem to find its way to treating pregnancy as related to gender. If there was no perfect fit between sex and harm, the court said, no foul. In a perverse way, the pregnancy decision fit Ruth Bader Ginsburg's litigation strategy that only similar things had to be treated similarly. But perfect equality was not going to help pregnant women. Or Paulette Barnes.

MacKinnon's analysis showed the way out. Pregnancy is one of the few "disabilities" only women have. The decision makers, MacKinnon concluded, saw pregnancy as hierarchically beneath the disabilities that were not linked to being female. In thinking outside the box of Ginsburg's conventional sex-discrimination theory, MacKinnon saw more deeply into what was really going on. The wrongdoing is not in treating women differently from men, even though that generally results in keeping women down and making them unequal. The wrongdoing is in treating men *as the standard for comparison in the first place*. The civil rights violation is in treating women as *lesser beings*. Just go directly to it. Does the behavior, in MacKinnon's formulation, "help to perpetuate women's subordinate place in the workplace and in society as a whole?"

Sex at Work Is Not Private

MacKinnon's understanding of harassment as subordination is so contemporary it could have been written with a hashtag. It set off a slow but steady transformation of analysis of all sexual relations. As time would tell, MacKinnon's insights on why sexual harassment was a violation of women's rights at work were so powerful they illuminated how sexual behavior kept women down everywhere.

But she had set herself a hard task. For starters, to be "discrimination," the existing law held that sexual behavior has to be seen as collective, not individual or "personal." The New York unemployment department described Wood's resistance to her boss's advances as a matter of personal choice; after all, maybe another woman would have liked being the subject of the physics professor's attentions. (The referee in her unemployment hearing concluded that Wood had an apparently quirky "antipathy" for the superior who mimicked masturbation when he saw her.[7] Fancy that.)

MacKinnon undertook to interrogate the decision-maker's conception of sexual behavior in the workplace as personal or individual. First, she read the court's calling harassment "personal" as meaning "private." If private, its argument went, a man seeking sex at work was simply manifesting a homey behavior that happened to occur at work. The Civil Rights Act and the unemployment compensation laws all apply only to relationships at work, and the harassment had nothing to do with the man's role as employer. Without yielding on whether sex at home is actually also political, MacKinnon first moves the disputed behavior out of the employer's suggested realm of the "personal." The incidents occur at work, she notes, in a relationship hierarchically defined by work, and the price is paid at work. Workers are behaving in the context of the workplace, not importing private behaviors from home. When an employer manifests personal behavior in the workplace, employees are sucked in.

Second, sexual harassment is motivated by a vision of women, collectively, as inferior to their male counterparts and subject to their whims. It is therefore discriminatory. Women are also, across the board, overwhelmingly working in jobs subordinate to men's jobs. They earn less, have lower status and less security, and often work in personal service positions—nurses, secretaries—in an environment that mirrors the power structure of the patriarchal family. Harassing behavior against women demeans them, pains them, makes the effort to do their jobs harder or impossible, and thus collectively disempowers them. Because they hold inferior positions, they are vulnerable, and thus the inequality of women is a cause of the harassment. Because the harassment makes them quit and transfer and suffer, inequality is also the effect of the harassment.

Of course, the global insight that sex can be examined for its discriminatory impact will inevitably leak into the home and all aspects of the sexual relationship. There was no equality law like the Civil Rights Acts of 1964 and 1972 that applied in the home or outside of work, so work was the first frontier. But it would not be the last.

Sex and Race

In rejecting the method of evaluating female plaintiffs according to how men in similar circumstances are treated, as the Ginsburg strategy prescribed, MacKinnon set in motion a way of thinking that meshed, later, with the effort to recognize that some people suffer from multiple sources of inequality. Women are not, as Ginsburg's theory assumed, all the same and the same as men on the inside, only being unjustly treated differently on the outside. The members of the group, women, obviously aren't all the same at all, despite being characterized at one level by their sex. Black women, for example, may suffer from discrimination different from that suffered by black men or by white women.

The earliest case makes the problem clear. In 1976 the plaintiff, one Emma DeGraffenreid, along with several other black women, sued General Motors for discrimination on the grounds that GM segregated its workforce by race and gender.[8] Although there were jobs in one department for black men and jobs in another for white women, there were no jobs for the black female plaintiffs.[9] The trial court rejected the suit, ruling that the Civil Rights Act did not protect black women against combined discrimination of race and gender. Reading the opinion in DeGraffenreid, a young UCLA law professor named Kimberlé Crenshaw was inspired to give the name "intersectionality" to the way disadvantage can be experienced along multiple planes. Crenshaw recognized that the Ginsburg method, using white men as the standard for comparison, led to the ridiculous ruling in DeGraffenreid. Black women are doubly removed from the model of the white male applied by Ginsburg, so the courts were doubly reluctant to call their treatment discrimination. But, applying MacKinnon's lens of dominance and subordination, the intersectional victims are not only invisible to the law, they are doubly oppressed: "MacKinnon's arguments on behalf of all women," Crenshaw says, "are fully applicable in the query posed by Black female plaintiffs, namely: Why must Black women be like white women or Black men to win the protection that Black men or white women received under antidiscrimination law?"[10]

The Intersection of Theory and Practice

While MacKinnon was formulating her first version of these arguments for a law school paper, Paulette Barnes was appealing her sex discrimination case to the DC Court of Appeals. Barnes, a young, determined, capable woman, was the perfect "first."[11] Her harasser, also an African American, was, of all things, the head of Equal Employment Opportunity at the Environmental Protection Agency. Although the case was not strictly a race case, from the time of slavery, stereotypes and myths that justified black women's sexual abuse justified their sexual harassment;[12] that the tormentor is black doesn't cleanse the behavior of its racist history.

Barnes had said no to her supervisor's demand for sex and been effectively fired. So the case posed the purest version of sexual harassment as a civil rights violation. But, as we saw, the trial court had rejected Barnes's claim that her civil rights had been violated. The supervisor's behavior had stemmed from his attraction to her as an individual. When the DC Circuit Court reconvened after Christmas, in 1975, the panel on appeal would be Judges David Bazelon, a liberal Truman appointee, Spottswood W. Robinson, the first African American on any DC federal court—and Catharine MacKinnon's father, George MacKinnon.

Catharine was in DC for Christmas break, and Judge MacKinnon had given her access to his office so she could use its Lexis legal-research system in her search for case law relevant to workplace sex abuse for her paper. At this time, there was of course no legal category for sexual harassment. As Catharine MacKinnon tells it, she was working at the Lexis machine over the holidays when a woman she did not know approached her.[13] The woman, MacKinnon recalled, told her she was working with Judge Robinson. We understand, she'd said, you've written something about sexual byplay at work.[14] MacKinnon gave the stranger her only copy of her unfinished paper. Some days later, her father left an envelope containing the paper on a chair at home. She says she never discussed the pending *Barnes* case with her father, Judge MacKinnon.

Two weeks later, Barnes's lawyers stood up to argue her appeal. Barnes had reason to be optimistic. David Bazelon was a lion of the left, and if anyone understood the power of the Civil Rights Act, it was Spottswood Robinson, who before his judgeship was a member of the all-star litigation team at the NAACP. In 1975 Robinson's chambers were also unique in that both of his law clerks were women. That triggered a buzz; with two women working in the same chambers there would surely be catfights, one sexist commentator suggested. Judge Bazelon also had a female clerk, making for an unprecedented presence of women on the DC Circuit as a whole.[15]

When Paulette Barnes filed her appeal, it was not obvious even to Judge Robinson that firing someone for refusing sex was discrimination.[16] Coming out of the civil rights movement, Robinson was naturally protective about what would qualify as a legitimate civil rights violation. Robinson's law clerk, Susan Low Bloch, a feminist whose résumé was even then full of ceiling-blasting female firsts, had real doubts. *Does making a pass amount to sex discrimination?* she asked herself.[17] Bloch's feminism, rooted in the argument of *The*

Feminine Mystique on the need to liberate women from the constraints of the home, was above all focused on women's equal access to the formal public world. The Civil Rights Act forbade an employer from denying employment on the basis of sex. Even among liberals, it seemed, making the connection between sex acts and inequality was going to be an uphill battle. After oral argument, liberal Bazelon was also disinclined to credit the civil rights argument. And Republican Nixon appointee MacKinnon was certainly not interested.

But — perhaps after reading MacKinnon's paper — Robinson recognized the wrong done to Barnes and decided to develop an argument to persuade his brethren. It took him months to formulate, but in the end, his draft opinion swung Bazelon to his side. Robinson's opinion was everything Catharine MacKinnon and the Dear Sisters at Cornell could have wished.

This civil rights veteran saw right through the court's suggestion that a rule must apply to all women to constitute sex discrimination. Don't tell me she was fired because she wouldn't have sex with the boss, he ruled. That analysis stops one big step short. "But for her womanhood," he wrote, "for aught that appears, her participation in sexual activity would never have been solicited."[18] Judge Robinson made similarly short work of the argument that only actions based *solely* on sex were illegal. Congress considered that formulation, he reminded his readers, and rejected it. And for good reason. It would have made the law meaningless if a discriminator could conceal their invidious purpose through a mask of "Oh, I don't mind employing black people, I just don't want to employ black people married to white people. I'm not a racist." Robinson's understanding of the law is that it prohibits discrimination based on sex "plus" any other factor, as long as the role of sex is significant. And the language of the law was identical for sex as for race.

Judge Robinson explained that he went to these great lengths to clarify the role of sex in the discrimination case because he was so concerned about the "implications" of the lower court's talk of "inharmonious personal relationships." What happened to Paulette

Barnes was not an unfortunate failure of mutual attraction. It was an illegal abuse of power over a protected class. Once sex in the workplace was reframed as a potential abuse of power to which only — and all — women were vulnerable because they were women, the lens shifted, crucially.

Even Judge MacKinnon ultimately went along with applying the Civil Rights Act to sex. The decision would be unanimous. But Judge MacKinnon buried in the seeming victory a bombshell of a weakness. MacKinnon, earlier in his career a longtime lawyer for the big Minneapolis firm Investors Diversified Services, was primed to protect companies if nothing else. Why should an employer have any responsibility for an acting-out supervisor who demanded sex? In the area of law that deals with such questions, called, archaically, master and servant, "servants" who act out like Barnes's supervisor did are held solely responsible for their behavior. If a servant is acting on his own, the master is without liability for any harms committed.

Judge MacKinnon's concurring opinion put hurdles in the way of a plaintiff attempting to get a judgment against an employer. The employee could sue the individual harasser, sure. But in order to implicate the employer in the supervisor's wrongdoing, MacKinnon suggested, the harasser had to be shown as acting for the boss or with the boss's knowledge. Maybe Barnes could prove that the EPA knew about what her boss was doing by making the case that other management personnel had harassed her, misled her, and retaliated against her when she complained. Maybe. But, MacKinnon concluded, employers can protect themselves from liability by doing three things: posting a sexual harassment policy; providing a "workable mechanism for reporting, including the employer warning the supervisor or noting that the advances were unwanted"; and "protect[ing] the complainant's identity."

The EPA settled with Barnes. She got a great job at the Federal Aviation Administration and became one of its few female air traffic controllers.[19]

But Judge MacKinnon's concurrence offered future plaintiffs a bad deal. If the courts ultimately followed his lead, the defendant who really matters — the employer — would usually be exempt from liability, and employers, as bank robber Willie Sutton said about banks, are where the money is. A decade after Judge MacKinnon's concurrence in *Barnes*, the Supreme Court would take up his invitation to gut the promise of his colleague's pathbreaking decision.

3

Redefining Sex
1979–91

Sex Is a Political Event

In 1979 Yale University Press published MacKinnon's book *Sexual Harassment of Working Women: A Case of Sex Discrimination.* Getting sex harassment recognized as a violation of the Civil Rights Act was a huge accomplishment, a game changer. But by this point, MacKinnon was gunning for much bigger game. If sex at work imitates sex at home, she wrote, what does that tell us about sex at home? "Many men go home every night to a person they fully consider themselves to be relating to 'as an individual,' unconscious of how their feelings, attitudes and treatment of her might contribute to her subordination and to that of women as a whole ... to view work relations between women and men this way focuses attention upon *the operation of socially defined sex roles even in the closest personal relations,* relations in which people are accustomed to thinking of themselves as most 'themselves,' hence most free."[1] In the brilliance of MacKinnon's gaze, harassment at work simply revealed the dominance embedded in sexual behaviors everywhere, including in the privacy of the home. Or, put another way, not only is sex at work political, not personal, but sex at home is political, too.

Sexual Harassment of Working Women was, to paraphrase Abraham Lincoln, the little book that started a big war.[2] MacKinnon's protean arguments led the DC Circuit to find in the *Barnes* case that sexual harassment at work violates the Civil Rights Act. But once sex was opened up to analysis as an exercise in dominance and subordination, the result turned out to be even more momentous.

We are, in the #MeToo movement today, met on a battlefield of that war. Because sexual harassment is also about sex everywhere, sex harassment actually matters *more* than even most kinds of sex discrimination at work.[3] In the years after the publication of *Sexual Harassment of Working Women,* MacKinnon turned her focus to the fraught questions of pornography and rape. Relentlessly and consistently, she would ask the same question: How do human beings interact in the realm of sex under conditions of inequality? Sexual harassment, as Catharine MacKinnon critically understood, is about unequal power: abusers extract sex for the arousal and affirmation of experiencing their power, and dominant actors extract sex as a reward for their dominance. But the dominant extract many gains from the subordinate in our, and most, societies — loot, cheap labor, racial oppression. Why is sex particularly meaningful?

It may seem obvious, but it is important to say that in actual sex (ordinarily) two people touch. They breach the distance between two embodied selves. Similarly, the sexual offender either touches the victim directly on her — or his — body or in simulated touching, as in forced viewing of sex acts or sexual texts or aurally, as in sexual phone calls. Unlike many forms of sex discrimination — discriminatory hiring or promotion policies, unequal pay — sexual harassment is fundamentally a physical assault, and, in Western countries, physical assault is an egregious political act.

Back in 2012 the commentator and NASCAR fan Nancy Qualls-Shehata explained the idea perfectly. She was watching CNN when a story came on about NASCAR driver Tony Stewart, who was shown greeting DeLana Harvick, the wife of a fellow driver, by coming up from behind her and grabbing her ass. The story treated Stewart, known for this sort of behavior, with a kind of "Tony strikes again" indulgence. "At the beach," a sports reporter wrote, "parents teach children to never turn their backs on the ocean. After all, you never know when a big wave is going [to] come up and wipe out someone from behind. At NASCAR tracks, parents should probably teach their children something similar about turning their backs on Tony Stewart."[4] The message for her own daughter, as for all girls and women, Qualls-Shehata knew, was clear: "Sweetie, your body is not your own, and any good ole boy can grab your butt and no one will stop him." She countered, "I wouldn't allow any kid, boy or girl, to do such a thing to another kid, boy or girl. This is simple decency and respect for another human being's dignity."[5] Qualls-Shehata knew what lesson to take from the incident. Physical bodies have politics. One's body is or is not one's own. Owning your body is central to your dignity. Anyone who argues that any touching short of rape is trivial is missing the point that Qualls-Shehata grasped immediately.

That the physical is the political is not a new concept. The core of chattel slavery was that the slave did not own her own body. That's why the abolitionists called slavery "man stealing," to signify the immorality of the practice. For centuries, English law, which is the source material of most American legal thinking, honored the space between two bodies (the bodies of slaves, of course, were exempt) by making assault (threatening or intending to commit an unwanted touch) and battery (unwanted touching), a tort, or wrong. If the unwanted touching was intentional, it was also a crime. In protecting the body from unwanted touching, the laws of tort and crime recognize a principle at the foundation of the Western Enlightenment: However unequal a society may be, everyone is equal in one fundamental way—their bodies are their own. In politics, the classic statement of this principle is usually attributed to Thomas Hobbes, the father of modern liberal political thought. "Look at men," Hobbes said in 1642, "as if they had just emerged from the earth like mushrooms."[6] All equal, even in strength, everyone in the state of nature has one primary agenda: to protect his (or her, more on this below) physical self from his neighbor. How do they solve the problem? By founding the state. Because each man (using Hobbes's terms) owns himself, he gets to be a player in the game we call founding the state. Here's the second point: the state (and other social institutions) exists first and foremost to protect people's right to control access to their bodies. People who have sufficient sovereignty over their physical selves to found the state are "citizens." As such, they submit to the authority of the state. The relationship between the individual and the state is thus consensual.

Hobbes's state of nature was hypothetical. Yet the ideal of equal self-ownership is the foundation of all of Western political thought. And that is where the problem with ass-grabbing behavior comes in. In the history of the West, if women can't keep others out of and off their bodies, if "their bodies are not their own," as the NASCAR story would have it, they cannot be citizens. That's why sexual harassment is worse than unequal pay.

It is not a coincidence that the actual society around Hobbes was changing with regard to female self-ownership at exactly the time Hobbes was writing. Across Europe, wherever the Protestant Reformation touched down after 1517, women started defying patriarchal traditions. One such upstart even gave rise to the Reformation version of an internet meme. Calvinist elders in Geneva, Switzerland, accused a woman from Lyons of having sex with her fiancé before marriage. "Paris est au Roi" (Paris is the king's), the defiant sex rebel replied, invoking a common slogan, "et mon corps est à moi." My body belongs to me.[7] In Lyons, as in Protestant towns all over southeast France, there was a sexual revolution going on. Daughters, even of respectable families, were dancing, strolling with young men, writing love poetry, and marrying whom they wished.[8] Their bodies belonged to them after all.

Not that everything was rosy. The same seventeenth-century Englishmen so concerned with justifying rulership as consensual were at that very moment engaged in the most egregious act of bodily violation: the slave trade.

The treatment of slave women as freely violable objects of sexual lust having reproductive value is one of the core political violations of the slave system. The slave narratives, which are the "movement literature of abolition,"[9] reveal the powerful dynamic of female self-ownership. Harriet Jacobs's classic, *Incidents in the Life of a Slave Girl: Written by Herself* (the explicit claim of authorship reflects peoples' denial that a slave or fugitive slave could own her own words) tells of the young woman who defied her rapacious master and took a white lover, because it was "less degrading," she wrote, "to give one's self, than to submit to compulsion."[10] When her master punished her by consigning her to hard labor, she ran away, hiding in a crawl space so small she was unable to stand up. By the time she escaped, she was permanently crippled.

It is no coincidence that many of the lead plaintiffs in the incipient workplace-sexual-harassment drama — Paulette Barnes and, as we will see, Sandra Burke and Mechelle Vinson and many others — were black women. They carried with them the vulnerability of the noxious hangover of slavery and they understood the price of submission. Even a century after the Civil War, black women knew the value of owning your own body.

In the wake of Betty Friedan's *Feminine Mystique*, second-wave feminists were not crazy about Hobbes's theory. He was arguing that consent to form the state was legitimate, even if the consent was technically offered in conditions of extreme threat and fear. The problem with Hobbes's analysis can be illustrated in a classic 1940s radio sketch by the comedian Jack Benny. The sketch involves Benny being confronted by an armed robber.

Robber to Benny: Your money or your life?

Long silence.

Benny, finally: I'm thinking it over!

The joke, of course, is that the choice would be clear to most people (hand over the money and live). But the former is not acceptable to Benny, a legendary tightwad. The notion of consent is not meaningful here, where the alternative to consent is so awful.

Women living in unequal conditions of fear and threat didn't have, despite Hobbes's thinking, the same relationship to the state as men did. In certain contexts, their consent was not meaningful.

For that reason, feminism could not accept, for example, the proposal, implicit in some of Hobbes's writing, that marriage is a one-time consensual bargain in which women give up all further claims to self-ownership. The most graphic example of this one-and-done theory is that a woman's loss of bargaining power justified, for centuries, the idea that a man could not be subject to the charge of rape with respect to his wife. The battle against the so-called "marital exception" to the law of rape was one of modern feminists' earliest battles. If women own their own bodies in the private sphere of marriage, it follows that they own them everywhere, including in the workplace.

The fight to extend the notion of meaningful physical self-ownership has been ground zero at every stage of feminism. The movement to resist marital rape and the movement to resist sexual harassment at work were the branches of the Hobbesian tree. The tree is the understanding that sex is access to the body, a political event, subject to the laws of politics. Hobbes wasn't perfect, and feminism had to set his theory into the context of the inequality of bargaining power in women's lives. But it was a start.

You Cannot Separate Sex from Power

MacKinnon, however, was not satisfied with building an argument on old liberal theories like ownership of one's body and the conditions of legitimate consent. In the 1970s and 1980s, an incredibly creative time for her, she constructed a new theory of feminism.[11] She began as all theorists begin, with an inquiry into how something can best be understood. How best to learn about women's lives, to formulate a theory about their place in society? We learn about women's lives, according to MacKinnon, from listening to them. That's what she was doing in Ithaca that fateful night in 1975, when she signed up for the Cornell group's newsletter. Gathering women's stories, she learned of a relentless and pervasive regime of male dominance. What does it mean to be a male or a female? she then asked. Her answer: the categories of male and female are created through "the eroticization of dominance and submission."[12]

She listened to countless "women's accounts of sexual use and abuse by men," and concluded that "you cannot separate sex from power . . . The male sexual role . . . centers on aggressive intrusion on those with less power. Such acts of dominance are experienced as sexually arousing, as sex itself. They therefore are. The new knowledge on the sexual violation of women by men thus frames an inquiry into the place of sexuality in gender and of gender in sexuality. A feminist theory of sexuality based on these data locates sexuality within a theory of gender inequality, meaning the social hierarchy of men over women."[13]

MacKinnon's theory allows her full access to so-called "personal relationships," which, as we have seen, was the first legal defense to claims of sexual harassment. In MacKinnon's analysis, rather than being a place beyond politics, the personal is the essence of politics: "The very place (home, body) . . . that feminism finds central to women's subjection form[s] the core of privacy doctrine . . . when women are segregated in private, one at a time, a law of privacy will tend to protect the right of men 'to be let alone,' to oppress us one at a time."[14]

Overlapping sexual arousal with dominance and intrusion, she fatally weakens the power of consent to legitimate sexual contacts. Consent is a power central to all liberal theory from sex to the formation of the state. To MacKinnon, "to consent means, in law, to be rolled by power."[15]

This framing of male sexuality as aggressive intrusion on those with less power earned MacKinnon the most potent punishment the male-dominated academic community could impose: she could not get a job. For twelve years, this most fruitful of scholarly writers wandered from visitorship to visitorship, with no reliable salary, no security, and no honor. One of the leading lights of the Yale faculty, Owen M. Fiss, called her rejection "a stunning indictment of American academic life."[16] And truthfully, only with the emergence of the current #MeToo movement has the connection between sex and male aggression been fully made to the public. The sheer number of #MeToo testimonies to men experiencing sex only or often as aggression reproduces the covert conversations in so many consciousness-raising groups that MacKinnon found in her early research.[17] All those years ago.

Rape Is the Practice

When we think about sexual, or, indeed, any unwanted physical access especially aimed at women, the first thing that comes to mind is the most sexed of unwanted contacts, rape. And indeed at the very same moment second-wave feminism was organizing around sexual harassment at work, activists were shining the spotlight on rape. In 1970 Susan Brownmiller, a freelance writer and member of the New York Radical Women, changed her mind about rape.[18] She had previously, she says, adopted the mind-set of heroic defense lawyers, the civil rights movement, sympathy for the accused. Rape was rare, something unusual, psychopathic, and not likely to happen to her or to most women.

Like Lin Farley at Cornell, Brownmiller came to her new understanding via consciousness-raising groups. She listened to her female acquaintances describe their experiences of rape, how common it was, how inconsistent their stories were to Brownmiller's notion of rape as rare, as outside the realm of normal experience. Then she went to a speak-out and heard total strangers tell their rape stories in public. She began to see how thoroughly women's experience of life was shaped and inflected by their vulnerability to the access to their bodies we call being raped. Brownmiller spent the next five years in the reading rooms of the New York Public Library, writing a powerhouse history of rape. Like MacKinnon's *Sexual Harassment of Working Women*, Brownmiller's 1975 blockbuster book, *Against Our Will*, set the ground rules for feminism's engagement with that definitional act of sexual abuse.

Rape, Brownmiller argued, is a unique and effective means by which men keep women in check. Men have the capacity to rape, and women are, accordingly, vulnerable. With that starting point, she extracted from her historical studies a handful of focus areas: rape in war, in revolutions, in the context of slavery and indigenous peoples, conventional rape defendants (the "Police-Blotter Rapist"), the role of race in rape, rape by authority figures, and finally the victims: the settings, the crimes, and the women fighting back. Even in times of peace rape was endemic, she concluded, and usually involved someone the victim knew.

The reception was tumultuous. Although the *New York Times* gave the book a positive review, Amanda Heller of the *Atlantic Monthly* declared that in places Brownmiller was given to "a kind of feminist pornography that overwhelms the book's more thoughtful passages."[19] Most tellingly, within months critics leveled scathing criticism of Brownmiller's treatment of black men accused of rape. Angela Davis, in *Women, Race and Class,* described *Against Our Will* as pervaded by racist ideas and Brownmiller as merely more "subtle" than earlier racist ideologues.[20] MacKinnon had a different focus as well. Defining rape as violence, not sex, MacKinnon says, enables people to avoid any critique of sexuality while being against rape.[21] MacKinnon was not going to make that distinction.

Diane Johnson, writing for the *New York Review of Books,* thought Brownmiller would discourage women from fighting an uphill battle against Brownmiller's world of pervasive rape. Also, Johnson worried, Brownmiller would alienate men, whom Brownmiller tags with broad responsibility for the pervasiveness of rape. News flash: women were already discouraged and fearful of alienating men. Shortly after the time Brownmiller's book was published in the mid-1970s, aspiring actress Cynthia Burr met with an up-and-coming Buffalo music promoter and moviemaker named Harvey Weinstein in New York. Her manager had thought it would be a good idea. After greeting her in the lobby of an old office building, Weinstein attempted to kiss her in an elevator, she claims, and later forced her to perform oral sex on him in a hallway. "The way he forced me made me feel really bad about myself," she remembers.

"What are you going to do when you are a girl just trying to make it as an actress? Nobody would have believed me," said Burr.[22]

Brownmiller was singled out as one of *Time* magazine's "Women of the Year" in 1975. The feminist movement turned its attention to the many ways the law stripped women of any meaningful protection against rape, rather than playing its appointed role of protecting their bodies. As a direct result of the activism, by 1979 several states had passed laws making rape a crime even in marriage; that year, Massachusetts was the first to convict a man for spousal rape. Brownmiller did not exactly lead the charge on acquaintance rape, the most common form of rape. She devotes only a few pages of a long book to the subject. But she had gotten people talking about rape in various contexts, and slowly the culture began to recognize what we now call date rape. In 1975 women in Philadelphia organized a march to "Take Back the Night" after a young woman was killed walking home at night; Take Back the Night soon became a national movement against rape and violence against women.

Legislatures began to abolish the requirement that prosecutors, in winning a conviction for sexual assault, had to prove that the victim resisted with force, a ridiculous and harmful concept that ignores the reality we saw in Tanya Harrell's story of simply being reduced to tears. Feminist activists began looking into what distinguished rape from other acts of sex. At about the same time as activists were organizing around sexual harassment, rape became the center of feminist attention as to how women should make their bodies "their own." While not as ambitious as MacKinnon's theory, the effort to control access to one's body with meaningful legal and cultural tools was certainly a step forward, linking Enlightenment claims to "citizenship" of the body with 1970s feminism.

Brownmiller embarked on a two-year college tour, at the end of which she turned to the matter she had taken up toward the end of *Against Our Will*: pornography. "The case against pornography," Brownmiller wrote, with eerie prescience, is "central to the fight against rape, and if it angers a large part of the liberal population to be so informed, then I would question in turn the political understanding of such liberals and their true concern for the rights of women."[23] The feminist move against pornography revealed as nothing before the chasm between traditional liberal thought and the rights of women.

Pornography Angers the Liberal Population

In 1977 the antipornography movement seemed uncontroversially embedded in the feminist movement of the time. The boldface names of New York feminism, Adrienne Rich, Grace Paley, Gloria Steinem, Shere Hite, Lois Gould, Barbara Deming, Karla Jay, Andrea Dworkin, Letty Cottin Pogrebin, and Robin Morgan, were mightily provoked. The porn industry was starting to inflect the larger culture. Movies like *Deep Throat* were suddenly attracting a mainstream New York audience. Promotion for the Rolling Stones' 1976 album *Black and Blue* included a Los Angeles billboard showing a woman covered in bruises: "I'm *Black and Blue* from the Rolling Stones . . . and I Love It!"

Catharine MacKinnon read Andrea Dworkin's 1974 book *Woman Hating* with its riveting analysis of pornography, including a powerful reading of the trendy pornographic book *Story of O.* "Pornography," Dworkin wrote, "like fairy tale, tells us who we are. It is the structure of male and female mind, the content of our shared erotic identity, the map of each inch and mile of our oppression and despair. Here we move beyond childhood terror. Here the fear is clammy and real, and rightly so. Here we are compelled to ask the real questions: why are we defined in these ways, and how can we bear it?"[24] MacKinnon had seen the political significance in *Story of O* and had been told her reaction was a little crazy. Reading Dworkin, she says, "gave me my mind back."[25] Women Against Pornography organized huge demonstrations, first in 1976 in San Francisco's porn-heavy Tenderloin district. In September 1979, seven hundred women attended a New York antipornography conference; thousands participated in a March on Times Square the following month. In 1977 feminist author Robin Morgan put forward the slogan "Pornography is the theory, rape is the practice,"[26] which did what great slogans do. It mobilized the language in the army of resistance, tying the portrayal of sexual violence to its enactment in real life. One Linda Boreman, publicly known as Linda Lovelace, published a memoir, *Ordeal*, in which she described being forced into making the edgy 1972 porn film *Deep Throat* with an actual gun to her head.[27]

Porn movie actors weren't the only ones with a gun to their heads. As Linda Lovelace revealed her story of coercion, music booker Harvey Weinstein was upstate making a slasher film in his hometown of Buffalo. His intern, a twenty-four-year-old communications student named Paula Wachowiak, took him some checks to sign. He greeted her in a towel, took off the towel, and asked for a massage. When she balked, he suggested that she could really benefit from being part of his movie project. Ultimately he seemed to take her refusal in stride. On her last day at work, he got out of his car to ask her, "Was seeing me naked the highlight of your internship?" Wachowiak never did go into moviemaking.[28]

By the early 1980s MacKinnon was teaching at the University of Minnesota Law School and arranged a visitorship for Dworkin to coteach a course on pornography.[29] Activists in Minneapolis learned of the class and asked the pair for help in resisting the spread of pornography in their town. Unsurprisingly, given MacKinnon's successful legal framing of sexual harassment as a civil rights violation, the two drafted a bill to provide civil rights protection for participants in pornography.

The Minneapolis Ordinance declared that "pornography is central in creating and maintaining the civil inequality of the sexes. Pornography is a systematic practice of exploitation and subordination based on sex which differentially harms women." The bill defined pornography as "the sexually explicit subordination of women, graphically depicted, whether in pictures or in words" adding that the depiction also includes a list of conditions, such as that "(i) women are presented dehumanized as sexual objects, things or commodities; or (ii) women are presented as sexual objects who en-

joy pain or humiliation," and a list of other vicious practices like being tied up or cut up or mutilated.[30]

Causes of action included coercion into pornography, forcing
pornography on a person, assault or physical attack due to pornography, and trafficking in pornography. Under the trafficking provision, people with a claim could sue not only makers but sellers,
exhibitors, and distributors. MacKinnon and Dworkin contended
that three classes of people — women acting in pornography, women
forced to reenact pornographic scenes in real life, and women in
the society where pornography portrayed women as subordinate
and dehumanized — were hurt. They arranged for women who had
experienced harm from pornography to testify before various city
councils. People just showed up to testify.

The measure passed in Minneapolis, but the mayor vetoed it.
In 1984 the city of Indianapolis passed an antipornography bill into
law, its version emphasizing the presentation of women as victims
of violence — in pain, raped, penetrated, cut up.[31]

MacKinnon and Dworkin justified the bills as exceptions to the
First Amendment protection of speech and images.[32] Pornography,
they argued, was more like an act than it was protected speech. The
ordinance sought to protect adult women, as a group, from the violence and abuse pornography targeted them for as well as the dimi-
nution of their legal and sociological status as women; that is, from
the discriminatory stigma that befalls women *as women* as a result
of pornography. Pornography is a practice, MacKinnon argued, of
discrimination on the basis of sex.

It is almost never fair to say, but in this case, the shit really did
hit the fan. There had been dissenters from the Women Against
Pornography movement from the beginning, including Deirdre
English, the editor of *Mother Jones*; a famous Radicalesbian activist, Gayle Rubin; and a San Francisco–based sadomasochism group,
Samois. By 1982 opponents of WAP had gathered enough adherents
to convene a fractious academic conference on sexuality at Barnard College. Feminism was always full of fractious academic con-
ferences, but this time the division was of a different magnitude.

Those opposed to pornography regulation bridged the gap between theory and practice through a community familiar to MacKinnon and Dworkin: lawyers. Starting with Ruth Bader Ginsburg at the ACLU Women's Rights Project in 1972, lawyers had always been central to liberal feminism. There weren't a dozen women on law faculties in 1971. But by the 1980s there were enough female lawyers and law professors to make a task force, in this case the Feminist Anti-Censorship Task Force (FACT), led by liberal law professor Sylvia Law and ACLU LGBT rights director Nan Hunter. When the ACLU challenged the constitutionality of the Indianapolis ordinance, FACT weighed in as a friend of the court to urge the court to strike down the antipornography law.

The new law, FACT said,[33] violated the constitutional guarantees of free speech. It would allow the government to impose a prior restraint on the production and distribution of print and pictures, and the work that might be found offensive is so loosely described as to be "virtually limitless." What was, for example a "scenario of . . . abasement," which the law would proscribe? Worse, Law and Hunter continued, how could anyone presume to judge sex? One woman's abasement is another woman's enjoyment. And by playing into the traditional double standard that women are sexually reluctant while men are promiscuous, the law also violates the Fourteenth Amendment, which forbids discrimination based on sex. It "delegitimates and makes socially invisible" women "who find sexually explicit images of women 'in positions of display' or 'penetrated by objects' to be erotic, liberating or educational" and "reinforces the stereotypical view that 'good' women do not seek and enjoy sex." Such an unconstitutional law could only be justified if it prevented serious and imminent harm. Here, FACT said, the proponents' social science studies purporting to show a connection between pornography and negative attitudes and behaviors toward women was radically unpersuasive. Only a few very violent images may do harm, and the ordinance extended well beyond that narrow class.

Many women central to feminism, from the author of second-wave feminism, Betty Friedan herself, to the author of one of the very first casebooks about sex discrimination, Susan Deller Ross, signed the FACT brief.[34] The trial court and the United States Court of Appeals for the Seventh Circuit struck down the Indianapolis ordinance as unconstitutional, and the Supreme Court summarily affirmed. MacKinnon said of the FACT brief, "At this point, for me, the women's movement that I had known came to an end."[35]

Sexual Liberation and Gender Equality

The tectonic change we call the sexual revolution, represented in the porn wars, was a factor in the feminist movement from the beginning. In 1950, for good or ill, American culture and law as derived from its British heritage treated sex as it had been framed for centuries, as confined to heterosexual monogamous marriage. In every state, there were laws against sex outside of marriage — adultery, fornication, sodomy, both homosexual and not — divorce was difficult to obtain, abortion was criminal, and birth control constrained. It is this 1950s vision of proper sexuality that conservatives and Republicans purported to embrace, with increasing intensity as the Republican Party moved to the right. The sexual revolution emerged from this model of human sexual relations. Freudian psychology, with its proponents' emphasis on the perils of repression, spread virally throughout the United States after Sigmund Freud visited in 1909.[36] The twentieth century also saw increasing interest in the scientific study of human sexuality, like the Kinsey Report, and the separation of the law of sex from its origins in religious teachings.[37]

The pace of sexual revolution accelerated to warp speed in the 1950s and '60s. In 1962 the elite American Law Institute produced a Model Penal Code, which withdrew the sanction of criminal law from what had traditionally been understood as sexual sins.[38] Slowly the laws against adultery and fornication fell by the wayside. Starting in 1957, the Supreme Court issued a series of opinions cutting down the prohibitions against obscenity under a newly robust interpretation of freedom of speech and expression. Reformers

took on the religiously bounded world of divorce law. The requirement to prove abuse or adultery in order to be granted a divorce
had led to widespread fraud on the part of people trying to establish
fault. Well-intentioned legal scholars proposed a model of divorce
without fault. California passed the new law in 1969. Both feminism
and the sexual revolution were deeply indebted to all these developments and above all to the invention of reliable birth control.

Consequence-free sex liberated sex and led to the sexual revolution mightily valued in the FACT brief. It also liberated women
from the biggest consequence of sex — pregnancy — and enabled
them to pursue ambitious lives as described, if admittedly mostly
available for white women, in *The Feminine Mystique.*

The promise for women was a sexual life free of the obligations
and hierarchical assumptions of traditional marriage. Considering
how fast society was changing, it is not surprising that well-intentioned feminists were of at least two minds about the sexual revolution. On the one hand, in 1972 Dr. Alex Comfort promised his
readers "the joy of sex" in a famous book by that title. Instead of the
rosy vision of men and women, as equal partners, finding their sexual bliss in a universe of available orgasms, however, MacKinnon
describes the sexual social changes of the 1960s not as leading to
greater equality but as "freeing male aggression." Women liberated
from the prescribed traditional sexual constraints by this process
had not more freedom, but "freer access to being subordinated."[39]
Only the range of potential oppressors had changed. In any event,
the two visions of feminism — what was called sexual liberation and
sexual equality — collided with a bang over the antipornography ordinance, and sexual liberation won.

Even after the liberationists beat the pornography ordinance,
the equality-driven movement to rein in sexual harassment at work
continued to gather steam, as if the two issues could be cleanly sep-
arated. However, the movement to shift sexual relations from the
realm of the personal to that of the political certainly slowed. The
position of many of the participants in FACT was that they were
opposed to pornography but even more opposed to invoking the

power of the state to stop it. They wanted actions like demonstrations, critical writings and enforcement of existing laws directly addressed to matters like sexual violence as their weapons.[40] Liberalism had a long and storied history in resisting the power of the
state, particularly where expression was concerned, and many of
the FACT supporters came from that honorable tradition.

The scholars and journalists and tastemakers weren't just worried about free speech in battling the MacKinnon/Dworkin ordinance, however. The resistance to the pornography ordinance
quickly moved into the familiar arguments that sex was private and
a matter of personal taste. "Women are agents," the ordinance opponents asserted, "and not merely victims, who make decisions and
act on them, and who desire, seek out and enjoy sexuality."[41] In a
trice, they went from withholding judgment to suggesting that any
sexual depiction might be positive. Influential public intellectual
Susan Sontag had speculated in her much discussed essay on pornography from the 1960s, that "peoples' consciousness varies," and
sex is so extreme anyway.[42] Let a thousand flowers bloom. Male aggression, subordination, it's all good. Indeed, pornography might
be positive, defenders asserted: "Many women fantasize about being ravished . . . If we fantasize a partner taking complete control
of a sexual encounter, then we are absolved from responsibility for
our abandoned behavior."[43] Even violent pornography, the ACLU's
Nadine Strossen added, citing male critic David Richards, might be
useful: "Susan Sontag has noted that violent pornography expresses
something about the sometimes extreme nature of sexual ecstasy
and the fantasies we experience in having sex."[44] Feminists, like the
"pro life" movement, gave themselves a great name: "sex-positive
feminists." What's not to like?

There were many formal feminist achievements after the pornography ordinance went down among competing visions of a feminist future. But the fundamental divide — a book coming out of the
Barnard conference had been called "Pleasure and Danger" — was
now revealed, and ultimately would open a deep split in the movement. Equality feminists were pushing to have every aspect of the

sexual relationship — like all human relationships — subjected to the lens of politics. Liberal and libertarian feminists were resisting at every level, to maintain a preserve in which some aspects of sex would be veiled from political view.

The FACT briefers won the legal battles. MacKinnon's effort to extend to other realms her critique of sex, so fruitful in the movement against sex harassment at work, had stalled.

But by the 1980s the men who controlled the media were not fooled by feminism's falter. Whether resisting sexual harassment at work or highlighting the harm from pornography, feminism was identified as the enemy. By 1986, stories about women being more likely to be killed by terrorists than find a husband after forty began to displace coverage of the slow integration of the white-collar workplace. Instead of *9 to 5*, in 1987 Hollywood produced *Fatal Attraction*, the morality tale of the homicidal single woman who can only be stopped with a gunshot to the chest. In 1991 the journalist Susan Faludi gathered together the evidence of resistance to feminism at all levels in a best-selling book, *Backlash*, giving a name to the phenomenon. As we have seen, MacKinnon's antipornography stance and framing of sex as male aggression resulted in her being largely ostracized from secure work in academia throughout the 1980s; she was finally offered a tenured position at the University of Michigan in 1990, where she remains today. Even now, however, she is reluctant to tell people where she lives.

4

Mechelle Vinson's Supreme Trial 1986

Bittersweet Victory

In the 1980s, while academic feminists were exchanging quotations on the extreme possibilities of human sexual tastes, Mechelle Vinson, yet another African American sexual harassment plaintiff, was delivering newspapers and working at a food store, trying to keep food on the table.[1] By 1985 she didn't have enough money even to make a long-distance call to her lawyer to ask about the status of her suit against her former employer, Meritor Savings Bank, in Washington, DC.

Vinson had begun working at the bank, then a branch of Capital City Federal Savings, in 1974. She was an attractive nineteen-year-old. She had counted herself lucky to run into the sociable branch manager, Sidney Taylor, on the street, where he gave her a job application.

Taylor was a character: after getting out of the army he had gone to work at the bank as a messenger and a janitor and worked his way up to branch manager. He was proud of his part in building the branch from $7 million in assets to $16 million. A practiced schmoozer belonging to dozens of civic clubs, he cut a popular figure in the neighborhood served by his branch. He was the first black branch assistant vice president in the Capital City system.

The little local bank had always seemed like an island of harmony and order in Mechelle's childhood. Married at fifteen, she had dropped out of school only to see the marriage unravel. Oh, God, she needed that job.

The moment Vinson finished her probationary period as a teller trainee, Sidney Taylor, now her supervisor at the bank, took her out to dinner and demanded she have sex with him. That's how it started.[2] Taylor made repeated demands for sexual favors,[3] usually at the bank, both during and after business hours; she estimated that over the next several years she had intercourse with him some forty or fifty times. Taylor consistently abused her verbally and physically, including approximately a dozen incidents of what she described as forcible intercourse, or rape. At least three of those episodes took place in a bank vault. In addition, Taylor fondled her in front of other employees, followed her into the women's restroom when she went there alone, and exposed himself to her. Taylor also touched and fondled other women employees of the bank. He exhibited pornographic images to the bank's female employees, making lewd suggestions. When these women asked Vinson, who by then had risen to assistant manager and so was their supervisor, to intervene, Vinson testified that Taylor told her: "This is my office and I will do what I like; if they don't like it, they can get the hell out — that is my way of relaxing them."[4]

Mechelle Vinson was not Paulette Barnes, who had just said no to her harasser. Vinson had put up with Taylor's harassment and abuse for four years. Finally, in 1978 she took sick leave from her job. Two months later Taylor fired her for excessive time off work. She had good reason to be sick (and tired), she thought. She told her divorce lawyer, who knew activist lawyer Pat Barry, and Barry filed a sexual harassment suit against both Taylor and Meritor. And so began Mechelle Vinson's trip to the Supreme Court of the United States.

Because Vinson did not have Paulette Barnes's clean facts — she did not refuse sex and get fired for it, which the DC Circuit had now ruled was illegal — it would take a judge of some insight to see that Taylor's empire at the bank branch represented a different kind of civil rights violation. Taylor not only demanded sex in exchange for employment, he also ran, as MacKinnon had suggested in her then-new book on the subject, a hostile work environment, like the physics department at Cornell where Carmita Wood had worked until she could take it no longer and quit.

On the surface, the judge in the case before the DC District Court, John Garrett Penn, had a background similar to the author of the *Barnes* decision, Judge Spottswood Robinson. Born in Pittsfield, Massachusetts, where his father was a machinist, Penn came from one of about five hundred black families in a city of fifty-five thousand residents. He switched his major at the University of Massachusetts from chemistry to become a lawyer. Penn was, he later said, particularly inspired by the decision in *Brown v. Board of Education,* which was decided the year he graduated college. He got to the federal court by way of a judgeship in the local DC courts.[5]

But Judge Penn was a disaster for Mechelle Vinson and the legal challenge to abuse. Unwilling to recognize the novel claim of hostile-environment discrimination, he excluded evidence presented in the case that Taylor had been harassing and assaulting her and many women at the workplace. Vinson would have had a case only if Taylor had demanded sex as a quid pro quo for Vinson's job. Vinson had stayed in the position, receiving promotions in the course of her employment. Penn issued his decision in 1980. After finding the Civil Rights Act did not protect women from a hostile workplace, Judge Penn gratuitously tagged Vinson with both making up the abuse and, weirdly, asking for it: "If [respondent] and Taylor did engage in an intimate or sexual relationship during the time of [respondent's] employment with [the bank], that relationship was

a voluntary one having nothing to do with her continued employment at [the bank] or her advancement or promotions at that institution."[6] When the cash-strapped Vinson asked the trial court to
provide the transcript so she would not have to pay hundreds of
dollars to have it transcribed for appeal, he denied her that recourse
too. This case, he wrote, "would not present any substantial question." Vinson's lawyer thus went to the DC Circuit for her appeal
with but fragments of the transcript.[7]

Right after Judge Penn ruled in Vinson's case, the agency in
charge of employment discrimination, the federal Equal Employment Opportunity Commission, amended its guidelines and advised that conduct that creates a hostile working environment violated the Civil Rights Act and that the employer was liable if a
supervisor was involved.[8] Shortly after the EEOC adopted the theory of the hostile work environment, another hostile-environment
case arrived at the DC Circuit.[9] This time, Sandra G. Bundy, a fortysomething vocational rehabilitation specialist and the third African
American woman in our story of early sexual harassment law, was
suing the DC Department of Corrections. Shortly after Bundy began work a few years before, her coworker, Delbert Jackson, began
asking her to have sex. After Jackson was promoted, the next two
men who supervised Bundy followed suit, one calling her at home
after obtaining her unlisted number. When she complained to the
department's director of community services, he said any man in
his right mind would want to rape Bundy and pressed Bundy to
have sex with him.[10] Bundy kept saying no.

Like Judge Penn, the trial judge in Bundy's case, George Hart,
rejected Bundy's claim that the behavior she'd been subjected to
violated the Civil Rights Act. Hart, a white Republican appointee
with a history of going easy on white-collar criminals but imposing
maximum sentences on other criminal defendants, was at least predictable.[11] Bundy's treatment was just a silly boys' game, Hart concluded, nothing to be taken seriously and certainly not illegal.

On appeal, the DC Circuit took Hart's opinion apart. Making

use of a passage from Catharine MacKinnon's book, Judge J. Skelly Wright found that sexual harassment that created a hostile work environment violated the Civil Rights Act. Women didn't have to resist so forcefully that they triggered a firing in order to suffer from sex discrimination. Between *Barnes* and *Bundy*, both of MacKinnon's theories were now the law, if not of the land then at least of the DC Circuit.

So Mechelle Vinson reached the court of appeals in 1982 with a new EEOC regulation in her favor and in the wake of a brand-new decision by the same court recognizing Sandra Bundy's hostile-environment claim. Better still, Judge Robinson, who had persuaded his brethren to recognize the claim of sexual harassment in the *Barnes* case and had been on the panel in *Bundy*, was again on the panel of three judges in Vinson's appeal. The argument seemed to go well. Then, unbelievably, three years passed without a peep out of the court. Vinson entered nursing school but, trying to pay her bills, had to drop out.

Finally, in 1985 Robinson delivered the unanimous opinion of the DC Circuit in Vinson's case. Between the new guidelines from the EEOC and the recent decision in *Bundy*, Vinson's was now an easy case. The Civil Rights Act did not just cover harassment where a woman got fired if she didn't put out. It covered behavior that made the workplace into a hostile environment. The asking for sex, as Judge Robinson put it, placed the female employee into an "intolerable position." Then Judge Robinson took a slap back at Judge Penn for his shocking defamation of Mechelle Vinson as a sexual "volunteer." Even if you could know that the sex was "voluntary" in some sense, it would not matter. The law was not going to penalize Vinson for *any* response she made after her boss put her in such an intolerable position. The appeals court had clearly absorbed Catharine MacKinnon's critical insight that sex can be understood only with a clear picture of the conditions of power surrounding it.

The court then went further and held that the employer was liable for harassment by any supervisor regardless of whether the bank knew or could have known about it. This was a rejection of Judge MacKinnon's suggestion, in his concurring opinion in *Barnes*, the first harassment case. Since *Barnes*, however, another federal court, the Eleventh Circuit, out of Atlanta,[12] had followed MacKinnon's analysis and let the employer off. The DC Circuit was thus in a position of conflict. The Supreme Court steps in most often when two of the lower courts disagree. After all, you can't have different federal law for different Americans depending on whether they live in Georgia or the District of Columbia.

The bank then did a very clever thing to ensure it would get the attention of the Supreme Court, hoping that the highest court, which had not yet ruled on the matter, would be more sympathetic to the employer. After losing unanimously before the panel of three judges, the bank asked all thirteen of the judges on the DC Circuit to reconsider the case, something called review en banc. The move looked irrational, because the DC Circuit was mostly composed of liberals in 1985, and between *Vinson* and the two other cases — *Barnes* and *Bundy* — many of the thirteen judges had gone on record supporting the claim for sexual harassment. Predictably, the full panel denied the bank a rehearing, 10 to 3.

But a political shift was under way. During the three years from 1982 to 1985 while Judge Robinson delayed delivering the opinion in Vinson's case, newly elected Republican president Ronald Reagan had begun making appointments to the court. In 1982 he put conservative law professors Robert Bork and Antonin Scalia on the DC Circuit. In 1983 he added Ken Starr, who would later demonstrate great interest in the subject of sexual harassment as the independent counsel in the investigation of President Bill Clinton's relationship with Monica Lewinsky. A Carter appointee, the liberal black feminist Eleanor Holmes Norton, who had been following the sex harassment movement from the early 1970s to her agency's recent guidelines, was replaced as chair of the Equal Employment Opportunity Commission by a conservative black assistant secretary of education, one Clarence Thomas, whose story unfolds in the next chapter. Four of the five members of the EEOC from Democratic administrations were gone by 1985.[13]

So the bank got what it wanted from its appeal to the whole circuit — a passionate dissent from the three Reagan appointees, written by Robert Bork.[14] Bork's dissent contains all the arguments that have been developed right up to the present moment to stymie women seeking redress for sexual abuse. First, Mechelle Vinson was a shameless seductress, Bork implied, alluding to evidence the bank had submitted about her "provocative" clothing and her sexual fantasies and sexual life, often shared with her fellow employees. Second, offices are not asexual places; allowing hostile-environment claims would generate an avalanche of such claims, many from unreliable temptresses like Vinson, who would "see fit" after the fact to complain about the sex. Must the bosses "insure" against any such claims? Such a regime would be costly and outrageous. Like Judge MacKinnon concurring in the *Barnes* case, Bork argued that the Supreme Court should hold the employer harmless from liability for the acts of its supervisors. Even if employers were not liable, he concluded, the suits would multiply, burying the federal courts. Then he pitched his audience of nine directly: the Supreme Court has never addressed whether sex harassment that created a hostile environment was a good claim. Five months later the court agreed to hear the case. Vinson's inexperienced but faithful lawyer, Patricia J. Barry, felt a chill.

The environment got colder when Clarence Thomas, trailing a memorandum he had written for the Reagan transition opposing the claim of hostile-environment discrimination in Holmes Norton's EEOC guidelines altogether,[15] and another Reagan appointee, Rosalie Gaull Silberman, flipped the EEOC in support of the bank. Representing the agency responsible for workplace discrimination, the solicitor general of the United States filed a brief against Vinson. If the Supreme Court examines the record as a whole, it will see that there is no way a claim of discrimination has been stated, the United States suggested. The administration's brief characterized Vinson as being a voluntary participant in her treatment by means of her sexually suggestive dress and conduct, thus contributing to the poisonous atmosphere she decries. She never went to the police and only complained, the brief concluded, because she had been fired for unrelated misconduct. Courts should be reluctant to recognize hostile-environment claims, the administration advised, since plaintiffs are so tempted to use them as sexual revenge and issues of credibility are so hard to resolve. In any event, following Judge MacKinnon's concurrence in *Barnes*, the bank should not be held liable for its employees' conduct. The chief enforcement agency of the Civil Rights Act, under its new chairman Clarence Thomas, was now on record that courts should scrutinize women's dress and speech if they sued, not believe their reports of abuse, and not hold the employer responsible.[16]

Pat Barry knew she was in over her head in representing Vinson before the Supreme Court. She also knew who could best make the argument in support of Vinson's claim — Catharine MacKinnon. MacKinnon, then living pretty much off the grid at a cabin in California, undertook the task. Basically unemployed at the time, she would write the brief with no library, no computer, no salary, and maybe worst of all, no complete trial transcript. Being MacKinnon, one thing in her argument would be perfectly clear. Nothing Vinson did in the circumstances in which she found herself could possibly be used in defense of the harasser or the bank. In her brief, MacKinnon called Judge Penn's bizarre hypothetical statement (and the solicitor general's brief on behalf of the EEOC) that if Vinson had sex with her boss, it was voluntary, "not a statement of fact," but "an assassination of character."[17]

Turns out there was only one justice set on reversal of the DC Circuit decision: Lewis Powell. After all, Powell wrote on his law clerk's initial case memo, "most of it [the sexual behavior Vinson complained about] was voluntary," and Vinson never reported the rapes "to the bank or to the police." Above all, Powell was clear, the Supreme Court should release the employer from any special liability for the supervisor under the Civil Rights Act unless the employer knew or should have known what Taylor was up to. When the justices met after the oral arguments, however, Powell found himself voting alone.[18] This was something of a surprise to Powell. He might reasonably have expected at least the most conservative member of the court, William Rehnquist, and probably the chief justice, Warren Burger, to be opposed to the expansive interpretation of the Civil Rights Act. Powell's notes reflect what is now common knowledge about Burger — often, when he found he would be in the minority, he switched his vote to the majority, so that as chief he could pick who wrote the opinion. By the time everyone had voted, Chief Warren Burger had indeed joined the majority,[19] and he had an unexpectedly enticing choice for the opinion — the normally conservative William Rehnquist.

In the end, Rehnquist's opinion was so hostile to *Vinson's* action that even Powell changed his mind and decided to join his conservative colleague.

On the critical matter, Rehnquist stayed with the majority: the Civil Rights Act of 1964 forbade sexual harassment creating a hostile work environment, just as it forbade racial harassment to the same end. The EEOC guidelines on that point, which agency, even under Clarence Thomas's leadership, had not abandoned, were now law. But as to Mechelle Vinson, her case would be sent back to the trial court, with instructions to retry it under the new theory the court had just affirmed. The justices were of one mind that the trial court had not gotten it right. The lower court had to give Vinson a chance to prove her hostile-environment claim. Rehnquist was particularly savage with the trial judge's statement that if Vinson had had sexual relations with Taylor, they were voluntary, calling the incoherent speculation a "finding," in scare quotes. Despite the US government's invitation to consider most plaintiffs lying temptresses in postcoital denial or revenge, "The correct inquiry" the Supreme Court ruled, "is whether respondent, by her conduct, indicated that the alleged sexual advances were unwelcome, not whether her actual participation in sexual intercourse was voluntary." But Rehnquist's opinion took away a lot of what the court of appeals had given Vinson. The trial court would be allowed to consider her alleged "sexually provocative" dress and sexual comportment, distasteful as the Supreme Court obviously considered the whole discussion.

Most seriously, Rehnquist wrote, the brief the solicitor general filed for the EEOC was right. The bank could not be held liable for its supervisor's harassment, without any bad act from the company itself. Since the record in *Vinson* was such a mess, he declined to set down a rule for when the employer would be liable, "but we do agree with the EEOC that Congress wanted courts to look to agency principles for guidance in this area." Rehnquist referred the court to the old common law of masters and servants Judge MacKinnon had suggested all those years ago. As the masters, employers would not always be held liable, Rehnquist continued, but neither would the employee's failure to complain about the harassment always be fatal to her.

The four liberal justices immediately bailed. Justice Stevens remonstrated that employers had been held strictly liable for quid pro quo discrimination, as in Paulette Barnes's case, for years. Most cases involve some mixture of the two claims, and it would be a godawful mess if the standards were different. Thurgood Marshall announced he would be circulating a dissent. Brennan and Blackmun joined Marshall. If the liberals could get a fifth, there would be a majority to hold the bank strictly liable.

Here's where it gets really interesting: Rehnquist sent a memo to the whole court that he would make a sixth vote if Marshall could get a fifth. He didn't want to be the crucial fifth justice (it's called "making a court") for holding employers strictly liable for employees' acts of workplace harassment, but he was uncharacteristically unwilling to be in dissent on this sexual harassment case. He had hopes to be chief justice, and the Senate, which would have to confirm his elevation, was in the hands of the Democrats. And so everyone waited for the crucial swing vote: Sandra Day O'Connor, the first and at that time only woman on the Supreme Court, or the

FWOTSC, as she slyly called herself. Two weeks later, O'Connor signed on to Rehnquist's opinion: employers would not be strictly liable for the acts of their Sidney Taylors.

Indeed, the bank seemed to be perfectly happy with its sexist supervisor; Taylor was still working there eight years after Mechelle Vinson had taken sick leave. After the Supreme Court case, he was caught embezzling. That was considered a serious offense, and the bank fired him.

Meritor v. Vinson established for the nation that sexual harassment creating a hostile work environment is a violation of the Civil Rights Act of 1964. Before the Supreme Court's ruling in the case on June 19, 1986, it was anything but clear whether Taylor's behavior — and the behavior of countless others — was "natural" and a "private" fact of life. In the workplace, at least, the formerly "natural" and "private" sexual conduct was hereafter subject to the law. Since the ruling in *Vinson,* sexual harassment creating a hostile work environment is illegal. For a million reasons — ambition, fear, economic need, racial vulnerability, psychological vulnerability — women fail to assert their right to a harassment-free work environment. But the right is there, like an unexploded land mine.

After the Supreme Court sent her case back for another trial, Mechelle Vinson settled with the bank and used the money to go to nursing school. She told the lawyer who negotiated the settlement that she could at least feel she was doing something to help people, even if she wasn't fighting the bank for yet another round.[20]

Meritor v. Vinson looks like a victory. But it was a dark victory. If only O'Connor had swung the other way. Strict liability makes the employer, which is in the best position to control its high-ranking employees, like supervisors, movie producers, morning anchors, chefs, and shop floor managers, watchful. Instead, employers and employment lawyers set about erecting a scaffolding of protection so they would not have to watch. They sent out policies formally forbidding harassment, they embarked upon training about what to do and not do, they set up human resources departments with procedures in place for lodging complaints — all to show a court, some day, that the employer was not responsible for how its people behaved. Then they stopped watching.

The Incalculable Courage of Black Women

Paulette Barnes, Sandra Bundy, Mechelle Vinson. Although there were white plaintiffs in the handful of cases from the early years,[21] black women fought sexual harassment in the workplace in numbers out of proportion to the general population. They were subject to the disadvantages society attached to their gender. And to their race. And to the intersection of both. Yet they disproportionately led the resistance. As white interns, employees, and aspiring actresses all took it from Harvey Weinstein during the 1970s and early 1980s, these vulnerable women of color stepped up. Why?

There were so many reasons not to. Every aspect of their identity — race, class, gender — conspired to expose these women to poverty. Black women stood on the lowest rung of the ladder of inequality. They did not have a cushion of financial security against the inevitable cost of resisting the harassment. Just look at the facts.

When Paulette Barnes was hired at the EPA, she took an entry-level position, under the federal government category GS-5, paid today at $28,000. Sandra Bundy came to the DC Corrections Department at an even lower level, GS-4. With five children from five marriages, and a bankruptcy in her immediate past, Bundy was at the edge of survival.[22] Mechelle Vinson was a nineteen-year-old high school dropout with a failing teen marriage. It is impossible to understand these women's situations outside of the intersection of gender, race, and class. Their tenuous financial circumstances and entry-level employment were a product of all of these factors.

In a largely segregated American workplace, the early plaintiffs were tormented by black men. When deciding to fight back, then, they had the unique conflict of loyalties between their membership in a racially oppressed group and their right not to be harassed because of sex. In calling out black men on the subject of sex, these women opened themselves up to charges that they were perpetuating a long history of black men being viewed by whites as sexual outlaws. On the ground, however, maybe it was less intimidating than taking on the white patriarchy. Although none of the black male defendants played the race card in the early cases, it was certainly in the deck. And the racial tension was sharpened given that the early black plaintiffs had white lawyers.

As the government brief against Mechelle Vinson shows, black women were in turn heirs to a long tradition in white America of being seen as promiscuous liars. Historian K. Sue Jewell reports that black women were represented as "Jezebels" at least since the institution of slavery, and against all evidence.[23] Thus their claims of sexual abuse, even in the context of the #MeToo movement, have not had the same attention as white women's claims. "Part of it, unfortunately, has to do with whether or not we see black women and girls as worthy of care and worthy of protection," the *Washington Post*'s global opinions editor Karen Attiah commented in 2017.[24] At all levels of the case, decision makers were obsessed with Mechelle Vinson's choice of clothing. They were particularly eager to use it against her to press her to settle after the Supreme Court ruled. "It's always relevant because if you're a black woman you're put in a particular social position by people who know that if you say something others won't take it seriously," MacKinnon has observed. "You're defined as sexually available [. . .] They don't even think of it as a violation," she concludes. "The definition is deep into the white supremacy mindset and black women know that mindset."[25]

With these obstacles pitted against them, where did these black women get the courage? By the 1970s, African Americans had spearheaded decades of racial civil rights activism. The activism emerged from and was nourished by a robust network of churchgoing. Thus was brought to civil rights activism a practice of calling out and testifying against oppression.[26] When Paulette Barnes's boss at the EPA demanded she have sex with him, her first thought was that it was some kind of racial discrimination.[27] Given black women's history in America and Barnes's subordinate position, that wasn't off the mark.

But Barnes had something most other victims of sexual harassment did not have: she lived in Washington, DC. In 1970 the District had a population that was 71 percent black. That percentage had been climbing since before the Great Migration in 1920, but rose especially between 1950 and 1960.[28] DC wasn't a model of racial equality, but the District did desegregate the schools after the *Brown* cases, and there were entry-level government jobs like the one Barnes had.[29] And DC was home to Howard University — a beacon of black higher education, established in 1867 and the source of the legal army that led the civil rights movement — Charles Houston taught at Howard; Thurgood Marshall, Spottswood Robinson, and a host of others were students there.

As during the Civil War, in the mid-twentieth century many in the national government were at the center of civil rights activism against the racial oppression centered in the states. As the movement took increasingly to the streets in the 1960s, President Kennedy asked a group of lawyers, leaders of the bar, including scores of African American lawyers, to set up an organization especially directed at bringing the racial civil rights struggle into the courts. With a handful of staff and the services of idealistic volunteer attorneys from the community, the Lawyers' Committee for Civil Rights Under Law was born.[30] When Paulette Barnes thought she had been the victim of race discrimination in the District of Columbia, the Lawyers' Committee was there, and, as we've seen, it was to the Lawyers' Committee that she went for help.[31] The movements against oppression do not just intersect; they build on the ones that went before.

None of these realities of working while black and female seemed to penetrate the consciousness of the monied, privileged white first woman on the Supreme Court, Sandra Day O'Connor, when she provided the crucial fifth vote to let the employers off the hook in *Meritor v. Vinson*. Had she joined the liberal foursome,

Brennan, Marshall, Stevens, and Blackmun, employers would have been strictly liable for the workplaces where their female employees labored. The banks, federal departments, and universities would have had to hire with care, make sure their supervisors knew the rules against harassment, and be on the lookout for any situations likely to produce lawsuits. Instead, by voting to protect employers, Justice O'Connor joined a decision that put the burden of stopping sexual harassment on the least powerful players, the disproportionately black, working-class women employees. They had to figure out how to complain, they had to risk complaining while still on the job, they had to trust in human resources departments ultimately answerable to the bosses. Nothing speaks louder of the dangers in self-referential white feminism than the crucial vote of the first woman Supreme Court justice in *Meritor v. Vinson.*

Litigating Sexual Harassment Claims

Once the Supreme Court found for Vinson, there ensued a robust stream of litigation about sex in the workplace. The lower courts struggled particularly with two questions *Meritor* left open: (1) under what circumstances could the employer be held responsible (since, according to the opinion, employers were not strictly responsible) and (2) how bad the harassing behavior had to be to amount to a hostile environment. Predictably, the lower-court opinions were all over the map. How much did the employers have to know about their employees' sexual acting out at work? How hard did the harassed employee have to work to rope the employer in to liability for its managers' conduct?

In a pair of relatively garden-variety cases that finally went to the Supreme Court (a secretary who was alternately threatened to provide and implored for sex by a department manager, and a marketer propositioned and threatened by a vice president two levels up), the Seventh Circuit sitting en banc produced *eight* different opinions.[32]

In 1998 the Supreme Court took review of the Seventh Circuit's eight-opinion decision and made another stab at establishing a standard for employer liability. Holding affirmatively that "an employer is subject to vicarious liability to a victimized employee for an actionable hostile environment created by a supervisor with immediate (or successively higher) authority over the employee," the Supreme Court then cut back on the good news: "a defending employer may raise an affirmative defense to liability or damages" provided that the employer exercised "reasonable care to prevent and correct promptly any sexually harassing behavior, and that the plaintiff employee unreasonably failed to take advantage of any preventive or corrective opportunities provided by the employer or to avoid harm otherwise."[33]

As we have seen, the employer's duty to prevent harassment the Supreme Court outlined in 1998 has been interpreted by lower courts to include three possible elements: formal antiharassment policies, antiharassment training, and miscellaneous preventative measures like posting the policies and requiring managers to sign off on them.[34] And before you could say "corrupt employer toady," every company over fifteen employees in America that had not set up an HR department in 1986 after *Vinson* set one up. They published formal policies and established structures to investigate accusations.[35]

Employers held antiharassment training programs often run by their lawyers. But lawyers and consultants who conduct training represent the employer and may therefore predictably hesitate to give advice to employees that will have the effect of structuring and preserving a cause of action against the employer. Should the case go to court, the human resources department will be the witness for the employer. Studies reflect that HR employees are embarrassed, they are untrained, they are unsympathetic with the accused, they fear disrupting the workplace, and they are reluctant to label something as discrimination.[36] High-profile employment lawyer Nancy Erika Smith characterizes HR's role in sex harassment cases as protecting the abusive men who run — or just work for — the company.[37]

But regardless of the defects in the procedures, after the decisions interpreting *Meritor v. Vinson*, any complaining employee had to start there, or no employers' deep pockets would ever be available to them. It's a real catch-22.

Since *Meritor*, academics have studied the effectiveness of the employer's defensive institutions to alert the employer that it has a problem. A 1995 study showed that employees were not complaining at any higher rates than they had in 1980, six years before *Meritor* even came down.[38] As of 2003, scholar Joanna Grossman reported, "cookie-cutter sexual harassment policies and procedures do not seem to have any reliably negative effect on the incidence of harassment."[39]

The entire seemingly useless system is set up alongside the strategies real people actually use when harassment surfaces. Here's what studies show people (women) really do.[40] They ignore the harassment, pretend it is not happening, reinterpret it as not harassment, and blame themselves. More healthily they avoid the harasser if they can, or appease him if they cannot. They talk to friends. Some women even confront the harasser before they go to HR.

As we will see, after forty years of silence, starting in October 2017, eighty-two women from the entertainment world would come forward to tell their stories of Harvey Weinstein's harassing ways.[41] But as evidence of how useless the system was, we must look at the decades *before* October 2017 to see what these women did when abused. In 1991 Laura Madden, then an employee, kept asking herself if Weinstein's assault was something she'd brought on herself. Madden told a friend about the incident. Actress Ashley Judd told her mother. Actress Sophie Dix, who told everyone in her circle — friends, family, people in the film she was in — that Harvey Weinstein attacked her, watched her career go downhill. So did Rosanna Arquette, who rejected him. Angie Everhardt told several people on the boat in the Venetian waters at the Venice Film Festival. "No one wanted to do anything about it because everyone was afraid of Harvey."[42] Actress Lauren Holly informed industry contacts. Lena Headey got into her car and cried.

The court's requirement that an employee complain to the boss — or his HR department — in order to sue the company mandated that the employee do the one thing she was least likely to do under the circumstances.

It Has to Get So Bad

The courts were equally ineffective in reining in most bad conduct. While the Supreme Court was considering Mechelle Vinson's case, Charles Hardy, the president of Forklift Systems of Nashville, Tennessee,[43] often told his manager, Teresa Harris, "You're a woman, what do you know?" and "We need a man as the rental manager." At least once, he told her she was "a dumb-ass woman." He proposed that the two of them go to the Holiday Inn to negotiate her raise. And it wasn't only Harris. Hardy asked other female employees to retrieve coins from his front pants pocket and threw stuff on the ground in front of them and then asked them to bend over and pick it up. In mid-August 1987 Harris complained to Hardy about his conduct. Hardy said he was surprised that Harris was offended, claimed he was only joking, and apologized. Shortly thereafter, while Harris was arranging a deal with one of Forklift's customers, he asked her, again in front of other employees, "What did you do, promise to bugger the guy?"[44] On October 1, Harris collected her paycheck and quit. Then she sued. Hardy had never touched her. Except through her eyes and ears.

The lower courts ruled against Harris. Sure, Hardy was obnoxious and a reasonable woman would be offended by his behavior. But the standard had to be higher than that. Echoing back to the conservative arguments in Mechelle Vinson's case five years before, the courts worried that they'd be flooded with tearful women. No woman could sue, they ruled, unless the behavior would interfere with a reasonable woman's work performance. They didn't think Harris would reasonably have suffered severe psychological injury from Hardy's badinage. Apparently, the court thought, having the

boss ask you if you were buggering a customer in front of the customer would not interfere with a woman's work performance or in-
jure her severely.

In 1993 the Supreme Court reversed, unanimously. A plaintiff
should not have to endure severe psychological injury to state a
claim for harassment. But how bad *did* it have to get? Although the
court had just sworn in the leading expert on sex discrimination in
the world, Justice Ruth Bader Ginsburg, Chief Justice Rehnquist assigned the opinion to his *first* woman, Sandra Day O'Connor. And
once again, as in her majority-producing vote in *Meritor v. Vinson,*
O'Connor produced an opinion that was formally on the side of the
woman, but actually not helpful. To state a claim, the behavior had
to be sufficiently "severe or pervasive" to create a discriminatorily
hostile or abusive working environment. (In the opinion, Justice
O'Connor describes the question about buggering as asking about
"some sex.") Um, no, newly appointed Justice Ginsburg responded,
in her first writing for the high court. Why not just ask if the offending behavior makes it harder for a reasonable person to do her
job at the Forklift desk? Since Ginsburg agreed with the unanimous
decision to reverse the lower court decision, her opinion is technically a concurrence. And so "severe and pervasive" became the order of the day.

Again the company settled. Was Hardy's behavior "severe and
pervasive"? Since 1993 the lower courts have had ample opportunity
to explain what Justice O'Connor's language means. And it's not
pretty. Most federal courts require actual sexual touching, which
would be assault and battery in any state, and also that the severe
touching be repeated several times or by several people or both.
The opinions in which the courts were not offended makes for re-
volting reading.[45]

Patting on the buttocks, grabbing the plaintiff's crotch, making her watch while he "self-stimulated," attempted kissing — not
enough. A forty-year-old coworker followed two seventeen-year-
olds, blowing kisses, making obscene gestures, touching one on the

chest, kissing, hugging, asking the other for dates — not severe and pervasive, another district court ruled. Touching, touching, touching, attempted kisses, I LOVE YOU signs — the cases are overflowing with sexual behavior the courts considered trivial or isolated.[46]

But the country was about to undergo a national televised tutorial in just what a severely and pervasively abusive workplace looks like.

5

Anita Hill and Clarence Thomas
Confirming Harassment
1991

Filling Civil Rights Hero Thurgood Marshall's Seat

Five years after the Supreme Court decision in *Meritor v. Vinson*, University of Oklahoma law professor Anita Hill learned that her harassing former boss at the EEOC, Clarence Thomas, was next in line for a seat on the United States Supreme Court. It took a while, but finally Hill's conscience got the best of her, and she started talking about her experience with Thomas to more and more people who might pass it on to the Senate Judiciary Committee. Predictably, someone passed it on.[1]

The Judiciary Committee didn't want to hear from her. The Republicans on the committee, a minority at that time, certainly didn't want to hear bad things about their nominee for the Supreme Court vacancy. Committee chairman Joe Biden did not want his hearings disrupted. Nor, to varying degrees, did Democratic members Howard Metzenbaum, Dennis DeConcini, Patrick Leahy, Howell Heflin, Paul Simon, or Herb Kohl want to hear from Anita Hill. Ted Kennedy, especially, did not.[2]

At first, this behavior seems odd. In 1986 the Democrats had taken over the Senate for the first time since the Reagan Revolution in 1980, and in 1987 they waged a stunning and successful campaign to defeat Supreme Court nominee Robert Bork. Bork mattered: he would likely have been the crucial fifth vote to overturn or severely limit abortion rights. As Reagan put one justice after another on the court, the margin in support of *Roe v. Wade* had kept narrowing. Now it was down to four reliable votes.

It's not at all clear that Bork's record opposing abortion by itself would have brought the judge down. The Senate had easily confirmed Justice Scalia, for example, and Scalia had held the same view. True, the Bork nomination was presented as more frankly anti-abortion than Scalia's, but Bork also denied there were constitutional protections for birth control. Birth control was at the heart of the sexual revolution, which obviously benefited men. Without it, sex would once again be heavily confined to traditional marriage, the conservative framework for sex. Liberal men in the Senate certainly didn't want that to happen.

After Bork, and with Ronald Reagan nearing the end of his term, Democrats hoped that the election of 1988 might be the end of the Republican nomination train. In many ways, for feminists, any Democratic president would do. Unlike the Republicans, the Democrats' platform supported abortion rights; they weren't going to overturn *Roe.* Democrats had a real contender, a brilliant and handsome John F. Kennedy wannabe in Colorado cowboy boots, Senator Gary Hart. At one point in 1987 Hart was polling ahead of Vice President George H. W. Bush by double digits.

One wonders how different post-1960s American political history would be if John F. Kennedy had kept his fly zipped. Hart, who came of age in the Kennedy era, idolized the handsome, dashing president.[3] But like JFK and his brother Ted Kennedy, the pro-choice candidate Hart had a woman problem. According to news sources he had been screwing around for years after he married his wife, Lee, in 1958.[4] When the *New York Times* political reporter E. J. Dionne Jr. asked Hart about the rumors in 1987, the candidate was indignant. He challenged the press to follow him around and see how boring his life was. A few days later, an anonymous woman called the editor of the *Miami Herald,* asking if the paper would pay for incriminating photographs. Instead *Herald* editor Jim McGee flew to DC and staked out Hart's townhouse. The next night he caught the candidate returning to the townhouse accompanied by Florida party girl Donna Rice. McGee never saw her leave and assumed she was still there the next morning.[5] But Hart's campaign was over. And the *Herald* reporters were strutting around like Woodward and Bernstein. It was the first time a presidential candidate had been derailed by a sex scandal not involving the death of the woman in question. Betty Friedan was quoted as saying it was the last time a candidate would get away with treating women like bimbos. The Democrats nominated the scandal-free governor of Massachusetts, Michael Dukakis. George H. W. Bush beat him by eight points.

With the 1988 presidential election, the Republicans had four more years to shape the Supreme Court. Bush's first appointment, New Hampshire moderate David Souter, sailed through confirmation in the Senate, but Bush's conservative supporters were irate, believing that the chance to put a movement conservative like Bork on the court had been missed. Bush promised them the next nomination would be theirs. Problem was, like Bork, most candidates favored by the conservatives left an ideological paper trail, and Bush was determined that his nominee not suffer Bork's fate. The Bush White House well knew that a campaign against a black judge to succeed Thurgood Marshall would be a lot harder for liberals to pull off. Not surprisingly, given the Republican Party's pursuit of their racist Southern strategy since 1968, there were not a lot of black Republicans to choose from. Clarence Thomas, newly appointed to the DC Circuit, was on a very short list.

Clarence Thomas, a Short History

Born in 1948 to an impoverished woman in Pin Point, Georgia, Thomas was one of the first generation of black Americans to come

of age after the desegregation decision in *Brown* in 1954.⁶ Deserted
by his father, from the age of six he and his brother lived with his
grandfather. In the poor and segregated South, Thomas's grandfather had gotten a leg up. Starting with a pushcart, Myers Anderson
developed a fuel and ice delivery business and built himself a tidy
bungalow.⁷ He sent his grandsons to a segregated but exemplary
Catholic parochial school. Contemporaries reported the loveless,
excessively strict upbringing his strong-willed grandfather provided
Thomas, and his mother, who was sidelined, spoke of the stubborn,
willful character her son developed in turn. But Anderson's industry and commitment allowed his advantages to be passed on to the
next generation. Clarence thought he might become a priest. Two
years into high school, he transferred to a newly integrated Catholic seminary and then went to a small town in Missouri for another
year of study for the priesthood. He was one of two black students.
He found the racial prejudice he encountered there so intense that
he left both the seminary and the Catholic religion. His grandfather
took this as a denunciation and cut him off, but it was 1968, and a
progressive Catholic college, Holy Cross, in Worcester, Massachusetts, gave him a scholarship. He graduated ninth in his class at Holy
Cross, proving himself, he said, to those who had denigrated him
as a mere affirmative action baby. The day after graduation, he married his first wife.

Although Thomas has denied it, he was admitted to Yale Law
School just as the school embarked on an ambitious program of
affirmative action. Affirmative action or not, Thomas again felt
disparaged by his white classmates. After Yale, he thought he'd go
into private practice and make a lot of money. To his surprise,
the big Georgia law firms hadn't even desegregated, let alone embraced affirmative action. He got no offers. Which turned out to
be a blessing in disguise, because when old-school Rockefeller
Republican John Danforth, the attorney general of Missouri,
went to his alma mater, Yale, looking for a black lawyer to add
to his staff, Thomas was a natural choice. Thomas, who had previously identified as a Democrat, moved to Jefferson City, Mis-

souri, with his wife and new baby son. And registered as a Republican.

Three years later, Danforth went to the United States Senate, and Thomas, briefly, to Monsanto Chemical in Missouri. But in 1979 Danforth, ever mindful of the racial makeup of his office, invited Thomas to DC. Thomas accepted, but only after Danforth promised he'd be working on issues like the environment, nothing to do with race. When Thomas got to DC, he continued his journey rightward, reading the works of the black conservative intellectual Thomas Sowell and networking with an obscure black conservative think tank run by one J.A. ("Jay") Parker. One year after Thomas reached out to Parker, Reagan counselor Edwin Meese picked Parker to head the Reagan administration transition team at the EEOC. Would Thomas help Parker set the agenda for the agency under new conservative leadership? Reagan's Morning in America would be a new day in Washington, too.

As we've seen, one of several memos Thomas wrote for the Reagan transition concerned the new EEOC guidelines Mechelle Vinson had used in the lower courts, rules that categorized unwelcome sexual attention creating a hostile environment as sex discrimination. The amended guidelines would lead to a barrage of trivial complaints, Thomas's transition memo suggested, adding that such efforts to rein in workplace harassment were largely futile. Although working on matters of discrimination, Thomas was vocal in his intent not to move into the new administration to work on race matters. He wanted to succeed without regard to race; that was the touchstone.

But when the Reaganites offered him the job of assistant secretary for civil rights in the Department of Education, he could not resist the lure of the big job. Meanwhile, he and his wife divorced, and he moved onto the couch in his friend Gil Hardy's apartment. Was Thomas staffing up at the new job? Hardy wondered. He had a recommendation for his temporary roommate: an associate at Hardy's law firm wanted to go into government. Her name was Anita Hill. In July 1981 Thomas hired her.[8]

Anita Hill, a Short History

Anita Hill was born in a tiny cluster of houses called Lone Tree, Oklahoma, two years after the Supreme Court decision in *Brown*. She was the youngest of thirteen children of a farm family, one of the few black farm families left in America in 1955. Because Anita was the youngest, born after a four-year hiatus following decades in which her mother birthed babies every other year, she was the doted on pet of the family. Unlike her other siblings, she got a full dose of her mother's undivided attention. She used it to play endless word games, suggesting combinations of letters that might or might not be actual words, until her mother begged her to stop. The quiet, bespectacled, bookish little girl walked a half mile to the bus stop to travel to the local elementary school, where grades one through four studied together in a room with one teacher and grades five through eight gathered in a second room with another. There were few children in the area, and the school served pupils both black and white. Weekends, she and her mother sowed and harvested peanuts—backbreaking, filthy work. "We were," Hill wrote in her memoir, "farm people. Our family outings consisted of going to church and prayer meeting, visiting nearby relatives, the yearly all-black rodeo."[9]

Hill went on to attend the recently integrated Morris High School in the small (white) town nearby, where she graduated first in her class in 1973. From there it was a short road to Oklahoma State University in Stillwater, and then to Yale. Neither of her parents had graduated from high school. Although she found Yale intimidating at first and never felt quite at home throughout her time there, she adjusted to law school, made friends, and set a course for herself, first to work off the student debt she had accumulated. She moved to DC, went to work for a law firm, and palled around with old friends from Yale living in DC and with other associates at the law firm.

But she was not happy at Wald, Harkrader & Ross. No one mentored her, she did not receive plum assignments, and her first performance reviews were mixed. One day on a walk to work, a senior associate at the firm, Gilbert Hardy, who had recruited her from Yale, invited her to a party at his place. There she met Clarence Thomas. A few weeks later Thomas offered her a job as his assistant.

Anita Hill and Clarence Thomas

Hill had been working as Thomas's personal assistant at the Department of Education for less than a year when President Reagan nominated him to be the new chairman of the EEOC. Shortly after he was confirmed, in May 1982, Hill followed him to the new job. Ten months later, in March 1983, Hill traveled with Thomas to Tulsa, Oklahoma, where Thomas was speaking at the law school of Oral Roberts University. During her visit, the law school dean, Charles Kothe, a great friend of Thomas's, invited her to join the faculty there. Oral Roberts was so deeply enmeshed with the fundamentalist movement that the American Bar Association was threatening to deny its accreditation. It would hardly be an obvious career move for Hill. But she accepted. By July 1983 Anita Hill was gone from Clarence Thomas's life. They had worked together for exactly two years.

After Hill left for Tulsa, Thomas's star continued to rise. Renominated to the chairmanship, he stayed at the EEOC until 1990. During that time, the EEOC moved distinctly to the right, culminating in its role in the Justice Department brief siding with the bank in *Meritor v. Vinson*. When George H. W. Bush succeeded Reagan in 1988, Thomas pursued a strategic plan to put himself in the running for the Supreme Court.[10] First he had to find his way to the intermediate court, the feeder for the high tribunal, the DC Circuit. His campaign for the circuit court seat was a preview of the ultimate campaign. He mobilized his conservative allies, and he made a series of courtesy calls on the NAACP and other civil rights groups he had ignored up to that time. The campaign went like clockwork, even capturing the support of the fragile "centrist" Democrats led by Georgia's own senator Sam Nunn. Who could resist the striver from Pin Point? Thomas had not been on the DC Circuit two years when Thurgood Marshall announced he would step down.

Marshall, a shrewd thinker even at the end of his life, did not want to be replaced by a conservative, whatever his skin color. "There's no difference," Marshall told the press at his farewell appearance, "between a white snake and a black snake. They'll both bite."[11] But from the standpoint of the Bush administration there was every reason to nominate an African American who would be conservative enough to satisfy Bush's increasingly restive right wing.[12] Thomas was perfect. Bush, like many elites a sucker for someone else's Horatio Alger story, loved the Pin Point, Georgia, tale. But the White House was taking no chances. It hired a pricey private consulting firm led by Kenneth Duberstein, Ronald Reagan's former chief of staff, to run the nomination.

For the first weeks of Thomas's nomination, the decision paid off handsomely.[13] Critically, the NAACP held its fire, telling a friendly reporter only that it would consider Bush's nominee without undue haste.[14] The NAACP's silence silenced other groups — the ones that had taken down Robert Bork with surgical precision. When savvier players, like Barbara Arnwine of the Lawyer's Committee, started pressuring groups on the left — divided and paralyzed by the optics of opposing a seemingly qualified black nominee — the Republicans, not taken by surprise this time, fought a brilliant ground game. White fundamentalists like Gary Bauer helped organize a "spontaneous" demonstration of blacks from Thomas's hometown to march on Washington, and other white fundamentalists working with the White House created an ad campaign to portray the opposition to Thomas as racism of the left.[15] The Senate Judiciary Committee hearings were scheduled to begin as soon as Congress reconvened, in September 1991.

The Gathering Storm

On Labor Day weekend, Floyd Brown, a conservative activist, released a TV attack ad, "Who Will Judge the Judge?"[16] Brown was responsible for the infamous commercial in the 1988 presidential campaign blaming the "soft on crime" Massachusetts governor Michael Dukakis for a furlough program that enabled the release from prison of a black inmate, first-degree murderer Willie Horton, who did not return from furlough and committed a series of crimes including rape before he was captured. Horton's threatening mug shot was prominently featured in the ad, which drew charges of racism. The Bush campaign distanced itself from Brown at the time, but the Republicans' scorched-earth strategy was laid down. This time, Brown's ad proclaimed itself as "a shot across the bow." If the liberal special interest groups and their allies on Capitol Hill want to have a battle, we're ready to go. After a brief paean to Pin Point, the spot shifted to "liberal Senate Democrats. How many of these Democrats could stand up to scrutiny?" the ad asked. "Teddy Kennedy? Suspended from Harvard for cheating, left the scene of the crime at Chappaquiddick where Mary Jo Kopechne died?"

The ad then showed a tabloid newspaper headline, "Teddy's Sexy Romp." As Thomas was about to go to hearing, Kennedy's nephew, William Kennedy Smith, was about to go to trial for rape allegedly committed against a woman he picked up in a bar in Palm Beach in March. The senator was a key witness in the rape case, because it was he who had gathered up the defendant and his cousin, Ted's son Patrick Kennedy, to go drinking until the wee hours of the morning. Kennedy had just returned to Washington after testifying before a Palm Beach grand jury. The ad took a shorter swipe at "Joe Biden, found guilty of plagiarism during his presidential campaign." Over the holiday weekend the Democrats were spending all their fuel defending Teddy Kennedy in the face of renewed media attention on the senator's philandering behavior. There is no reason to believe that Brown or any of the Republicans had any hint of Thomas's still-unannounced sexual harassment troubles. They just wanted to neutralize resistance to Thomas's nomination from Kennedy and other liberal Democrats in advance of the Supreme Court confirmation.

They had good reason. Last time, less than an hour after President Reagan nominated Robert Bork in 1987, Senator Kennedy fired the opening shot: "Robert Bork's America is a land in which women would be forced into back-alley abortions, blacks would sit at segregated lunch counters, rogue police would break down citizens' doors in midnight raids . . ."[17] Years later, journalist Michael Kelly reported in 1990, Bork was still furious, and even Kennedy's partner in stopping Bork, Joe Biden, called the speech "unfair."[18]

Four years after Bork's failed nomination, on Tuesday, September 10, 1991, Clarence Thomas sat down at the witness table for his Senate confirmation hearings. Each senator on the committee, mostly Democrats in a majority-Democratic Senate, could ask him questions. He expected to be asked about many things: his personal story, his education, his experience, and most of all his thinking on controversial legal issues. Chief among them were the perennials — abortion and affirmative action. His writings and decisions had already shown him as a conservative on most subjects. His goal was to get through the hearings without giving liberals any additional ammunition by which to derail his nomination.

He had no reason to believe that he would be asked to answer for his behavior toward his assistant from years ago, Anita Hill.[19] Since Hill had gone off to teach in Oklahoma in 1983, he had won confirmation to the DC Court of Appeals, without a peep from her. But unbeknownst to Clarence Thomas, as the news of his nomination spread to Norman, Oklahoma, that summer, the thought of his appointment to the high court was starting to give Hill pause. In July she made one of her periodic phone calls to an old Yale friend, Gary Phillips. When he asked her what she thought of her former boss's ascension, she told him she had left her job with Thomas because of his years-long campaign of vulgar and relentless sexual harassment. Phillips was not the first person Hill had told; she had confided at the time and over the years to others.

But Phillips was the first DC player to hear Hill's story. A lawyer at the Federal Communications Commission, he mentioned his conversation with Hill to his bridge club, although he did not name her. After all, Hill hadn't asked him to keep the story quiet. A card player shared it at a Washington dinner party. Someone called the famed liberal lobbyist Nan Aron from the Alliance for Justice, who figured it out and alerted a friend at Judiciary Committee member Howard Metzenbaum's office. Bill Corr, chief counsel to a Judiciary subcommittee chaired by Metzenbaum, was not eager to bother the senator, who was over seventy and notoriously straitlaced. Someone else hinted to another Metzenbaum aide. Meanwhile, a Kennedy aide, Ricki Seidman, had gotten wind of something involving Thomas and trips to Oklahoma. With agonizing slowness, in August the story started to gather steam.

On September 5, Metzenbaum's office dispatched a young black female NYU Law School grad, Gail Laster, to—news flash—call Anita Hill directly. Then Senate staffers located a staff member, James Brudney, who actually knew Anita Hill at Yale; she agreed to speak with him. In a telephone interview, she laid out the basic facts of her experience with Clarence Thomas, how in the office he discussed in lascivious detail the pornography he watched, describing women with huge breasts and people having sex with animals. He commented on Hill's appearance, pressed her for dates, boasted of his sexual prowess, and generally subjected his employees to an endless stream of dirty sex talk. In one instance, he went to his desk for a soda, picked up the can, and said, "Who has put pubic hair on my Coke?"

As James Brudney, offstage on the morning of September 10, was getting this salacious story from the former Yale classmate he vaguely remembered, Clarence Thomas took the witness seat. Across the green draped table, the members of the Senate Judiciary Committee looked out, ready to decide if Clarence Thomas should sit for life on the highest court in the land.

Who Will Judge the Judges?

JOSEPH BIDEN, CHAIRMAN

Early in Joe Biden's first term as the senator from Delaware, in 1972, his bighearted fellow senator Ted Kennedy popped into his office.[20] Everyone in the Senate was being particularly solicitous of the young new member. A month after Biden was elected, his beloved wife and young daughter were killed in a horrible automobile accident; his two young sons, injured in the crash, were still hospitalized. Come to the Senate gym, Joe, Kennedy proposed. I don't feel like working out, Biden answered. Not that kind of gym, Kennedy answered. This is an old-man's gym, get a massage, sit in the steam. You need to meet your colleagues. And so Biden went. Senator Barbara Mikulski ("Do I look like a gym rat to you?"[21]) later remembered the Senate gym as the place where the guys roamed around the steam room making deals. Two decades later, as the Anita Hill charges surfaced, Republican John Danforth and Joe Biden ran into each other in the collegial locker room, and Biden gave Danforth his word that any hearing on Anita Hill's accusations would be very quick. When urged by Mikulski and his female colleagues from the House to take Hill's accusations seriously and set up proper hearings, Biden pointed his finger at the women and said he had made a commitment to his Republican colleague to expedite the hearing.[22] Keeping his locker room promise to Danforth was more important to Biden than any accusation from Anita Hill.

President of his high school class, Biden was known as someone who cared passionately about being liked and was powerfully disinclined to judge his friends for personal indiscretions.[23] In 1971, at the age of twenty-eight, a desperately marginal Democratic Party had asked him to run against the incumbent Republican for the Delaware Senate seat. With the overconfident senator paying no attention to the race, the likable Biden scored an upset and became a member of the Senate club. Biden may look like a liberal now, but for most of his career he was known as something of a centrist Democrat. A Catholic from an anti-abortion state, he supported *Roe v. Wade* but opposed using federal funds to pay for abortion.

Late in the summer of 1987 Biden had been the subject of hostile press coverage of his unsuccessful run for the presidential nomination. After taking down Gary Hart for his philandering, the press caught Biden using a chunk of a speech from British politician Neil

Kinnock without crediting Kinnock. Then they nosed around in his (unimpressive) law school record and found an instance in which he had been accused of plagiarism (he was later cleared). Two decades later, Biden recalled feeling he'd been dishonored unfairly and badly treated by an unsympathetic media. In his 2007 memoir, *Promises to Keep,* he calls the Washington press corps the "Big Feet." When he sat down to run the hearings on the Clarence Thomas nomination, the dishonor still smarted. Biden didn't like a nasty fight, and the last thing he and the other Democrats wanted was an attack by a lily-white Senate on the character of a black nominee.

Biden considered himself a friend to women. He certainly had reason to be, since his whole life was made possible by women who had put his career first. Before she died in 1972, his young first wife, Neilia, ran their real estate business, raised their three children all under the age of five, and managed his organizational and entertainment efforts as Biden was just getting started in politics. Her well-to-do family quietly made it possible for him to pay the bills while running for the Senate.[24] All of Joe's campaigns, starting with his run for high school class president, were managed by his sister, Valerie. When he decided to take his Senate seat after the accident, while his two young sons were still in the hospital, Val moved in to take care of the family. Her first marriage ending, Biden's sister fetched the boys from school and organized the meals and all the medical care.

Three years after Biden's terrible loss, he saw a picture of a beautiful blonde on a billboard in the Wilmington, Delaware, airport. *Now that's just the kind of woman I'd like to meet,* he thought to himself, looking at her photograph. When he met her, he found out she cared nothing for politics. But once married to Joe, Jill Biden became as skillful and supportive as the other important women in his life. By 1991 Biden had been working for a year with a Senate Judiciary staffer on a crime bill to address domestic violence against women. The senator was horrified by reports of women being raped or assaulted in the home. By the time of the Clarence Thomas hearings, Biden had not gotten very far with the initiative. He was surprised that the "inside the Beltway women's groups" did not rally behind him. They didn't trust him, he believed, because he was not fully pro-choice.[25]

Kind, accustomed to supportive women, obsessed with being liked, and suspicious of the media and of organized political feminists, Biden was a mixed bag for chairman of the Senate Judiciary Committee when Anita Hill finally decided to go public with her harassment allegations against Clarence Thomas.

TED KENNEDY

Michael Kelly's classic 1990 article about the senator, "Ted Kennedy on the Rocks," foreshadowed Kennedy's performance in the Judiciary Committee's Hill/Thomas hearings one year later.

In 1987 Kennedy had been the man. Without Kennedy's aggressive personal lobbying (with the help of hundreds of civil rights leaders and liberal activists) against the Bork nomination, the candidate probably would have been confirmed. But that was then.

By 1991 Kennedy was, as Kelly portrayed him so graphically—"The skin has gone from red roses to gin blossoms. The tracery of burst capillaries shines faintly through the scaly scarlet patches that cover the bloated, mottled cheeks"—on the rocks.[26] Kennedy's drinking, Kelly reports, started in earnest after Teddy's second brother, Robert Kennedy, was murdered in 1968. But the philandering was ancestral. The family patriarch, Joseph P. Kennedy, was a legendary womanizer, flaunting a Hollywood screen star mistress and hitting on his sons' dates when well past his sell-by. Kelly relays that Ted Kennedy was having sex with other women almost from the day he married his first wife, Joan, in 1958. Certainly by 1979, journalist Suzanna Lessard, writing about Kennedy's unsuccessful presidential run, could reliably state that "within the world of politics and journalism, Kennedy's womanizing is widely known—to the many women who have been approached themselves, for example, and to reporters and others who have been around Kennedy and have seen the pattern in action. While I was talking to people for this article, it seemed as if almost everybody in that world had another anecdote to offer."[27]

Kelly detailed some of those anecdotes. The most memorable is a 1985 episode that the journalist called "Brasserie I," after the classic DC power broker watering hole. (The implication that there were more Brasserie incidents was intentional.) A "pretty" waitress at the Brasserie confirmed that Kennedy and his sidekick, Senator Chris Dodd, had summoned her to a private room at the restaurant. "The six-foot-two, 225-plus-pound Kennedy grabs the five-foot-three, 103-pound waitress and throws her on the table. She lands on her back, scattering crystal, plates and cutlery and the lit candles. Several glasses and a crystal candlestick are broken. Kennedy then picks her up from the table and throws her on Dodd, who is sprawled in a chair . . . Kennedy jumps on top and begins rubbing his genital area against hers, supporting his weight on the arms of the chair. As he is doing this, [a supervisor] enters the room." The women "start to scream, drawing one or two dishwashers. Startled, Kennedy leaps up. He laughs. Bruised, shaken and angry over what she considered a sexual assault, the waitress runs from the room. Kennedy, Dodd and their dates leave shortly thereafter, following a friendly argument between the senators over the check." And that's just Brasserie I.[28]

By 1991 Kennedy's record of liberal activism on women's issues had been seriously tarnished by his long and sordid reputation for sexual misdeeds. As the Hill/Thomas hearings played out, Ted Kennedy was largely silent.

THE REST

Turns out the fourteen members of the Judiciary Committee were not men inclined to sympathize with media-driven accusations of bad behavior. On the Democratic side, Senator Howard Metzenbaum of Ohio, who could be rabid in his public criticism of congressional colleagues' antics, got caught owning a DC restaurant that didn't pay all its taxes. Vermont's rock-solid Senator Patrick Leahy had to quit the Intelligence Committee when it was discovered he shared with a reporter a document the committee had deemed confidential. Arizona's Dennis DeConcini was one of the "Keating Five" — senators who were accused of improperly helping fallen thrift executive Charles Keating. At the very least, the Senate Ethics Committee had concluded, DeConcini's actions gave the impression of impropriety.[29]

Dance Like Everyone's Watching

Luckily for all these vulnerable liberals, nothing in the first round of hearings on Thomas's nomination remotely approximated the fight over Robert Bork. The most dramatic moment in the hearings came on September 11, the second day, when Patrick Leahy pressed Thomas on how it was possible he hadn't given much thought to the abortion decision, *Roe v. Wade*, which was handed down while he was in law school.[30] Nope, Thomas answered, never did.

Meanwhile, however, behind the scenes, Metzenbaum aide James Brudney took the Anita Hill story to Harriet Grant, the chief counsel to Senator Biden's nominations unit. Grant was less than interested in Anita Hill's story. If the witness were that eager to come forward, Grant said, she should just call the Senate herself. Hill thought this procedure somewhat strange. But on September 12, as Thomas testified on, she did talk to Grant, indicating her desire not to be publicly identified. To her credit, Grant impressed on Hill that it would be impossible for her to remain anonymous; she would have to confront Thomas directly. Grant informed Biden's chief counsel, Ron Klain, about her conversation with Hill, and Klain immediately went to Biden. Can't look into it unless Thomas gets a chance to confront his accuser, Biden said.

The hearings droned on, Biden's inquiries so extensive and convoluted Thomas seemed unable to remember exactly what the question was when it came time for him to answer.[31] On Friday, the thirteenth, Thomas wrapped up, and the following week interest groups started presenting their witnesses for and against him. Unlike with the Bork process, there weren't many opponents. On Tuesday the seventeenth the octogenarian Erwin Griswold, the former dean of Harvard Law School, had the temerity to suggest Thomas was unqualified for the Supreme Court,[32] but no one else wanted to be heard picking that fight. All seemed quiet on the confirmation front.

If liberals unhappy with Thomas's conservative jurisprudence ever got wind of what Anita Hill was murmuring behind the scenes, however, there would be the fight of a lifetime. And that's exactly what happened. Brudney, the Metzenbaum aide, was trying to walk Hill through the legal questions in her claims, like whether sexual harassment had to involve unwanted touching. He called in a classic player from the early days of feminism, Professor Susan Deller Ross, author of the casebook on women and the law that anchored the course MacKinnon took at Yale Law School all those years ago. And Ross called Judith Lichtman, who had represented the first harassment plaintiff, Paulette Barnes, after her boss fired her for not putting out. With Lichtman and her activists at their backs, staffers sympathetic to victims of workplace harassment, working at the offices of paralyzed or indifferent Democratic senators, became more and more agitated. Hill said she hadn't understood before why it was necessary to come forward, but she was now willing to do so. Someone had to push Biden. It fell to Leahy. After Leahy spoke to the chairman, Biden agreed. He would send the FBI to talk to Anita Hill.

But when she heard this, Hill balked. She would talk to the FBI, but she insisted on telling her story in her own words as well. On Monday, September 23, Hill's four-page typed statement rolled off the congressional fax machine in all its graphic detail. The statement culminated in Hill's memory of Thomas telling her that if she ever talked, it could ruin his career. Harriet Grant took a copy to the counsel for Republican senator Strom Thurmond, and Biden informed the White House. Two days later, on September 25, the White House contacted Clarence Thomas. New charges had arisen, and the FBI would be coming to talk to him.

Everyone's Watching

The hearings, however, were over by then, and the committee scheduled a vote on Thomas for Friday, September 27.

As the date for the vote approached, Biden still hadn't distributed Hill's statement to the rest of the Judiciary Committee. Seeing the days tick past toward the vote on confirmation, and now committed to her path, Hill began to rattle her own network. A friend told liberal Illinois senator Paul Simon. A Hill friend had reached out to Harvard professor Charles Ogletree, who told his Harvard colleague Laurence Tribe. Tribe, not shy, called Biden. Finally, Biden decided to share Hill's statement with all his Democratic colleagues on the committee. They were reading that statement when they filed in to vote that Friday. NPR Supreme Court reporter Nina Totenberg was there. What were they all looking at? Totenberg wondered.[33] Then the committee vote broke 7 to 7, much less support for Thomas than court observers had anticipated. At the time, Supreme Court nominees on track for confirmation attracted robust bipartisan support. Still, the committee voted unanimously to send Thomas's nomination to the full Senate, without its endorsement. And then Senator Biden made an odd speech about how the committee's deadlock was completely unrelated to the nominee's character. Knowing that the nominee's character had not been at issue during the hearings, Totenberg was baffled. "I smelled dead fish stinking here," she recalls, "and I started beating the bushes really hard." She was in the bushes for a week, but it didn't take Totenberg long to find out what was behind the sudden drop in support for Clarence Thomas.

By the time Totenberg got to Anita Hill herself, she was pretty sure the law professor was a serious woman with a fine record. But Hill refused to talk to Totenberg unless she had obtained a copy of Hill's affidavit. Hill wasn't going to leak the official developments to the press. And Charles Ogletree, now Hill's main legal adviser, had assured Hill that Totenberg wouldn't be able to get access to the document. Totenberg knew differently. "I'm a reporter!" she recalls. "This is catnip. Remember, I was married to a former United States senator. I'm calling." She got the affidavit, and she got an interview with Anita Hill. But she wasn't about to go public with it before talking to the Judiciary Committee chairman, and Joe Biden wouldn't take her phone calls. For thirty-six hours, she tried to rouse Chairman Biden. Or anyone on his staff. Meanwhile, *Newsday*'s Timothy Phelps was hot on her trail.

Totenberg was reluctant to go forward with the story, explaining her timidity at the time as issuing from the nature of Hill's allegations. It would have been different, she says, if the charge was financial, rather than sexual, wrongdoing. "Being a woman," Totenberg thought, "isn't a help here." She knew who would be on the hook for exposing the source who had given her the affidavit: between her and Timothy Phelps, they were going to go after her. But Totenberg had made up her mind. Phelps was coming out on Saturday with a story over the *Newsday/Washington Post* wire. Totenberg broadcast her interview with Anita Hill on Sunday, October 6. The full Senate was scheduled to vote on Thomas's nomination two days later.

As she foresaw, being a woman did not help Nina Totenberg. On Monday, October 7, while the Senate was digesting the implications of her revelation, Totenberg went on *Nightline*, joined by liberal senator Paul Simon and Republican Alan Simpson. Simpson laid into her the whole show, accusing her of being unethical and unprincipled. Simpson was so furious he followed Totenberg out of the studio to her car, pulled open the car door, and, from his full height of six feet plus, screamed at her for a long two minutes or more. Finally, she got out of the car, she recalls, pulled herself up to her full five feet, five inches, looked up at the big, tall senator from Wyoming, and said, "Senator, you are a fucking bully." When the car finally pulled away from the scene, her driver had some advice for Totenberg. "Lady," he said to the reporter, "you need to get yourself a gun."

By Tuesday, the day of the Senate vote, it became clear even to Biden that Thomas might not have enough Democratic votes to be confirmed. There would have to be hearings. A handful of Democratic leaders, including Danforth and Biden, met in the office of Majority Leader George Mitchell to negotiate the terms of the now inevitable Hill/Thomas hearings. And there, the refined senator and man of the cloth John Danforth erupted in an uncontrolled outburst of male rage; in his own words, a "threatening, shocking" outburst, shouting, red in the face, profane, and completely inconsistent with any norms of the Senate he served.[34] Even after Chairman Biden and Leader Mitchell gave him everything he demanded — a short, two-day hearing, to start immediately on Friday, no inquiry into any other aspects of the nominee's sexual practices, and an immediate vote the following Tuesday — he was seething. Having rolled the Democrats like a sushi chef to get a limited, fast-track hearing, Danforth nonetheless went to the floor of the Senate and unleashed another tirade, this time on the person or persons responsible for leaking the affidavit to the press, in violation of Senate rules.

The hearings were scheduled for Friday, October 11. And so Anita Hill prepared to go to Washington. The Republicans were screaming mad. The Democrats would do anything to assuage their colleagues' male rage. Nobody's child, Hill was going to need some help.

Janet Napolitano, later governor of Arizona and secretary of Homeland Security, was sitting in her law office in Phoenix that week in September 1991 when the famed liberal constitutional scholar and senior partner John Frank poked his head around her office door. "I'm going to Washington to help Anita Hill," he said.[35] "Want to come?" Did she ever. After all, had she not been there for Frank when he testified against Robert Bork in the summer of 1987? That time, the anti-Bork forces had been preparing at length and in depth for weeks before the hearings. And now, four years later, they were going to have to do in forty-eight hours what it had taken them weeks to do in the Bork hearings. The opposition to

Thomas, whom Frank considered just as undesirable as Bork, had never gotten off the ground. Although the senators had had information about Hill's charges for weeks and in some cases months, they were indifferent to or unwilling to face the issue. Now Frank and Napolitano had to take the red-eye to meet their client for the first time. Her friend and lawyer Ogletree would be there, defending Hill and bravely risking his status at Harvard Law School, where he was up for tenure.

By the time Frank and Napolitano got to the capital city, the White House team had already unleashed the attack on Hill. They had their narrative: she was a sex-crazed fantasist, driven by frustrated desire for the attentions of Clarence Thomas.[36] All week, Thomas's allies — Phyllis Berry, who had worked for Thomas at the EEOC, Hill's former dean Charles Kothe — barraged the press with the fantasy story. Late Thursday night, the Hill team got a message from Chairman Biden. Danforth had demanded that Thomas make his statement first. And Biden had said sure.

The Hill/Thomas hearings lasted but three days. Televised throughout, they left the impression that the confrontation had gone on for weeks. But the reality is: Thomas testified for an hour Friday morning, Hill spoke afterward. Thomas gave a surprise rebuttal appearance Friday night and testified all day Saturday. Sunday, both sides presented third-party witnesses.

In Thomas's opening statement Friday morning, he flatly denied having said anything that Hill alleged. Then he warned Chairman Biden that he would not take any questions about his sex life. That was "private," he (and Danforth) contended. Biden agreed,[37] and thereby gave away the only line of questioning the Democrats could have used to offset Thomas's denials of wrongdoing. And then the nominee stepped down.

Hill was on the witness stand for seven hours. By all accounts, she was unexpectedly effective. She opened by sharing with Chairman Biden that her extensive family had not been able to get into the hearing room; the proceedings were so hurried and abrupt.[38]

The nation watched as her tall and dignified mother and father came in and embraced their youngest daughter. And then she told her story. What follows is an excerpt:

> After a brief discussion of work, he would turn the conversation to a discussion of sexual matters. His conversations were very vivid. He spoke about acts that he had seen in pornographic films involving such matters as women having sex with animals, and films showing group sex or rape scenes. He talked about pornographic materials depicting individuals with large penises, or large breasts, involved in various sex acts.
>
> On several occasions Thomas told me graphically of his own sexual prowess. Because I was extremely uncomfortable talking about sex with him at all, and particularly in such a graphic way, I told him that I did not want to talk about these subjects. I would also try to change the subject to education matters or to nonsexual personal matters, such as his background or his beliefs. My efforts to change the subject were rarely successful.[39]

Off and on for two years, Clarence Thomas, her boss, had deluged her with sex talk, questions about her sex life, descriptions of his sexual prowess, opinions about her dress, and vivid depictions of the pornographic movies he had watched.

Republican committee member Senator Arlen Specter of Pennsylvania had been assigned the job of cross-examining Hill. He was a longtime former prosecutor, and he jumped at the chance to show off his skills. He was armed with an affidavit from a passing acquaintance of Hill's, management consultant John Doggett, who suggested Hill had fantasized a sexual relationship with him as well. Ultimately, when he appeared before the committee, Doggett self-destructed so spectacularly[40] that even the studiedly neutral mainstream media quoted sources describing him as "cocky and pompous," a man whose "ego tends to overpower his judgment,"[41] the *New York Times* concluding that his testimony was "bizarre" or "at best irrelevant."[42] The Senate staff knew that two separate women had come forward to offer to testify about Doggett's sexually offensive conduct when they worked with him. But Biden refused to let in the refutation witnesses. Before his own rambling, and mostly irrelevant, testimony could be refuted, at midnight on Sunday, the "Doggett" version had done its work. When Anita Hill left the hearing room after seven on Friday, Arlen Specter accused her of perjury, for fantasizing her relationship with Thomas.

Nonetheless, Hill's matter-of-fact presentation of the explosive story was, according to the reports on the six o'clock news that Friday, an unequivocal success. After she'd wrapped up her testimony, her team thought her story would dominate again at ten and be the lead story in the next morning's paper. They went off to have dinner.[43] Napolitano was sitting alone in the hearing room when the door suddenly opened and the White House's handler Boyden Gray walked in, followed by the nominee and the entire Judiciary Committee.

There had been some question about whether the hearing would resume after Hill finished at 7:40 p.m. The Democrats wanted to break, but the White House's Duberstein insisted. He threw a fit in the committee scheduling meeting and, once again, Chairman Biden let Duberstein dictate procedure. Shortly after eight, Clarence Thomas sat down and began answering friendly questions from the Republicans on the panel. Orrin Hatch, particularly, pressed him for a reaction to the racial stereotype of the oversexed black man. Finally, Thomas erupted. The whole proceeding, he thundered, was nothing more than a "high-tech lynching for uppity blacks." Hot, angry, and indignant: Clarence Thomas was holding back no more.

"I could count votes," Napolitano recalls, sitting there, a thirty-three-year-old law firm associate with no allies on the Judiciary Committee at all. "And I could see that any serious effort to get at the truth of what Anita was saying just floated away. It was a perfectly staged piece of political theater."[44] The overnight polls shifted immediately to Thomas.

Thomas came back for a full day Saturday. He continued to deny everything Hill had alleged. The Democrats continued to dance around the issue. Biden let anything the Republicans wanted to suggest into the record; Kennedy emerged briefly to defend Hill and then lapsed back into complete silence; and Leahy came to realize he was in an epic fight, but that it was way too late to land any blows. The Republicans continued to spin visions of Anita Hill as an "erotomaniac" to the press. On Sunday morning, Hill adviser Wendy Sherman called someone she knew in Biden's office and said, "'What are you all doing, don't you understand what is happening here?' I warned Biden," she says. "We all warned Biden. The United States Senate was still very much a boys' club."[45]

The Republicans were making Hill out to be a liar. Why was it all about Hill? Hill's side had easy access to a number of witnesses who could validate her story by testifying to Thomas's long, extensive, and well-established habit of consuming pornography. There was an adult-film rental place near his office at the EEOC. But none of that mattered. For a decade pornography had been classified as a matter of individual choice, simply a way for a person to exercise his or her taste in erotic gratification, sex-positive. And Biden had agreed with Danforth that the committee wouldn't look into Thomas's "private" life. Without explicitly saying so, senators on both sides of the party line conducted themselves as if Thomas's "personal" behavior was out of bounds.[46]

But the hearings ground on, with one Republican senator after another suggesting, in statements or to the press outside, the most scurrilous things about the private life of Anita Hill, and the Democrats just watched it all go by. On Sunday, the four friends Hill had confided in contemporaneously appeared in DC to support her story, and a long list of women who had worked with Thomas came to support him. Although the Hill team was dispirited by Sunday night, they had an ace in the hole: another accuser, Angela Wright. And Wright herself had a corroborating witness, Rose Jourdain. The Hill team thought Wright would take the chair on Monday.

Angela Wright, another black woman, had worked for Thomas as his director of public affairs at the EEOC for a year in 1984–85 before he fired her.[47] When the Hill story broke, she was working as an assistant metro editor at the *Charlotte Observer*. In an eerie echo of Hill's approach/avoidance dance with the Senate committee, Wright was reluctant to come forward. But for her submission to demonstrate her journalistic aptitude at the paper, she had written a column not for publication describing Thomas's workplace behavior. And someone had sent it to Mark Schwartz, a Judiciary Committee staff member. Biden told Duberstein, the committee subpoenaed Wright, and Duberstein went to work to discredit this second woman. Wright flew to Washington Friday, the day Hill was starting to speak before the committee. By Sunday, the Republicans had assembled a full attack on Wright's employment record and were determined to stop her from testifying.

The committee caucused late Sunday and, as Biden later reported to his staff, the members voted not to call Wright. Everything about the decision not to put Wright on the stand is now disputed in the much-examined confirmation hearings. Biden's people say the deal was that her deposition, unexamined and unrebutted, would be read into the record. DeConcini says he has no memory of knowing about her before he voted on Thomas's appointment. "If there had been a second woman," he says, "I might have voted against Thomas."[48] Wright says she was ready to testify and angry at being dealt out.[49]

Anita Hill went back to Oklahoma. With the polling running toward him, Thomas gained eleven Democratic votes, enough to be confirmed by the Democratic-dominated Senate for a life-tenured seat on the United States Supreme Court. All but two Republicans (one of whom later became an independent) voted for Thomas. As Napolitano predicted, those Democrats included her Arizona senator, Dennis DeConcini, who voted for the Republican nominee. So did Thomas's fellow Georgians Sam Nunn and Wyche Fowler, and even the liberal senator from Illinois, Alan Dixon. After slow but steady progress in the courts, the rights and wrongs of sexual harassment, with a soupçon of pornography thrown in for good measure, had just met male political culture. Republicans would do anything for access to the levers of power, and the liberal Democrats included a critical mass of wusses and womanizers.

The Senate was not done yet. At the insistence of Republicans, especially Nina Totenberg's bully Alan Simpson, they hired a special counsel and held extensive hearings into who might have leaked Anita Hill's affidavit to the press. *I'm going to have to go to jail*, Totenberg thought.[50] She certainly wasn't going to give up her source. Orrin Hatch pounded on Senator Metzenbaum so hard with accusations that he was the source of the leak that Metzenbaum decided to retire. Metzenbaum staffer James Brudney had already interviewed for a teaching job that fall, and, getting it from Hill for what she'd endured and from the special counsel, left politics and went to Ohio to teach law school.[51] Two years later, when a Democratic administration nominated Janet Napolitano for the job of United States attorney in Arizona, a position requiring Senate confirmation, Alan Simpson opposed her so forcefully that the normally routine appointment had to go to the whole Senate, where moderate New Mexico Republican Pete Domenici defended the reputation of Napolitano, an old family friend.[52]

Joe Biden pronounced himself well satisfied with the outcome of the Thomas confirmation. Most everyone who'd watched, he said, had thought he'd been very fair.

Scribbling Women

Biden might have been happy with his performance, but two young women in the Washington bureau of the *Wall Street Journal* were not.[53] After Anita Hill told her story that first Friday morning of the Hill/Thomas hearings, reporter Jill Abramson got a phone call from her colleague and bestie Jane Mayer. "Jill, this is it!" she exclaimed. The two had long wanted to write a book together. "It has everything. It's great political drama. It has race, it has sex." The two journalists say it was the story, not the feminist history, that attracted them. But they both knew that women mattered. The *Journal*'s Washington Bureau, run at that time by Al Hunt, a liberal journalist married to Judy Woodruff, a White House reporter for PBS, had an unusually large number of women on the payroll. And, as female journalists, Abramson and Mayer had encountered and seen routine sexual harassment. Mayer had once rejected the sexual advances of a married colleague as gently as she could, resulting in his vendetta against her, played out in the office, where he did everything, she stated, short of "throw[ing] her down the stairs."

The two longtime female friends (they attended the tony Ethical Culture Fieldston School in New York together) were still a rarity as women at their status level in journalism. But they had always been stars. After Fieldston, Jill went to Harvard, and Jane, a year later, to Yale.

Abramson was not particularly interested in journalism during her college years, but in 1973, after her freshman year at Harvard, she was working on Nantucket when Robert Kennedy's son Joe was in a serious jeep accident. Nantucket was fogged in, and nothing was running. *Time* magazine's Boston bureau manager, a family friend, knew that Abramson was on the island with her parents. So she asked Abramson to see if she could find out anything about what had happened. Turns out the wife of the local doctor was a serious drinker, and while visiting Abramson's mother knocked back a few Salty Dogs of grapefruit juice and vodka. The gory details of the accident — maybe drugs, alcohol, Kennedys arriving to the rescue — came tumbling out. "I did not have to go off my porch," Abramson chuckles. "I just waited until she left and called *Time*." When she got back to Harvard the next fall the magazine rewarded her with a job as a stringer.

Abramson's Boston bureau chief, Sandra Burton, the first woman bureau chief in the history of *Time* magazine,[54] made sure Abramson learned the ropes. When Abramson graduated in 1976, an election year, Burton hired her for a year. The Boston bureau of *Time* — with three women reporters — was a veritable gender paradise in 1976. After the year at *Time*, Abramson joined a political PR firm and went to Arkansas to work for a promising Southern candidate for governor, Bill Clinton. There was talk of the candidate's affairs even then, but in 1978, well after the early sex harassment decisions in DC, Abramson did not see this as particularly unusual or risky behavior. Several years after Chappaquiddick and the Wayne Hays and Wilbur Mills scandals, the risks of sex in the political workplace were still not clear. The candidate's wife, Hillary Rodham, actually made more of an impression on the young political consultant, so smart and so central was she to every aspect of her husband's campaign.

By 1980 Abramson had signed on to legal journalist Steven Brill's new magazine, the *American Lawyer.* She was not alone. Brill hired a lot of strong women reporters,[55] and he sent twentysomething Abramson, who had never run anything, to DC to manage a staff of sixty at another publication of his growing empire, the *Washington Lawyer.* "He was a tough boss, could be a bully," Abramson says, "but if you were talented and female he had plenty of time to mentor you and really push you into opportunities that I would never have thought to pursue." Washington bureau chief Al Hunt was the same way, she said, when she went to the *Wall Street Journal* in 1988. Once Anita Hill surfaced, Hunt was frantic to get a woman out to cover the hearings. With her background in legal reporting, Abramson was a natural.

So, it turned out, was Abramson's pal back at the office, Jane Mayer.[56] She had followed a straighter career path to journalism than Abramson, fueled along the way by a strong interest in power, its abuses, and its relationship to truth. What happens to people when they speak an "inconvenient" truth to power? Mayer happily stepped into the shoes of the prior *Time* stringer when she got to Yale. As bureau chief Sandra Burton had done for Abramson, Bonnie Angelo, a rare senior woman at *Time,* this time in the Connecticut bureau, put the ladder down for Mayer. Mayer went to Oxford to start a PhD just as Angelo went to run *Time's* London bureau. She hired Jane to string again. Quickly, Mayer decided she'd rather write than study history, and she quit her job to become a metro reporter for the local *Washington Star,* which *Time* had just acquired.

When the *Star* folded, the *Wall Street Journal* hired Mayer to cover the television industry. In 1983 Mayer convinced the *Journal* to send her to Beirut under the guise of doing a story about a TV camera-man, and while she was there Hezbollah militants attacked the US Marine barracks, with devastating effect. Her reporting convinced the paper she could do more than television coverage. They sent her to the White House.

"Don't think it wasn't still incredibly sexist at the *Journal*," she cautions. Women reporters weren't allowed to cover arms control, for instance, so when Reagan went to negotiate with Gorbachev in 1986, Mayer stayed home. "Why don't you do a feature about the First Lady's favorite designer, Adolfo?" her boss suggested. Instead of investigating ball gowns, Mayer turned her attention to President Reagan's scandalous sale of arms to Iran to fund the entirely illegal American support for the Contras, right-wing militias in Nicara-gua, and cowrote a best-selling book about it.

Then came the Thomas hearings. "One thing was clear," Jane Mayer remembers. "Clarence Thomas and Anita Hill could not both be telling the truth. They were both compelling witnesses and all had corroborators, and the corroborators were believable, so somebody was lying under oath."

When the hearing ended, the two saw Biden and the Democrats throwing up their hands and saying, Well, we'll never know the truth. The hell we won't, Abramson said. "We weren't out to avenge Anita Hill . . . we were prepared to write that book whichever way it came out," Mayer says. "Although," she adds, "it seemed more likely that he was lying." What they did know was that "if you report something enough you can find the truth." Basically, Mayer said, they "reconvened the hearings." It took almost four years. The in-trepid girl reporters talked to everyone other than now-confirmed Justice Thomas. Even Hill, who had said she wanted the experience behind her, talked to Abramson and Mayer. Most importantly, they tracked down all the witnesses who would have added the weight of repetition to Hill's side of the "he said/she said" narrative the Republicans had been so anxious to create—the owner of the porn video store in DC that Thomas frequented, a former colleague of Thomas's, Kaye Savage, who said he decorated his apartment walls with *Playboy* magazine centerfolds. The two journalists did all the work the FBI would have done, had Chairman Biden run the committee hearings like a normal inquiry.

Sexual harassment and abuse, it turns out, is rarely an activity that takes place exclusively in locations concealed from human witnesses, immune from investigation, and thus reduced to "he said/she said." Offenders typically repeat behaviors, so there are habit witnesses. Sometimes their actions involve public conduct, subject to human observation. They leave paper trails, they speak imprudently, they keep diaries, they use credit cards. On the rare occasion where two people tell completely inconsistent stories, investigative journalists are perfectly trained to, as Mayer says, "report something enough so that you find" where the truth lies. All they lack is subpoena power.

Mayer and Abramson figured out pretty quickly that their book would be a political event in itself. The Hill/Thomas hearings before an essentially all-male Senate had ignited a maelstrom in the election year 1992. By the summer before the election between Thomas sponsor George H. W. Bush and Bill Clinton, the polls indicated that the public believed Anita Hill, 44 percent to 34 percent.[57] Washington state senator Patty Murray watched the hearings on television and decided to run for the US Senate. Dianne Feinstein signed on to run for the unfinished term of California Republican John Seymour, and Barbara Boxer ran for the open California full-term seat, making California the first state represented by two women. Alan Dixon, the Illinois Democrat who had voted to confirm Clarence Thomas, lost the primary to an African American woman, Carol Moseley Braun, who went on to become the first African American woman in the high chamber.[58] Dixon was joined in defeat by another Democrat in the Clarence Thomas camp, Wyche Fowler of Georgia, who, losing support among women, went down by the skin of his teeth.[59] The media named 1992 the Year of the

Woman. (Dennis DeConcini, the only Democrat who voted for Thomas in committee, decided not to run again when his seat came up in 1994.)

In 1993 then-conservative pundit David Brock published *The Real Anita Hill,* a right-wing-sponsored compendium of every rumor and speculation the right could produce about the character of the woman who had dared tell her story of sexual harassment. Abramson and Mayer decimated him in their review of the book for the *New Yorker.* [60] (Nine years later, in his confessional, *Blinded by the Right,* Brock recanted and admitted his Anita Hill book was filled with lies.) But the image of Thomas as a liar was becoming embedded in the culture, and at critical junctures women were outraged by the result that he was confirmed while other women had been ready to testify against him.[61] And a weird thing was happening: Thomas's sponsor and mentor Senator John Danforth decided he'd write a book, too, and every time Mayer and Abramson's publication date got changed, Danforth changed his publication date. It was almost as if he had created the book expressly to offset theirs, whenever it appeared.[62]

After years of investigation, *Strange Justice* came out in 1994 and made the definitive case that it was Thomas who had lied. Thinking of themselves as documentarians and historians, coming from the most establishment of publications, Abramson and Mayer were actually surprised by the ferocious attacks on them that the book provoked. Mayer recalls being compared to Janet Cooke, the *Washington Post* reporter who had made up her Pulitzer Prize–winning article about an eight-year-old heroin addict. The vilification of Abramson and Mayer rounds out the Hill/Thomas hearings as a perfect harbinger of the scorched-earth tactics of the right.

But the partnership of the two pioneering woman journalists was also a harbinger of the forces lining up on the other side of the subject of sexual harassment and abuse. Just as they started writing the book, Mayer became pregnant with her first child. "Oh, no," she thought, "this is going to mess everything up and I'll be distracted." But Abramson said, "Don't worry about it." "That's the great thing,"

Mayer remembers, "about working with another woman who's had two kids." And so they didn't worry about it. Not even when they went to pitch the project to a TV studio, and Mayer was so enormous all she could fit into was a gigantic polka-dotted muu-muu. Where politicians, liberal and conservative, failed to vindicate women, the handful of early female journalists were going to do some heavy lifting.

Strange Justice was a finalist for the National Book Award, it was made into a TV movie, and it formed the basis for numerous revisionist portrayals of the Hill/Thomas hearings. Fourteen years after the book's release, *New Yorker* editor Hendrik Hertzberg, reviewing Thomas's memoir, *My Grandfather's Son*, in 2008, asserted as incontestable fact that "any doubt that his lies were lies was laid to rest by Jane Mayer and Jill Abramson in their 1994 book *Strange Justice.*"[63]

6

Bill Clinton, Monica Lewinsky, and Feminism's Swerve

1992–98

Bill and Hillary Clinton, an Introduction

As the nation was struggling with the aftermath of the Clarence Thomas confirmation in the run-up to the 1992 elections, a self-identified feminist was emerging as the Democratic candidate for president: skirt-chasing Arkansas governor Bill Clinton. The Clinton candidacy in fact involved two feminists, the youthful fortysomething Clinton and his Yale law school classmate and wife, Hillary Rodham Clinton, a partner in Arkansas's biggest law firm. Throughout his political career, Hillary had been so much a part of Bill's team that Clinton frequently boasted whoever elected him got "two for the price of one." After Yale, Arkansas native Bill Clinton had returned home in 1973 to pursue his political ambitions, and Hillary Rodham had followed, soon after to be wed.

Both Clintons were strongly tied in to the eastern establishment of money and opinion that was always central to the national Democratic Party. In the late 1980s, Bill was the head of the National Governors Association, a big step up the ladder leading from Little Rock to national office. Hillary had been making her way up through the prestigious American Bar Association. Shortly after she stepped down as the first chair of the ABA's groundbreaking Commission on Women in the Profession, she appeared with Anita Hill in a sold-out program at the ABA's 1992 annual meeting.[1] Anita Hill had made progress and "transformed consciousness," Clinton raved. Regardless of what was happening on Hillary Clinton's own home turf, there would be no tolerance for sexual harassment in the office at the 1992 ABA convention.

The Clintons were never constrained by a foolish consistency. As an antiwar college kid, Bill had worried about the impact his draft-dodging might have on his political future.[2] Hillary, the liberated counterculture commencement speaker at the all-female Wellesley College, had followed her man to Arkansas, cut her hair, and then started using his name. Running to recapture the governor's seat after losing his bid for reelection the first time in 1980, Bill had learned to pivot just enough to the right to embrace the local business behemoth Walmart and take on the teachers' union.[3]

These moves coincided with the Democratic Party's own move to the right. Following the Democrats' landslide defeat in the presidential election of 1984, some Democratic congressmen from what we now call red states — Al Gore of Tennessee, Sam Nunn of Georgia — and some staffers formed the Democratic Leadership Council in an attempt to pull the party to the right in order to reverse the Democrats' sliding fortunes and win back the white working and middle class. By the 1992 primary, white male Southern governor Bill Clinton, immediate past chair of the DLC, was a logical centrist candidate. But Clinton was a hard man to pin down. Centrist that he was, he was also the first presidential candidate to hold an open fundraising party in the rich and gay community of Los Angeles, where he promised to end the practice of barring gays from serving in the military.[4]

Clinton Under the Hidden Law of Adultery

The Clintons have attracted accusations of falsity from their earliest days on the national scene. The attacks would eventually encompass every imaginable hysterical accusation — stealing money, selling drugs, murder, child molestation. But the most potent attack on Bill Clinton was always about sex. On January 26, 1992, right before the critical New Hampshire vote in the Democratic primary, which would have solidified his position as the front-runner, rumors of Governor Bill Clinton's years-long affair with a state employee, Gennifer Flowers, a former cabaret dancer, exploded in the tabloid *Star.*[5] One election cycle earlier, in 1988, married Democratic front-runner Gary Hart had stepped aside in a heartbeat after the press caught him entering his DC townhouse with a party girl. But the vastly savvier (and nervier) Clinton campaign did something much smarter than Gary Hart did — instead of defying the press, it reached out to them. In the wake of the Gennifer Flowers story, television news show *60 Minutes,* still the gold standard of media in those waning pre-internet days, agreed to interview the candidate and, equally importantly, his wife, on the subject of his sex life. The interview would air right after the Super Bowl.

A record audience hung on through the boring last quarter of Super Bowl XXVI, with the Washington Redskins clearly in command over the Buffalo Bills,[6] to watch the upcoming drama. Sitting side by side on the cozy couch of a Boston television set, Hillary put her hand comfortingly on Bill's arm and Bill clasped his hands in front of him. Then host Steve Kroft started his tough interview.

Did he have an affair with Gennifer Flowers?

Clinton: "That allegation is false."

Are you categorically denying you ever had an affair with Gennifer Flowers?

"I said that before. And so has she."

Kroft was going to be in for a long session.

Clinton did admit to "causing pain in my marriage."

Kroft tried another angle. You've said your marriage had problems. Does that mean adultery? Are you prepared to say you've never had an extramarital affair?

Clinton dodged. "No married couple should ever discuss that with anyone but themselves . . . Are we going to engage in a game of 'gotcha?'"

Kroft tried one last time. "I think most Americans would agree that it's very admirable that you've stayed together . . . that you seem to have reached some sort of understanding and arrangement."

Bingo.

Bill Clinton erupted. "Wait a minute, wait a minute, wait a minute. You're looking at two people who love each other. This is not an arrangement or an understanding. This is a marriage."

And then Hillary, for the win:

"You know, I'm not sitting here," she volunteered, "some little woman, standing by my man like Tammy Wynette. I'm sitting here because I love him, and I respect him, and I honor what he's been through and what we've been through together. And, you know, if that's not enough for people — then, heck, don't vote for him."[7]

At a press conference at the Waldorf hotel in New York City the next day, Gennifer Flowers revealed she had been taping her phone conversations with the governor. She played a clip of one tape for the press. Pace Bill Clinton, the tapes seemed to show that the "allegation" of their affair was not "false."

The truth was out, but it did not matter. People didn't vote based on whether Clinton screwed around. Clinton came in second in the New Hampshire primary, labeled himself the Comeback Kid, and went on to win the nomination and the election. Just a few months earlier, in October 1992, a poll about Clarence Thomas revealed that people now believed Anita Hill, sure.[8] Arguably angry and motivated female voters were responsible for many outcomes in the Year of the Woman, including Bill's plurality victory in the election. But in a portent of things to come, when ABC News/*Washington Post* asked if the hearings should be reopened and Thomas's tenure reconsidered, the public demurred. We believe Anita Hill, the polls seemed to say, but not that any price should be paid for what Thomas did. Like Sidney Taylor, Mechelle Vinson's harassing boss at the bank, Justice Thomas would keep his job. Not being strictly liable for their Sidney Taylors, the bank, and other employers, would keep their money. When the time came to rein in horndog Democrat Bill Clinton, cheating on his feminist wife, in 1992, the public said the same thing.

The sexual revolution, which had vanquished the antipornography movement ten years before, was clearly in ascendance. Despite the role workplace harassment and pornography played in Mechelle Vinson's case and in Anita Hill's ordeal with Clarence Thomas, most people still felt America could accommodate both political gender equality and sexual libertinism in one culture.

In a 2017 book, *The Naughty Nineties: The Triumph of the American Libido,*[9] cultural chronicler and journalist David Friend explains why Clinton was the vital symbol of a society in which libertinism had definitively taken the field. From that start he uncovered a picture of the people raised in the 1960s, aka baby boomers, attaining substantial social power and at the same time creating, by chance and by intent, a culture rife with sexual content. "Every five to ten years the quantity and tolerability of sexually suggestive content in the culture increases exponentially," he suggested.[10] In addition to Bill Clinton's profligacy, a host of cultural items — sex-positive feminism, pornography on the World Wide Web, the sex-driven media — make up Friend's picture of a sexed-up world.

As Friend so astutely notes, most Americans made their first real acquaintance with Bill Clinton when they watched him lying about sex on TV in 1992. The episode squarely presented the Naughties with a difficult problem. What to do about the old-fashioned wrong of adultery in a sexually revolutionary world? Clinton took a leaf from the liberal feminists' arguments on pornography and told society it could just look away. Pundit Jonathan Rauch delivered the most telling analysis in 1998, nearing the end of Clinton's term. Like pornography on the web, Rauch says, adultery is everywhere. Americans didn't want to live in the suffocating world of the Republicans' religious, monogamous, heterosexual family values. But they didn't want the sexual anarchy of the free love movement either. So society invoked what Rauch named the hidden law of adultery: If you pretend not to do it, we'll pretend not to notice.[11]

Would America Pretend Not to See Monica Lewinsky?

With Hillary onstage beside him on *60 Minutes,* Clinton reminded society of a corollary of the hidden law: only the cuckolded spouse, usually a woman, gets to decide when to call the adulterer out.[12] The liberal Clintons' *60 Minutes* interview echoed the early response to adjudicated claims of sexual harassment, where sexual conduct was characterized as personal, not political or subject to legal review. Hillary Clinton gave her verdict on the allegations against her husband and suggested that that should be good enough. By 1992, in the courts of law deciding harassment suits, the sex-is-personal defense had soundly lost. But in politics, the Clintons were contending, alleged sexual misconduct was still a "personal" matter, and only the personal woman, the wife, was in a position to object. The voters could choose not to vote for Clinton, as Hillary suggested on *60 Minutes,* but the clear implication was that they would be making a mistake if they did so. She had judged her husband worthy, and that should have been enough for anybody.

A long train of Clinton accusers — Gennifer Flowers, the modestly positioned government employee who didn't like being erased from history; employee Paula Jones, who sued the president for sexual harassment, assault, and defamation in 1994; Kathleen Willey, who accused him of groping her in 1998; and Juanita Broaddrick, who in 1999 claimed that Clinton had raped her during his campaign for Arkansas governor in 1978 — made their cases against Clinton and were ignored. Because they were not his wife, they were not the right complainants. Hillary, who, we now know, was not the best judge of the seriousness of her husband's behavior, had covered him with a kind of cloak of sexual invisibility.

But the situation was unstable. Sex is not a human behavior immune from moral or political meaning. At the simplest level, often the sexual behavior involved the workplace. As we know, by 1986 the Supreme Court had ruled in *Meritor v. Vinson* that sexual harassment at work was not a purely private act. Sexual harassment at work was governed by the normal world of law, the Civil Rights Act, tort law. Paula Jones contended she was working the desk at an Arkansas state event when the then-governor summoned her to his hotel room and dropped his pants. In the first round, the trial court in *Jones v. Clinton* ruled that Paula Jones couldn't sue a sitting president during his term, but Jones's suit was reinstated by the court of appeals, and the reinstatement affirmed by the Supreme Court. The trial court took it up again. Nonetheless, for some months no one took Jones's suit seriously. If it did not get dismissed on the merits, Clinton could lie, and everyone would pretend to believe him. Perjury in a civil case rarely carries any serious penalty. The society could treat sexual harassment at work as a wrongful act and still refuse to attach real consequences to the wrongdoing. That's why plaintiffs in sexual harassment cases usually lose. Or don't sue at all.

As it turned out, Jones's case was a time bomb; it was socially acceptable for Clinton to lie about sex, as he usually did, but lying in a court of law can sometimes be recognized as perjury, and Clinton was no ordinary civil defendant in a sex case. A clear indication of the danger Jones's suit posed was that she was represented by lawyers from the substantial organization of Clinton haters on the right.

At first though Jones's suit wasn't the worst threat to Bill Clinton's presidency. That arose from a completely unrelated scandal, the Clintons' investment in a dicey real estate venture in Arkansas years before: Whitewater. When the real estate investment went belly-up, it took a federally regulated savings and loan bank down with it, which raised federal legal questions. On that slender thread of the Clintons' financial involvement with the real estate scheme, the Republican Congress organized an investigation. After much partisan pressure, an independent counsel, by then one Kenneth Starr, who had been appointed by a panel of mostly very conservative Republican-appointed judges, was supposed to be looking into Whitewater. There is no obvious connection between the Whitewater scandals and Jones's case. It took a staggering degree of irresponsible behavior and bad fortune on Clinton's part for the independent counsel to join forces with Paula Jones and blow up the Clinton presidency. But wherever Bill Clinton was, there was always a lot of gunpowder lying around.

The election—and reelection in 1996—of the adulterous Bill Clinton produced considerable payoffs for feminists. In 1993 Clinton nominated Ruth Bader Ginsburg—the Thurgood Marshall of the women's movement—to the Supreme Court. His Democratic Congress in 1994 passed the Violence Against Women Act, which he signed into law. He also signed the law protecting access to abortion clinics, a response to the increasingly aggressive tactics used by anti-abortion activists that had turned clinics into war zones. He filled the government with high-ranking women, from the attorney general to the surgeon general. In 1995 his cuckolded spouse went to Beijing to proclaim to the largest-ever international gathering on the subject of women that "human rights are women's rights, and women's rights are human rights." Sounds great, right?

Throughout their marriage, Hillary got to decide when the women in her husband's sphere were political subjects, with human rights, and when they were in the hidden, lawless realm of the personal. Who's missing in this picture of the covertly wandering husband and enabling wife? The other woman. In Bill Clinton's case, Gennifer Flowers, and the next one up—Paula Jones, a six-dollar-an-hour high school graduate working the registration desk—were dragging a heavy burden of social class when they complained of Bill Clinton's disregard for their rights as women and as human beings. So far, Paula Jones had gotten nowhere. But in 1995 Bill Clinton turned to a young White House intern, daughter of a bourgeois cancer doctor and a writer from LA. (Confined to the White House and surrounded by watchers, he did not have the same range of choices as in the obscure precincts of Little Rock.)

Born in 1973, Monica Lewinsky was not a boomer and apparently did not know the rules of the hidden law of adultery. After she and the president embarked upon a sexual relationship in the White House, she blabbed about it with open abandon. She told college friends, high school friends, a couple of shrinks, an old boyfriend, her aunt, a coworker. She even told her mother, whom she was living with at her apartment in DC's Watergate complex.[13] In 1996, after she'd been transferred out of the White House to the Pentagon, she told a sympathetic older woman at her new place of work, Linda Tripp, about the affair. Unbeknownst to Lewinsky, Tripp had a deep suspicion of President Clinton from her days in the White House as a holdover from the Bush years. She also had a tape recorder.

The Bare Facts

Lewinsky, by all her many accounts, had her first sexual contact with the president on the evening of Wednesday, November 15, 1995, while working in the West Wing. The government was shut down over a budget impasse. She and the president had been exchanging glances for a while during her internship, and on this first occasion, the president took her back into the private study off the oval office, and a windowless hallway where they kissed. Later that evening, they went back, and she gave him a blow job. Over the next year and a half, the president and Monica Lewinsky met and had direct physical sexual relations around ten times, most often in the first six months.[14] She performed oral sex on him, in and around his private offices off the Oval Office, in the bathroom, in the hallway. He fondled her, but he refused to have genital intercourse with her, although at least once he inserted a cigar into her vagina. When she was not at the White House, the president arranged encounters by calling her at home and inviting her to visit. On Friday, April 5, 1996, Evelyn Lieberman, a high-ranking aide with an eye for improper appearances, arranged to have Monica Lewinsky transferred from her White House job to the Department of Defense.

On Easter Sunday, April 7, 1996, Lewinsky went to the president for help, and she and the president had sexual contact in the hallway outside the Oval Office study and in the study itself. This was their last in-person sexual encounter for over ten months. But on Friday, February 28, 1997, the president had his personal secretary, Betty Currie, call Lewinsky to invite her to the White House for a radio address. After the address, Lewinsky and the president kissed by the bathroom. Lewinsky performed oral sex on him and he spilled a little semen on her dress. They met again for sex in March 1997, but that was it. Although they met in person a few more times, there was only smooching. During the sixteen months of their relationship, Lewinsky testified that she and the president also engaged in "phone sex" approximately fifteen times. The president initiated each phone-sex encounter by telephoning her.

Meanwhile, the courts had reinstated Paula Jones's lawsuit. By December 1997, both President Clinton and Monica Lewinsky knew someone had talked. Clinton called and told Lewinsky she was on the list of potential witnesses to be deposed in the previously unthreatening civil suit. So, under the hidden law of adultery, he suggested to Lewinsky that she give a cover story for her White House visits: she was "delivering documents." She signed a false affidavit to stave off the deposition.

Turns out Lewinsky's confidante, Linda Tripp, had been in touch with a conservative book agent, Lucianne Goldberg, a well-known Clinton hater. Through her, Tripp met with *Newsweek* reporter Michael Isikoff and Paula Jones's lawyers, who had put Lewinsky on the witness list. Tripp decided to deal directly with Independent Counsel Ken Starr,[15] and Starr sought and received permission to expand his investigation of the Whitewater banking deal to Clinton's subornation of perjury and obstruction of justice in the unrelated *Jones* suit. On January 16, 1998, just as Starr got his expanded authority, FBI agents and US attorneys under Starr's orders surrounded Lewinsky at the mall where she had gone to meet her friend Linda and detained her in a hotel room for twelve hours, trying to get her to turn against the president and wear a wire in further encounters with him. Her affidavit was perjury, they told her, and she could go to prison for decades for it. At times she contemplated suicide. But when they released her to go, she had not agreed to anything.

No matter. By the time Clinton sat for his deposition in the Paula Jones case, Independent Counsel Starr and Jones's lawyers had heard all about Monica Lewinsky. As he had done in matters related to sexual impropriety, Clinton lied. On January 17, 1998, the online gossip site Drudge Report revealed Lewinsky's existence and the content of her taped conversations with Linda Tripp. For seven months, the media, quickly including the mainstream media, lawyers for Paula Jones, and a host of other political actors, revealed various aspects of the Clinton/Lewinsky affair. President Clinton continued to deny — to his family, to his cabinet, and, in a televised press conference, to the American public — that he had "had sexual relations with that woman, Miss Lewinsky." While it was still her word against his, Clinton's defenders acted on a corollary to the hidden law of adultery: the other woman is target practice. In a campaign disturbingly reminiscent of the conservative's war on Anita Hill, the Clinton team orchestrated a series of attacks on the character of Monica Lewinsky. She was a "sexually demanding stalker," as one White House intimate put out. A key congressional ally, Charles Rangel, questioned whether she "played with a full deck."[16] When a private conversation of Hillary's was revealed years later, Americans learned that Monica was, in the spouse's estimation, just a "narcissistic loony toon" whom Bill had heroically tried to rid himself of.[17] The media gleefully unearthed the story of Lewinsky's earlier sexual affairs.

In June, Monica Lewinsky finally got a proper DC legal team, and her lawyers negotiated a full immunity from the false affidavit in exchange for her telling Ken Starr the whole story. The independent counsel brought her before a grand jury, where she testified under oath for days. Finally, on August 17, 1998, after learning that the independent counsel had a specimen of Clinton's DNA from the blue dress Lewinsky wore during one of their encounters, the president of the United States told the grand jury that he "may have been misleading."[18] That night, he told the American people that he had had "relations" with "Miss Lewinsky," which were, in his mealy-mouthed phrase, "not appropriate."

On September 9, 1998, Independent Counsel Ken Starr released a 445-page report to Congress, suggesting grounds for impeachment. The report, hands down the most salacious document ever printed by the Government Publishing Office, includes, in agonizing detail, Lewinsky's descriptions from the grand jury of each of her encounters with the president. The Republican-dominated House voted to make the report public.

Americans thus got a full dose of what happens when the hidden law of adultery no longer applies. Unable to hide, Americans had to decide if they cared whether President Clinton had been engaging in something resembling "sexual relations" with Miss Lewinsky. By and large, they did not care.[19] After the release of the Starr Report, 60 percent of Americans polled said the president had apologized enough, 59 percent approved of the way he was doing his job, and 70 percent expected him to serve out his term. In November 1998, for the first time in more than a half century, the president's party gained seats in the midterm election. Nonetheless, the House Republicans began the consideration of articles of impeachment, the constitutional device for removing a president from office.

On December 19, 1998, three months after the Starr Report, by a narrow partisan majority, the Republican-controlled House approved two of the Judiciary Committee's four proposed articles of impeachment, perjury and obstruction of justice in the Paula Jones case, and sent President Clinton to trial in the Senate. It was only the second time in American history that a president had been impeached and referred, as the Constitution requires, to the Senate for trial on the issue of his conviction. In the new post–hidden law regime, the publisher of *Hustler* magazine quickly revealed newly appointed Republican House of Representatives leader Bob Livingston's extramarital affairs. Livingston announced his resignation as Speaker and said he would resign his legislative seat entirely in six months. On February 12, 1999, by a majority vote that included five Republicans, the Senate acquitted the president.[20] They didn't get anywhere near the constitutional requirement of two-thirds to convict.

Feminism, in Game of Chicken with Liberal Ally Clinton, Swerves

What is the relationship between a sexually comfortable twenty-two-year-old intern, who was not threatened or coerced, and the president of the United States, who did not lose his office, doing in a book about harassment and abuse?

In March 1998, long before Clinton came clean, Gloria Steinem, the closest thing the feminist movement had to a spokesperson, opined in the authoritative *New York Times* opinion section, "If all the sexual allegations now swirling around the White House turn out to be true . . . feminists will still have been right to resist pressure by the right wing and the media to call for his resignation or impeachment."

Feminists should resist, Steinem argued, because the calls — and accusations of hypocrisy — were leveled only at feminists. Why, Steinem asks, aren't the critics of feminism also turning their fire on "environmentalists" who liked Clinton's environmental policy or "journalists" who approved of his defense of free speech to call for Clinton to step down? Why hound us feminists about how women are treated? Somehow *Gloria Steinem* missed the message that looking out for other women, especially young and vulnerable ones, is Feminist Job One.

And then, she continued, each of the other known accusations against Clinton involved him grabbing and kissing or offering his penis to his female supporters or employees *only one time!* He understood no meant no. Hadn't the Supreme Court said the harassment has to be severe and pervasive? Joining the many courts that dismissed such behavior as just a little harmless merriment, Steinem explained that it's not as if Clinton had made the women's lives a living hell for two years like Clarence Thomas did. Now that, Steinem said, was real harassment.

And finally, "Whatever it was, her relationship with President Clinton has never been called unwelcome, coerced or other than something she sought. The power imbalance between them increased the index of suspicion, but there is no evidence to suggest that Ms. Lewinsky's will was violated; quite the contrary."[21] So what if he lied about sex? In an eerie echo of the arguments against judging sexual behavior that go back to the pornography debate, Steinem suggested that it's the people judging the groping and the penis-showing and the involvement with the intern who were at fault. Maybe if we were more mature about sex, there would be no hidden law, and Clinton could just own his sexual behavior rather than having to lie about it.

In April, right after Steinem's op-ed, the unusually clear-eyed social observer Marjorie Williams described feminists as either silent or dismissive regarding Clinton and Lewinsky. The positions of "women in Congress—including several swept to power by female outrage over the Senate's treatment of Anita Hill . . . range from the procedural stonewall ('What is important for the American people to know is that there is a process in place to deal with these allegations,' in the words of Senator Barbara Boxer) to the creative inversion (What about Ken Starr's 'humiliation' of the women he dragged before the grand jury?, fumed Representative Nancy Pelosi) to the truly fanciful twist on gender politics ('Not so many years ago, a woman couldn't *be* a White House intern,' said a straight-faced Senator Carol Moseley-Braun on *Meet the Press*)."[22]

Reading the tale released by the Republicans that September, it is stunningly obvious that Clinton's sexual relations with the twenty-two-year-old certainly was not what she "sought," in Steinem's words. The question is: why would a person enter into sexual relations different from what she desired? In his widely praised book about the matter, *An Affair of State*, federal judge and legal scholar Richard Posner undertook to analyze the morality and legality of the events that had just transpired.[23] "Many radical feminists," he intoned, "believe that sex between a male superior and a female subordinate is sexual harassment per se because of the imbalance of power between them. Most Americans would reject this view if they read Monica Lewinsky's testimony."[24] Posner and many analysts get it wrong because they see only one reason a person would have undesirable sexual relations: coercion. The coercion may range from the application of force, as in rape, to an implicit threat or reward regarding the victim's livelihood, to the insistence that the person must work in a hostile sexual environment. Such exercises of power are the stick in unsought sexual relations. But understanding, as MacKinnon suggested all those years ago, that you cannot separate sex from the context in which it happens, we have a richer way of understanding what went wrong.

There are many ways to undermine a person's will besides force or threat. Bill Clinton did not apply the stick to Monica Lewinsky; she has said that from the beginning. Behaviors other than the stick may not be illegal harassment, but they are politically and morally wrong and present an important issue for a movement for women's equality. Marjorie Williams described this notion at the time as: "the hard-won consensus that men should not use social and economic power to recruit sex partners in the workplace, and that it's fair for both sexes to expect limits on how much sexual relations are allowed to distort the system of rewards. I'm talking, here, not about feminist legislative achievements, but about a shift in the extralegal realm of mores, the shift that followed and ratified the actual laws against specific forms of sexual harassment."[25] Who ever said that only illegal behavior is wrong?

Distorting the Rewards of Sex

In what sense was Clinton wrong? First, and most obviously, President Clinton risked what actually happened — the revelation of their sexual relationship, a revelation that did Monica Lewinsky untold harm. There is a good argument that he should have known of the risk. He had been outed for his long affair with Gennifer Flowers; he was the subject of a lawsuit for sexual harassment by Paula Jones, which he could not seem to get dismissed or delayed; and a hostile and determined investigator, Ken Starr, was dogging his every move. His silence in face of the risk of being found out and the price of that revelation for a twenty-two-year-old was deceitful. Lewinsky is obviously not without fault in the secret coming out. She apparently had some warning that the affair should remain secret, as she was tiptoeing around the West Wing and sneaking in on Sundays. Lewinsky's completely irrepressible talking about her sexual adventures played a big role in her exposure. But her behavior just reinforces how naive she was about what the media and the political environment Clinton lived in could do to her. He knew and she didn't. And when a person with superior knowledge deceives someone, they violate the will of the less informed person.

Admittedly, it took a devilish combination of circumstances for them to get caught. Monica talked, a right-wing Clinton hater sat in her area at the Pentagon, Kenneth Starr's operation had no bounds on its ambition to bring this president down. So a second and more pressing question is whether Clinton's sexual relations with Monica Lewinsky would have been politically and morally wrong, even if the two were not realistically at risk or even if they had never been caught. Remember, it was the sexual relations between the president and Monica Lewinsky, not the scandal that hit her later, which was the subject of Steinem's op-ed, in which she exonerated the president on behalf of movement feminism.

As Steinem says, Clinton did not use the stick of coercion or threat to establish a sexual relationship with the young employee. But he offered something much more insidious and directly related to what supposedly worried Steinem, the power imbalance. A power imbalance can be both a stick and a carrot, and he offered Lewinsky, in the most predictable way, the carrot. And what a carrot! Handsome, charismatic, surrounded only by subordinates, securely anchored in an unshakeable marriage, more than twice her age and the most powerful person in the entire country. How much did his power distort the system of rewards, as Marjorie Williams framed it? Because the independent counsel put the whole intimate story before a grand jury and then published the results, we know a lot. And then Lewinsky told the story again, in 1999, to celebrity biographer Andrew Morton.

From the very first time when he reached for her, she felt she had been transported to another realm: "In the inner office, the President stood close to her before wrapping his arms around her and holding her tightly. 'I remember,'" she told Morton, "'looking at him and seeing such a different person than the one I expected to see. There was such a softness and tenderness about him ... I can't believe I am here, standing here alone with the President of the United States' . . . he told her that she was beautiful and that her energy lit up a room. 'He probably says that to everybody but at the time he made me feel incredibly special.'" The second time she went to him he was in the Oval Office. "Oh my goodness," she thought, "I'm walking through the Oval Office." He was, she decided that night, "her sexual soulmate."[26]

Although, after the scandal broke, the White House and the media portrayed her as the aggressor, she told one of her pals that she and Clinton had been making eyes at each other and being a little bit flirty way before that. "She would see him in the halls. And one afternoon . . . he must have said something to her, you know," her friend Neysa Erbland reasoned, because it was so risky if she were wrong, and then "she — she lifted up her shirt and showed him her underwear."[27] Not coerced, certainly, but not entirely her idea either.

When she became a White House employee in December, she had access to the West Wing, and they soon set up a routine where he would call her, frequently after hours, and she would come to one of the covert places where they would have oral sex.[28] At these times Clinton was, as she described it to the grand jury, "very affectionate . . . We would tell jokes. We would talk about our childhoods. Talk about current events. I was always giving him my stupid ideas about what I thought should be done in the administration or different views on things. I think back on it and he always made me smile when I was with him."[29] She says she once told him "he was like rays of sunshine, but sunshine that made plants grow faster and that made colors more vibrant."[30] And so she began to fall in love with him. He reassured her that he never wanted her to feel theirs was only a sexual relationship. She gave him a nickname: Handsome. She allowed herself to fantasize that his marriage would not outlast his presidency and that she had a chance of marrying him.

Her deluded understanding of what was happening bubbled over to her friends. "It was happy, it was good. She talked about wanting to be able to see him more, wishing they could see each other freely. You know, she was crazy about him."[31] Even her contemporaries saw how unrealistic she was. "You're making a mistake," friend Catherine Allday Davis warned her. "Monica is loony!" Davis told mutual friend Ryan Schlunz. "I love her but geeeeeuz . . . sometimes I cannot even believe the stuff she gets herself into."[32]

He tried to break it off as early as February 1996, saying he felt guilty. She shed bitter tears that night. Her mother, Marcia Lewis, told biographer Andrew Morton that she was relieved at the breakup, which was only temporary as it turned out. This affair was too big for any of them to comprehend, let alone deal with sensibly. "I felt it was wrong," Lewinsky's mother shared with Morton. It frightened her because of the enormity of it. It was a terrible secret to bear. It was wrong and it was terrible, but Monica's mother actually gave a much better explanation of the politics of sex with a president than feminist icon Gloria Steinem did: "What do you do? March down to the White House, say I'm Monica's mom and I'm here to see the President, and shake my finger at him? Tell him to leave my little girl alone? That's absurd."[33]

When, five months after the affair had begun, Lewinsky was told she would be transferred out of the White House, her initial reaction was that "I was never going to see the president again." When he called her, she went to the White House to protest. "Why do they have to take you away from me? I trust you," she reports him saying. "I promise you if I win in November I'll bring you back like that."[34] And so began a year and a half of purgatory, as Lewinsky waited to be let back in. First she counted the days until the election. The day after the election, she went to a welcoming ceremony on the White House South Lawn, wearing the distinctive beret he had liked. She returned home fully expecting him to call her to the White House and tell her what he had arranged for her return. "I got everything ready," she told Andrew Morton. "I put out what I was going to wear and I had my hair cut. Then I sat — and I sat and I sat. I waited all weekend for him to call and it didn't happen."

Unsurprisingly, Clinton never did bring her back. Months later, Lewinsky's mom, Marcia, ran into Evelyn Lieberman at a political event and told her how sad Monica was that she had been booted. "It's a curse," Lieberman replied to the mother, "to be born beautiful."[35] The president would tell Lewinsky that he was working on it, or advise her to apply for this or that position, but she mysteriously never got in. The crying quotient increased exponentially as Lewinsky began to suspect she was being "strung along."[36] Despite Lieberman's best efforts to keep the beautiful, cursed young woman away from the president, however, he kept circling back. He called her, they had phone sex, he arranged for her to come to the White House occasionally, using his personal secretary to set up the meetings. He bought her presents, mostly tchotchkes from his vacations here and there, a hatpin or a dress from Martha's Vineyard. For a year and a half, when weeks passed and she did not hear from him, her mother testified, she cried. When he called her or called for her, she was happy. When he finally stopped the sexual exchanges, he told her that his wife and daughter were the priority. He didn't want to keep risking something that valuable for Monica Lewinsky.

And yet, even after it became clear that they were both in legal jeopardy and the gifts they had exchanged were incriminating, he sent her more gifts. When he saw her name on the witness list for the *Jones* case, it was December (1997), and there were presents. Didn't that seem weird? a special prosecutor asked her a few months later, as she testified before the grand jury. "You know," she answered, "I have come recently to look at that as sort of a strange situation, I think, in the course of the past few weeks, but at the time, I was — you know, I was in love with him, I was elated to get these presents and — at the same time that I was so scared about the Paula Jones thing, I was happy to be with him and — I — I didn't think about that."[37]

One month after he gave Lewinsky her Christmas gifts, Clinton told the American people to listen to him: "I did not have sex with that woman, Miss Lewinsky." Even this summary version of the record of her ignorance, her vulnerability, her suffering, and her family's helplessness reveals in the most graphic fashion the moral and political wrongdoing in distorting the rewards of sex as the president did.

Clinton was the ally, the most reliably supportive president feminists had ever had. His value trumped, they argued, the suffering of one delusional and undisciplined twenty-two-year-old. Even after the scandal essentially crippled the administration, the Clinton White House did participate in strengthening the penalties for sex trafficking and getting more money for Head Start.[38]

What an ally! But the price was high. If the Hill/Thomas hearings were a national teach-in on the wrongs of sexual harassment at work, the feminist swerve in face of Clinton's sexual behavior was a national teach-in on the triumph of sexual libertinism on the liberal left. It was the turning point of the movement against sexual harassment and abuse for the next two decades, an eternity in social movement time. Sure, as Livingston's outing reflected, the Republican men were no better, in private. But the right drove him out, leaving the retrograde religious vision of heterosexual marital sexuality as its model. The left, feminists' natural allies, gave them Clinton's libertinism. "When the dust of Clinton's presidency settles, the laws against sexual harassment will still be on the books," Williams acknowledged. "But the social sanctions against the behavior will be irretrievably damaged."[39]

7

Life Among the Ruins of the Feminist Collision with Bill Clinton

1998–2016

Manhattan Supergals

On January 30, 1998, just days after the Lewinsky story hit the press, Lisa Chase, an editor at the *New York Observer,* had the bright idea of holding a panel discussion at the fancy restaurant Le Bernardin for "ten Manhattan 'supergals'"[1] —including writers Katie Roiphe, Erica Jong, Marisa Bowe, Nancy Friday, designer Nicole Miller, former *Saturday Night Live* contributor Patricia Marx, and "retired dominatrix and writer" Susan Shellogg.[2] The gathering offered feminists, at least of the Manhattan variety, a peek into the post-Clinton-sex-scandal world. Chase assigned the piece after being out one night with female friends, when someone asked whether they would "fuck the President," and everyone present concluded they sure would. Chase thought the panel would reveal the kinds of conversations she'd been hearing all over the city.[3]

Patricia Marx liked Clinton better for having had a titillating affair; after all, he came off as kind of a hunk. Jong, for one, wanted a president who was "alive from the waist down," and Marx declared him "cute and getting cuter all the time." They pronounced Kenneth Starr (in Friday's words) "a big sissy," and speculated about whether Lewinsky had swallowed the president's semen. "Oh," volunteered Jong, "imagine swallowing the Presidential come."[4]

A few weeks later, reporting in the *New Yorker* on her evening at a White House state dinner, editor in chief Tina Brown allowed herself a similar excursion into sexual fantasy: "Now see your President, tall and absurdly debonair, as he dances with a radiant blonde, his wife . . . Amid the clichés about his charm, his glamour is undersung . . . Forget the dog-in-the-manger, down-in-the-mouth neo-puritanism of the op-ed tumbrel drivers, and see him instead as his guests do: a man in a dinner jacket with more heat than any star in the room."[5] In all his glamour, he was, as Chase describes him, "a JFK kind of person." Whew, JFK, the man who brought a string of women into the White House at all hours of the day and night.

Only Marisa Bowe, editor of the online magazine *Word,* paused in the merriment at Le Bernardin to notice that Monica Lewinsky looked "sad" in a recent picture making the rounds in the media. Katie Roiphe suggested that Lewinsky's very value lay in her lack of good looks. She made average women dream that they too could attract the amorous attentions of the president, Roiphe offered, unlike JFK's preference for bombshells like the incomparable Marilyn Monroe. Jong contributed the report that her dental hygienist thought Lewinsky had "gum disease."

Those were hot days at the trendy *New York Observer*: sex and power, that's what the paper was interested in. And how wonderful was it, every girl's dream, as one of the supergals said: "You can be the President, but you can fuck the President, too."

Or can you?

If You're a Celebrity the Courts Let You Do It

Amid the tumult surrounding the Lewinsky scandal, an important legal decision about Bill Clinton's sexual behavior was handed down. In April 1998, three months after the supergals met for drinks, the federal district court in Arkansas made a decision in *Jones v. Clinton*, which had been remanded to the trial court after the Supreme Court ruled that a sitting president was not immune from civil litigation: district judge Susan Webber Wright dismissed the case against Clinton without even going to trial. In order to do what she did, Judge Wright had to assume that, even if everything that Paula Jones said had happened between her and then-governor Clinton was true, Jones still had not stated a viable legal claim for damages against Clinton.

What did Paula Jones say?[6] Paula Jones said that, on May 8, 1991, she was, in her capacity as an Arkansas state employee, working the registration desk at an event in which Governor Bill Clinton was participating. After she met his bodyguard, Danny Ferguson, the governor, who had spotted her from some distance, sent Ferguson back to Jones's desk to ask her if she'd like to come to Clinton's suite in the hotel. After Jones came to the suite and announced herself, the governor shook her hand, invited her in, and closed the door. A few minutes of small talk ensued, which included the governor asking her about her job and mentioning that Dave Harrington, Jones's ultimate superior and a Clinton appointee, was his "good friend." The governor then unexpectedly reached over to her, took her hand, and pulled her toward him, so that their bodies were close together. She removed her hand from his and retreated several feet, but the governor approached her again and, while saying, "I love the way your hair flows down your back" and "I love your curves," put his hand on her leg, started sliding it toward her pelvic area, and bent down to attempt to kiss her on the neck, all without her consent.

"What are you doing?" Jones asked. She "escaped" from the governor's reach "by walking away from him." She was extremely upset and confused and, not knowing what to do, attempted to distract the governor by chatting about his wife. She sat down at the end of the sofa nearest the door, but Clinton approached the sofa where she had taken a seat and, as he sat down, "lowered his trousers and underwear, exposed his penis (which was erect) and told [her] to 'kiss it.'" "Horrified" by this, she "jumped up from the couch" and told the governor that she had to go, saying something to the effect that she had to get back to the registration desk. The governor, "while fondling his penis," said, "Well, I don't want to make you do anything you don't want to do," and then pulled up his pants and said, "If you get in trouble for leaving work, have Dave call me immediately and I'll take care of it." As she left the room (the door of which was not locked), the governor "detained" her momentarily, "looked sternly" at her, and said, "You are smart. Let's keep this between ourselves."

There are many other allegations in Jones's suit, including assertions of maltreatment by other supervisors after she turned the governor down, but Judge Wright found the other complaints inconsequential. Jones's claim the governor asked her to kiss his penis was, however, harder to discredit. By moving to dismiss, Clinton was saying that even if true, their encounter wasn't abusive enough to violate the law. And the judge agreed: "While the alleged incident in the hotel, if true, was certainly boorish and offensive . . . This is . . . not one of those exceptional cases in which a single incident of sexual harassment, such as an assault, was deemed sufficient to state a claim of hostile work environment sexual harassment . . . Considering the totality of the circumstances, it simply cannot be said that the conduct to which plaintiff was allegedly subjected was frequent, severe, or physically threatening, and the Court finds that defendants' actions as shown by the record do not constitute the kind of sustained and nontrivial conduct necessary for a claim of hostile work environment."[7]

From the time she'd come forward with her story, the public hadn't paid much attention to Paula Jones. She lived at the intersection of gender and class, a clerical employee making six dollars an hour in 1991. And, from the Supreme Court decision in *Meritor v. Vinson* in 1986 to Judge Wright's dismissal of her claim against the president in 1998, there were other cases where the courts gave a pass to a boss accused of isolated acts of sexual misconduct. But on the whole, and with a spike in complaints in 1991 after the Hill/

Thomas hearings, those twelve years before the decision in *Jones v. Clinton* had seen a slow but steady improvement in the status of civil rights action against sexual harassment. *Jones v. Clinton*, a high-profile decision involving the most powerful man in the world, sent a chill through the movement.[8] In 2016, when another powerful man, Donald Trump, was accused of boorish behavior, he and his handlers trotted out Paula Jones to sit in the gallery at his debate with presidential candidate Hillary Clinton. Unlike the priggish Ken Starr, 2016 Republican candidate Trump wanted to remind the voting public that even liberal celebrities did it.

The Feminist Movement Was Already Weakened When It Took the Hit

When the Clinton/Lewinsky sex scandal surfaced in 1998, the last thing organized feminism needed was another blow right at its perennial weak spot, sex. The conflict between easy access to sex and gender equality, always inherent in the feminist movement, had gone dormant in some respects after the pro-pornography side beat the MacKinnonites in the 1980s. Clinton's affair threatened to reopen the wound. No wonder so many movement feminists gladly signed on to the White House's portrayal of Monica Lewinsky as a sexual sophisticate from sunny California, determined to seduce the president of the United States. This version of the president's sexual partner would make the problem for feminism so much easier than the real inequality the record so graphically reveals.

And the movement, now more than thirty years old, was beset by so many other problems. The resistance to feminism, convincingly chronicled by Pulitzer Prize–winning journalist Susan Faludi in her book *Backlash*,[9] had begun to bleed the movement dry. Faludi writes that almost from the beginning in the 1960s, the normal forces of opposition to social change—traditional religion, conservative politics—had mobilized to resist feminist inroads. By 1982 a coalition of such forces had defeated ratification of the Equal Rights

Amendment, the constitutional provision intended to prohibit legal discrimination on the basis of sex. In 1980 the Republican Party
officially withdrew its support for the ERA and made opposition to
abortion central to its political platform. But at least the conservative political opposition was open in its enmity. Women belonged in
the home, ERA opponent and conservative activist Phyllis Schlafly
asserted. Human life begins at conception, and so a woman had to
carry every fertilized egg to birth regardless of her wishes or the
real cost to her. These opponents were not going to embrace feminism whether its adherents wanted to fuck the president or run for
president.

By 1991, however, Schlafly's movement had largely failed. Abortion was by then protected by two decades of Supreme Court decisions. ACLU lawyer Ruth Bader Ginsburg had basically transformed the old racial-equality amendments to apply to sex equality.
The real threat came from feminism's "frenemies," those enemies
masquerading as friends, particularly friends in the media. Frenemies would never argue that women should not serve on juries
or have access to abortion. The friendly threats to feminism were
numerous, but they could be roughly divided into two types: feminism had succeeded and women should be happy with what they
had achieved and go home, or feminism had succeeded and women
were miserable with what they had achieved and should thus go
back home. Regardless of which argument you pursued, the outcome was, as *Time* magazine asked, disingenuously, in the middle
of the Clinton affair, "Is Feminism Dead?"[10]

The frenemies homed in on feminism's vulnerability — equality
kills sexuality — like Luke Skywalker flying into the Death Star. Faludi was alerted to the existence of the backlash, which became her
subject, in 1986 when she happened to see the article in *Newsweek*
reporting that single women over forty were more likely to be killed
by a terrorist than find a (heterosexual) mate.[11] Good journalist that
she was, Faludi asked herself, could this possibly be true? Check-
ing the statistics, she found that *Newsweek* had made the assertion
based on one statistically dubious unpublished study.[12] Journalism

101 should have dictated the story be killed, but the idea was so appealing to the editors that no one checked the numbers. The more she looked at the coverage of feminism, the more hostility and bad data she identified. In 1991 *Backlash* won the National Book Critics Circle Award for nonfiction, and "backlash" became the generic name for the drumbeat of media stories intended to discourage organized activism for gender equality. But it didn't stop the backlash. The threat of sexual blackmail against any woman who demanded equal treatment was so potent that seven years after *Backlash*, *Newsweek*'s more robust competitor, *Time*, just dispensed with the terrorist and proclaimed the movement "dead."[13]

The more than thirty-year-old movement was certainly on the ropes. This is not shameful or surprising. Very few secular movements had ever tried to unite such a large and diverse population for social change — and for so long. Starting with a book aimed at white suburban housewives in 1963, the movement virtually exploded in the early years. From self-consciously leaderless, evanescent downtown collectives like the radical feminist 1960s Redstockings, to housewives in classic midwestern Muncie, Indiana, the message of "women's liberation" spread. Like the universe after the Big Bang, it spread and then it thinned out.

A microcosm of the movement can be seen in the history of the iconic feminist vehicle *Ms.* magazine. *Ms.* was founded in 1971 by Gloria Steinem and a roomful of other female New York journalists who wanted to create a women's magazine controlled by women. A 40-page excerpt of the "preview" issue was published as a pullout in the trendy *New York* magazine in December 1971. Within weeks, twenty-six thousand people had subscribed. The preview issue itself, which appeared in January 1972, sold out its initial offering of three hundred thousand copies in eight days.

Ms. magazine never had a secure financial plan, its advertisers were always jumpy, and by 1978 it could be sustained only as a not-for-profit. Steinem and a few others founded the Ms. Foundation for Women, at that point to support the magazine, which had always had more impact than income. In its heyday, *Ms.* helped set the agenda for American feminism. In 1977, just two years after Lin Farley and the Cornell women named sexual harassment, *Ms.* ran a cover story on the problem. The cover illustration featured a doll seated behind a desk, with a male hand reaching over its shoulder and down inside the front of its dress. (A faction of the magazine's editors didn't want to actually show it happening.)[14]

At its height in the early 1980s, *Ms.* reportedly had a monthly circulation of seven hundred thousand readers.[15] As *Ms.* grew in popularity and tried to maintain its appeal to a diverse readership, the magazine experienced every divide that rent the movement as a whole. Predictably, *Ms.* early on took fire from the left for not being ideologically pure enough.[16] In April 1985, for example, the editors ran an article, "Is One Woman's Sexuality Another Woman's Pornography?" Looking back, the editors present remembered a debate on the pornography article so intense that "some people never got over it." The magazine was also accused of prioritizing white women's issues. In 1986 one woman of color, a star contributing writer, Alice Walker, resigned. "A people of color cover once or twice a year is not enough. In real life, people of color occur with much more frequency. I do not feel welcome in the world you are projecting." Ominously, Walker resigned not just for herself but also for her daughter, Rebecca Walker, also a *Ms.* contributor, then age seventeen.[17]

Already rent by division, by 1987 *Ms.* faced, as the movement did, the price of its own success. In an effort to appeal to its diverse subscriber base, *Ms.* had become to some younger supporters bland, uncontroversial, boosterish, and unironic.[18] Like the movement, *Ms.*'s target audience was beginning to rise in the world of work the movement had begun to open up. Many of these women didn't need a collective organ to raise their consciousness. Predictably, competition arose — *Working Women, Savvy, New York Woman.*[19] The control group at *Ms.* kept seeking new owners — an obscure Australian company, Fairfax, first, and then professional publishers like Dale Lang — and they tried publishing without advertising, as ads got harder and harder to find. In 1997 a core group of women took it over again, this time as Liberty Media. They professed a plan to relaunch the magazine with a new emphasis on youth.[20]

In 1996, before the magazine's relaunch, an underpaid editor in the New York office, Jennifer Baumgardner, took a horrified look around at where the great success story of feminism's second wave had landed, and walked off the job: "I had loved it there more than anywhere since the womb, but by the time I left the sight of the harried editors, the stained and airless offices, and the constant crises had made me ill. After years of declining working conditions under hostile male owners — long hours, low pay, bungled editorial processes that alienated writers, a harrowing year of stiffing writers, and being asked to sit in for the beleaguered company receptionist so that the poor woman could go to the bathroom — I got out."[21] *Ms.* had, as Baumgardner put it, "battered women's movement syndrome." After drinking too much wine with her BFF Amy Richards, she and Richards decided to write a book.

Baumgardner and Richards recognized that by 1996, the waters of feminism were rising again, this time in a third wave. As the history of *Ms.* magazine reflects, thirty years after *The Feminine Mystique* ushered in the second wave, American females were spread across the firmament and pursuing as many visions of a good life as there were women in America. In 1992 Rebecca Walker (whose departure Alice Walker had announced in 1986) wrote an article for *Ms.:* "Becoming the Third Wave." In May 1992 Walker and Shannon Liss started the Third Wave Direct Action Corporation, with a mission "to fill a void in young women's leadership and to mobilize young people to become more involved socially and politically in their communities."[22] A picture of the founders, two women of color, two white — reflects a core commitment of the new group: the intersection of sex with race and class.[23] As of 2002, the board of Third Wave was half people of color. Anthologies of personal narratives, which offered the public face of the new wave movement, included stories from a rainbow of different races and cultures.[24]

Members of the organization, reconstituted in 1997 as the Third Wave Foundation, got membership cards asking, "My issues are

_____?" "No two cards," Baumgardner and Richards report, "have ever listed the same answer." Members listed "Jewish progressive life," "war crimes," "student financial aid," "interracial dating," "fat oppression," etcetera, etcetera. The new wave, Baumgardner and Richards reported in 2000, was still working on issues, including sexual harassment, "inherited from the Second Wave," but prominent third-wave issues included "equal access to the internet, HIV/AIDs awareness, child sexual abuse, self-mutilation, globalization, eating disorders, and body image." A robust "Girlie" movement centered in the new media "zines" of the 1990s arose to reclaim the word "girl." (Zines are small-circulation, self-published, and often inexpensive or free publications, usually about one subject, often a performance group.) Girlies were trying to breathe new life into feminism. Reacting to "an antifeminine, antijoy emphasis that they perceive as the legacy of Second Wave seriousness, Girlies have reclaimed girl culture, which is made up of such formerly disparaged things as knitting, the color pink, nail polish, and fun. They also claim their right to a cultural space once deemed the province of men; for example, rock n roll, porn and judgment-free pleasure and sex."[25]

Baumgardner characterizes the third wave as throwing open the gates to feminism. People did not have to go to NOW meetings or marches or write to their congressional representatives. They could make individual feminist decisions every day in their own lives on whether or not to have children, to work in the market or at home, to give their daughters Barbie dolls, to adorn themselves (or not) with makeup. Young feminists could create culture, rather than just criticizing it. They would have their own bands, publish scores of small zines to the in groups, and organize women's music tours, like the famous Lilith Fair.

By opening up feminism, which they took to be closed, to individuals who did not want to abide by a set of rules, the third wave vastly expanded the potential appeal of feminism, should the occasion arise when women needed to organize collectively again. "You're sexy, a wallflower, you shop at Calvin Klein, you are a stay-at-home mom, a big Hollywood producer, a beautiful bride all in white, an ex-wife raising three kids, or you shave, pluck, *and* wax," the Manifesta proclaims. Everybody's welcome. But nothing specific is required. "Institutions like NOW and *Ms.* magazine attenuated," Baumgardner explained in her retrospective on the wave, "in part because Third Wave feminists didn't need any members to be feminist."[26]

Much of the third wave involved yet another generation of daughters figuring out a way to distinguish themselves from their liberated mothers, from NOW and *Ms.*, just as the second-wave feminist founders — at least the white ones, since most women of color always had to work — had rejected their stay-at-home moms. But living a feminist life while rebelling against feminist mothers is tricky. "To do feminism differently from one's mother, to make choices that are our own, and not simply a reaction or a rejection, is the task of our generation," Baumgardner and Richards say.[27] When the old feminists like Gwendolyn Mink and Katha Pollitt suggested that the feminist movement should have been harder on President Clinton, the young feminists took Monica Lewinsky's word that she had started it. Her decision was "stupid" and her motives "delusional," they wrote, but nonetheless "the relationship was consensual." Young women are going to make mistakes, but that's their right. After all, "the effect of his presidential authority was not coercive but seductive — the aphrodisiac of power." Delusional and under an aphrodisiac, Monica was "an adult woman with responsibility for her actions."[28] The married leader of the free world, they admit, might not be as "emotionally available" as Lewinsky wanted, but she chose her choice. As for what feminism owed plaintiff Paula Jones, Baumgardner and Richards wrote, Judge Susan Webber Wright tossed her complaint against the president. Since the law "disagreed" that the president had engaged in "blatant sexual harassment when he asked a state employee to kiss his penis,"[29] that was that. Why, the heirs to twenty years of feminist legal reform asked, would feminism have an obligation to challenge what the law said?

Characterized by their heirs as overwhelmingly white, bourgeois, antijoy, and antifeminine, and still trying to lead a movement
where politics had devolved into the thousand different issue cards
the Third Wave Foundation got back, the leaders and spokespeople
of second-wave institutions like NOW and *Ms.* had their work cut
out for them in 1998. At that very moment, they were confronted
with the sexual acts of a charismatic Democratic president and his
twenty-two-year-old intern, just on the line of mature judgment.
No wonder they were so eager to defend the young woman's sexual agency and to belly up to the bar with third-wave feminists and
Manhattan supergals. And like any other mother's frantic efforts to
stay hip, it availed them nothing. The new third-wave generation
continued to treat their predecessors as people whose books were
out of print. Between the girly third wave and the exoneration of
the boorish president, the lesson for male liberals was that they had
nothing to fear from any version of feminism, whatever the wave.

Bill Clinton's Sex Scandal Put Hillary in the Senate, but It Put George W. Bush in the White House

The feminist bargain with Clinton looked good at first. The first
feminist to try her wings after the dust settled in 1998 was the First
Feminist, Hillary Clinton. Eight days after the Clinton/Lewinsky
"imbroglio," as Hillary called it, hit the news in January 1998, Hillary appeared on the *Today* show to testify to Bill's innocence. It was
all, as she famously suggested, "a vast right-wing conspiracy."[30]

At the time, Bill and Hillary polled evenly, with an impressive
65 percent favorability rating. As details of the Lewinsky testimony
and the Starr Report became public, Bill's numbers dropped, while
Hillary's remained constant. Nonetheless, she spent seven months
leading the campaign to defend him, including, by most accounts,
framing the narrative that Monica Lewinsky was a combination of
ungrateful beneficiary of Bill's famously good nature and delusional
stalker.[31] As her husband finally copped to his impropriety on August 17, 1998, Pew pollsters found two-thirds of the public applaud-

ing Hillary's decision to stand by her man. Respondents described her favorably as: "strong, intelligent, brave, loyal and good." (This was a big step up from 1996, where a common answer to the pollsters' questions about Hillary was "rhymes with rich.")[32]

By the November 1998 midterm elections, with impeachment proceedings still a few weeks away, Hillary had decided to use her new popularity as a victim to campaign for the Democratic congressional candidates. If the Dems suffered from Bill's scandal, after all, he might actually be impeached and tossed out. The Clintons needed the Democrats to do well in November. By all accounts, she was dynamite. She raised millions, spoke at thirty-four rallies, and racked up chits with senators from New York to California. Ominously, she outdrew crowds for Clinton's formerly faithful vice president, Al Gore.

Right after the 1998 midterms, New York senator Daniel Patrick Moynihan announced he would not run for reelection in 2000. To run for Senate in New York, state law requires only that candidates be in residence by election day. On July 8, 1999, Hillary Clinton stood at the side of the patrician Senator Moynihan and announced her candidacy for the New York Senate seat.[33]

When the feminist establishment threw in their lot with Bill Clinton in the spring and summer of 1998, they may have sincerely believed in their sex-positive "Manhattan supergals" idea of the world. Or they may have made a cold political calculation that they needed to defend Bill Clinton for the greater goals of the movement. Putting the much-maligned feminist Hillary Clinton in the Senate would be a payoff for backing Bill. The previous second in the "two for the price of one" would finally step out and into an independent political career. In November 2000 she was elected to the United States Senate from New York. By all accounts, Hillary Clinton's term and a half in the Senate was a big success.[34]

Feminist politicos had calculated, but math is hard. As Hillary was running for her Senate seat, Bill Clinton's two-term vice president Al Gore was staging his own run to succeed his boss as president of the United States. Anonymous sources from the Gore campaign complained to journalists throughout that Hillary Clinton's 2000 campaign was "sucking the oxygen" of Democratic support and money from the presidential race.[35] But Hillary Clinton wasn't even Al Gore's biggest Clinton problem. Bill Clinton was.

Poor Gore. In typical straight-arrow fashion, he had stuck by Clinton's months-long campaign of denial, defending his innocence in numerous, well-documented public statements and appearances. In 1999 the Republicans put up a billboard outside Gore's out-of-Washington headquarters in Nashville, Tennessee, showing Gore and Clinton hugging and quoting Gore calling Bill "One of America's Greatest Presidents." In March 2000, as Gore trailed Republican George W. Bush in the early polls, half of the voters who approved of Bill Clinton's job performance disapproved of him as a person. The "disaffected Clinton voters," the prestigious Gallup poll speculated, could cost Gore the election.[36] The devilish problem Gore faced was that the negative fallout from Clinton's sex scandal was almost exactly equal to the benefit from Clinton's job favorables. And the worst part was that the negative impact from Clinton was concentrated in the voters in swing states like Ohio and West Virginia.[37] And so the Gore campaign struggled every day.[38] Had Clinton been impeached, of course, Gore would have run as an incumbent after eight years of a rising economy: shoo-in.[39] Feminists had faced the same calculation as Gore in deciding whether to embrace Bill Clinton: backing Clinton would be worth the cost of living in the world of sex with interns in the White House if Democrats remained in control of the executive branch.

Gore lost. Looking back on the election of 2000, Stanford's Morris Fiorina wrote with two other eminent political scientists that "Clinton fatigue, broadly defined, probably directly cost Gore 3–4 percent of the vote, easily enough to lose the election."[40] Fiorina and his coauthors offered their "personal view" that, nonetheless, Gore could have used Clinton on the campaign trail to swing a tiny state — Arkansas, New Hampshire — and taken the election. Political author Roger Simon bluntly disagrees: "From the first day of campaigning to the last, Gore's polling shows the opposite. Clinton was a loser. Use him and lose."[41] On one point there is clear agreement among all the commentators, though. No Monica, no Gore defeat in 2000.

And what a defeat. On his first day in office, Republican president George W. Bush reinstated the policy that restricts foreign NGOs that receive US Agency for International Development family planning funds from using their own, non-US funds to provide legal abortion services, lobby their own governments for abortion law reform, or even provide accurate medical counseling or referrals regarding abortion.[42] Virtually nothing President Bush could do would have been worse for women. The Center for Reproductive Rights estimated that seventy-eight thousand women worldwide die every year from unsafe abortions.

In 2003 Congress passed for the third time a law limiting the medical procedures that could be used in performing certain abortions (anti-abortion activists call the procedures "partial-birth abortion"). The 1995 and 1997 versions of such federal bills had been vetoed by President Bill Clinton. But now George Bush signed the measure into law. And the constitutionality of the law began to wend its way to the United States Supreme Court. At first, the prospects for the anti-abortion law in court did not look promising. In 2003 the court, by a vote of 5 to 4, had struck down an almost identical law out of Nebraska, because it did not have an exception for preserving the health of the mother.[43] In 2005, however, the fifth, swing justice, Sandra Day O'Connor, announced her plans to retire, and in 2005 President George W. Bush replaced her with the passionately anti-abortion appeals court judge Samuel Alito. On April 18, 2007, the Supreme Court sustained the federal Partial-Birth Abortion Act.[44] The decision, *Gonzales v. Carhart,* was the first anti-abortion decision from the court since 1992. The vote was 5 to 4, with President Bush's appointee, Justice Alito, providing the crucial fifth vote. The crucial swing vote on the nine-member court now moved to Anthony Kennedy, who wrote the opinion in *Gonzales.*

The hit feminism took in *Gonzales v. Carhart* is palpable. It was the first decision since *Roe* to approve a limitation on abortion regardless of its impact on the mother's health. What good could such a restriction possibly do, the challengers asked? Even Congress is not allowed to pass laws just because it feels like it. In response, the bizarre opinion written by Justice Anthony Kennedy, now the swing vote, airily speculated that, contrary to all statistically grounded social science literature on the subject, some imaginary woman somewhere must regret having had an abortion. So any restriction, like outlawing a methodology that might discourage the imaginary regretful woman later, would be good. The decision in *Gonzales v. Carhart* arguably marks the first appearance of alternative facts in Supreme Court jurisprudence in decades. Like the Republicans on the Judiciary Committee, who imagined that Anita Hill must have been suffering from an erotic mania in 1991, a handful of old men in 2007 made women's lives worse by imagining what they must be thinking about abortion. The razor-thin election of George W. Bush made their fantasies the law of the land.

The Clinton Scandal Was the Making of Fox News, the Gift That Keeps on Giving

In October of 1996, just as Monica Lewinsky was counting the days until that year's presidential election was over so she could return to her post in the White House, media mogul Rupert Murdoch realized his long-term dream of starting a round-the-clock American news network. Fox News, the third cable news channel born in the heat of the new television technology, after NBC's MSNBC and Ted Turner's CNN, did not have an auspicious start. To run it, Murdoch hired former CNBC president Roger Ailes, who had just been humiliatingly passed over to run NBC's new cable channel. Ailes had been one of Richard Nixon's image makers in the run-up to the 1968 presidential victory, and he had worked the seam between conservative political consulting and conservative television production ever since.

Ailes's fondest dream was to run a conservative television network, which, he believed, was the key to reorienting the United States permanently away from liberal politics. With his nascent network, he had only the resources to hire performers like Sean Hannity, who "had never held a full-time job in television," and Bill O'Reilly, who, Ailes himself admitted, had been in the business twenty-five years without ever becoming a star.[45] Fox was fighting an antitrust suit against Time Warner, to force it to carry the network on its make-or-break service in New York, and Fox's Washington bureau news director had to wage a pitched battle for White House credentials. The viewership was minuscule.

Then, on Sunday, January 18, 1996, the commentator Matt Drudge posted an article on his website, the Drudge Report, about the president of the United States having a sexual affair with an intern. Eight days later, Clinton denied it. It was a godsend. Ailes told his best prospect, Brit Hume, he was going to launch a new show that night; Hume's program became one of the leading sources of stories about the pursuit of Bill Clinton. Fox viewership increased by 400 percent.[46] And the network found its purpose. Fox News was going to tell people how to think about what they were seeing. The Lewinsky affair was tailor-made for the network's political agenda—to make it "okay to despise the President."[47] Fox host Bill O'Reilly was Clinton's media Inspector Javert, pursuing him in the media as independent counsel Ken Starr did on the ground. Soon O'Reilly's show, *The O'Reilly Factor*, filled with the memorable characters of the Lewinsky scandal: Clinton's sleazy adviser Dick Morris, dismissed for discussing White House business with a prostitute, Linda Tripp's Svengali, Lucianne Goldberg, even Drudge himself. Fox watchers were so addicted to the scandal coverage that the Fox logo burned itself into their television screens as they left Fox on all night after broadcasting ceased. Twenty years later, Fox News had shaped the political landscape sufficiently to become the prime, if not the only, cause of the election of Donald Trump.

Note to Chickens: Once You Swerve, You're Dead Meat

Feminists, who would apparently rather be loved than feared, were neither. So for ten years after they assembled behind Bill Clinton, they got nothing. Unless it was also something the guys wanted.

First, Hillary tried the route the Manhattan supergals suggested — be the president. After all, almost from her arrival in the Senate, Hillary was the presumptive presidential front-runner. There was talk in 2004, but she ultimately decided to finish her first term in the Senate.[48] After her landslide reelection to the Senate in 2006, however, the 2008 presidential race was greased. As political commentator Ezra Klein astutely observed, Hillary was running as the prohibitive favorite, and, after she sucked up the talent, there were fairly few pools of political operatives with the seasoning to staff competing candidates at the national level.[49]

Senate Majority Leader Harry Reid, however, was not the least bit interested in Hillary Clinton in the crucial months of 2007. He had his eye on a new senator, the freshman from Illinois who had given such a stunning speech at the 2004 Democratic National Convention. Late in 2006 the majority leader called Barack Obama into his office for a heart to heart. Obama didn't like it in the Senate, he had noticed. But, he suggested, the new senator could run for president. Reid and Obama agree that Obama was a little taken aback by the majority leader's suggestion. What made Reid focus on Obama? Obama was like me, the senator with the famously hardscrabble youth told the press. He faced obstacles in his youth and so did I. And so Reid, the whitest of Anglo westerners, identified with Barack Obama in ways, he says, others may not have. Reid was hardly an avatar of political correctness. In a stunning glimpse into white people's thinking, Reid was reported as saying that part of Obama's appeal was that he was "light-skinned" and had a "Negro" accent only when he "wanted to."[50] (There was a flap; Reid apologized.) But the bottom line was Reid thought he had a winner. About Hillary Clinton he was not so sure. Although Reid purported to be neutral in the hard-fought primary between Obama and Clinton, he was not.

Obama's other Senate ally, former majority leader Tom Daschle, wasn't even in the Senate anymore. He lost his seat in 2004, partly, some thought, because of his role in preventing Bill Clinton's conviction in the Senate. Daschle's first detailed memory of Bill Clinton was of watching the *60 Minutes* episode where "he and Hillary [Clinton] responded to one of the early crises that they faced in the campaign, involving allegations of his personal life."[51] After Clinton won the presidency, he says, "you could see that the transition was rocky . . . There was also Whitewater right out of the box. That also caused a lot of people to be concerned that this President could have some ethical or legal questions down the road."

Above all, Daschle was sincerely heartbroken at the failure of the Clinton administration to pass some kind of national health care program in 1994, an initiative led, of course, by Hillary (two for the price of one) Clinton. Daschle spent about a third of his 2008 book, *Critical: What We Can Do About the Health Care Crisis,* published just in time for Hillary's first presidential run in 2008, analyzing what went wrong with the Clinton health care initiative, with a special focus on Hillary's lack of attention to the legislative branch.

Defeated in 2004, Daschle might not have seemed like much of a threat to Hillary Clinton's ambitions four years later. But when he left the Senate, his chief of staff, the highly regarded Pete Rouse, went over to the newbie from Illinois. As Ezra Klein reported in the *American Prospect* right after the election, Obama's whole primary team actually came directly out of Daschle's office. "His deputy campaign manager, Steve Hildebrand, managed Daschle's 2004 campaign. His director for battleground states, Jennifer O'Malley Dillon, and his director of communications, Dan Pfeiffer, were both deputy campaign managers for Daschle in 2004. Obama's foreign-policy director, Denis McDonough, was Daschle's foreign-policy adviser, and his finance director, Julianna Smoot, was head of Daschle's PAC. And in February of 2007—which is rather early for this sort of thing—Tom Daschle, who had served with Joe Biden and

Chris Dodd and John Edwards and Hillary Clinton, stepped forward and endorsed Barack Obama."[52] Daschle's old friends and colleagues from the Midwest — Richard Gephardt of Nebraska, Byron
Dorgan and Kent Conrad of North Dakota, along with dissidents
from further afield — Bill Nelson of Florida, even Barbara Boxer
of California, were secretly urging Obama to run against Hillary
Clinton.

Why the resistance to Clinton? John Heilemann and Mark Halperin, in their scoop- and scandal-filled blockbuster about the 2008
election, report that everyone, *everyone* in the DC governing classes
had heard about Bill Clinton's ongoing sexual affair with someone,
although the identity of the unnamed other party differed, depending on the account. Nothing had ever been proved to the Lewinsky level, but Hillary's natural allies from her dutiful service in the
Senate did not want another election about Bill Clinton's libido.
They disliked that prospect a lot more than they liked Hillary. Heilemann and Halperin focus particularly on Hillary's fellow New
Yorker, Senator Chuck Schumer, who, they say, knew all the details
from running in the same New York circles as the Clintons.[53] As
Obama started showing some promise of winning in a majority-
white country, Lion of the Senate Ted Kennedy and immediate past
Democratic presidential candidate John Kerry both endorsed the
male contender.

Elections are never only about one thing, not even something
as important as gender. Obviously, Clinton's vote to authorize then-
president George W. Bush to launch the disastrous Iraq War played
a big role in the primaries. So, too, did then–state senator Barack
Obama's speech against the war, delivered in an obscure local venue
in Chicago in 2002, but perfectly timed to set him up in contrast to
the hawkish Clinton. After Obama won the lily-white Iowa Democratic caucuses, the prospect of electing the first African American
president began to dawn on people. As Obama's racial symbolism
emerged, feminists began to imagine a postracial future as well. The
debates among feminists took the form, dating back to the nine-

teenth-century debates about suffrage, of whether black women should put their racial identity or gender identity first.

However, the generational divide in the feminist movement also erupted full-bore on the national scene. In what may be seen in hindsight as a crucial development, Barack Obama beat Hillary Clinton among female caucus goers in the overwhelmingly white Iowa primary contest.[54] Exit polls in Iowa also reflected a bright divide between caucus goers over and under forty-four, with Obama clearing the field in the under forty-four group and Hillary only winning definitively with people over sixty.[55] To produce that outcome, the female Iowa electorate had to divide similarly along the lines of age. The commentary often, if not always, followed the same cleavage.[56] Seventysomething second-wave icon Gloria Steinem gave a passionate appeal, in the *New York Times*, to all women to support Hillary as a historic opportunity. In an impressively comprehensive analysis of the feminist split in the *New Republic*, younger commentator Michelle Goldberg wrote, tellingly, "For young feminists, who have largely gone for Obama, their first encounter with Hillary came when she defended Bill from charges of philandering during the 1992 presidential campaign; for them, her case for leadership was never clear-cut."[57]

Toward the end of the primary, feminist opinion writers, of whatever wave or commitment, most notably *Salon*'s Rebecca Traister, later the author of a best-selling book on the election, began to write about the inexplicable ferocity of their men friends' hostility to Hillary's candidacy.[58] Avidly defending their freedom to choose Obama over Hillary, especially in defiance of the aging doyennes of the second wave, many young third-wave writers confessed to Traister their shock at the behavior of liberal young men. LaToya Peterson, who ran the blog *Racialicious*, actually had to say she never allowed anyone to call Hillary a "cunt."[59] In an effort to comfort Traister, Gloria Steinem told her it was a step forward that guys on the left were denying any sexist motives. In her day, Steinem shared, they would not have bothered.

As with the confirmation of Clarence Thomas, long after Hillary's deficit in the primaries was too deep to recover from, there was an upswelling of belated feminist indignation. And, like the Year of the Woman, it was too little and too late to help the female candidate. But again, like the election of a cognizable number of women to the Senate in 1992, the election contest between a woman and an African American man did coincide with some diversification of the face of the mainstream media. MSNBC tried to cover Hillary and wound up with a scandal over white male anchor Chris Matthews's obvious bias against her and in favor of Barack Obama. The network hired Rachel Maddow, a female and a lesbian woman (!) to anchor her own show. Even a woman of color — Tamron Hall — got some traction at MSNBC and NBC. They were followed at MSNBC by Melissa Harris-Perry and Joy Reid. Not in 2007, but afterwards, there were a few more women at mainstream outlets. And when women revved up their activism, those women were there to cover it. In 2007 Jill Abramson assigned *New York Times* culture reporter Jodi Kantor to political reporting.[60] She would cover the 2008 election campaign. Ten years later, she would break the Harvey Weinstein story.

In the near term, however, having swerved in 1998, the feminists and their female candidate in 2008 got nothing from the liberal men of the Democratic Party. Well, not nothing; just nothing more. Women had been pouring out of law schools, a natural feeder for political jobs, at record numbers every year since the Clinton administration. No matter: as of 2013 Barack Obama's administration employed just slightly fewer women in high-ranking administrative positions than Bill Clinton had. Twenty years before.[61]

8

Feminism Reborn
Online, On Campus
2003–11

Women on the Internet; or, Scribbling Women Part 2

The Revolution will be posted. At the height of the backlash against feminism in 1989, an Australian woman who thought American teen magazines were all "preserved in aspic," started a new magazine, *Sassy. Sassy* aimed at the hip girls who "felt like they were outsiders, but who could still pass for normal in the high school cafeteria."[1]

New York private high school girls Andi Zeisler and Lisa Jervis interned at *Sassy* when it was at its insurgent high point in the early 1990s. A few years later, Zeisler and Jervis were in Oakland, California, living from hand to mouth and working in sexist workplaces for little money. They watched in horror as the right-wing religious group Focus on the Family started a boycott of *Sassy* for encouraging teen sexuality (as if), advertisers pulled out, and *Sassy* got sold for the second time in 1994. The new owners fired the founding editor and the entire staff, and turned *Sassy* into what Zeisler calls "Bizarro Sassy," the very opposite of its irreverent self.[2] And Zeisler and Jervis saw the reliably feminist *Glamour* remade by 2000 as another *Cosmo* by the new editor Bonnie Fuller, another celebrity-mag alumnus. Now where could uppity girls looking for cool content go?

Avid consumers of popular culture, they knew there was an alternative — the little handmade paper missives, adorably called zines, xeroxed and sent via US Mail to a list of like-minded consumers. As luck would have it, when Zeisler was interning at *Sassy,* the offices were in the same building in lower Manhattan as *Ms.* magazine. Zeisler was always popping into the offices two floors up from *Sassy,* and she had noticed something. In its early years *Ms.* was very much a magazine about pop culture, with stories about getting Hollywood stars on board for the Equal Rights Amendment, say, and it often carried pop culture figures on the covers. But, she says, by 1995 *Ms.* had stopped engaging with pop culture and connecting with young feminists. ("I had nothing against it," *Slate* editor in chief and one of the founders of *Slate*'s women's-issues section, DoubleX, Jacob Weisberg, says of the original feminist publication. "It was a monthly, right? Just no one read it. It was old. Magazines have a life span and theirs was over."[3]) Zeisler decided to start something that mixed *Sassy* and *Ms.* "We really loved pop culture," she remembers, "but where was the feminist content?"[4] She could bitch, she decided, or start *Bitch,* a zine on feminism and popular culture.

In the first issue, Jervis included an editor's note: "This magazine is about thinking critically about every message the mass media sends; it's about loudly articulating what's wrong and what's right with what we see. This magazine is about speaking up. Will that make us bitchy? Yeah."[5] And so they did. And were. The premiere issue included "*Sassy*: Then and Now: How the Most Original Voice in Teen Girl Mags Got Stifled by a Big Bad Corporation"; "*Kids* and Sex: The Mixed Messages of Larry Clark's Film"; "Amazon Women in the Moon: A Look Back at the Early Days of MTV"; "Magazines We Hate: *Esquire*'s Women We Love Issue Is, Predictably, a Gagfest"; and "Subversion on a Massive Level: Gender as Constructed Spectacle in the Little-Seen film *Sleep with Me.*"

Almost immediately, Jervis and Zeisler got feedback: readers wanted them to bitch about what's wrong, but also to talk about what was right with respect to women. And so *Bitch* started making recommendations — for an underground filmmaker, and for Suzie Bright and her *Sexual State of the Union*; for comedian Margaret Cho. *Bitch* launched its first website in 1998, partnering with the digital arm of *Wired* magazine, *Hotwired,* and by 2003 *Bitch* was in the internet with both feet. So now an internet-savvy reader could go to *Bitch* May 2003 and see a review of Toys "R" Us as gender hell, or an interview with feminist philosopher of the body Susan Bordo. Or read a long-form piece about race in the film *Bringing Down the House,* starring Steve Martin and Queen Latifah. By 2016 the print quarterly had a circulation of eighty thousand and the online readership was nearly five million unique visitors each year. Bitch Media employed thirteen full- and part-time staff and numerous freelancers.[6]

Feminism on the internet, what a good idea, twentysomething Jessica Valenti said to herself as she labored to keep feminism's heartbeat going in 2004 at the NOW Legal Defense and Education Fund.[7] Bill Scher, her boss at the fund, who ran a liberal blog, advised her to start a blog of her own. "I was always complaining," she admits, "that there was a lot of feminism happening among my young friends, and we weren't getting any credit. There were some feminists blogging online, but they were more like keeping a journal. I gathered my sister and a couple of my friends to do it." *Sassy* was hugely formative when Valenti was young, and *Sassy* was what Valenti had in mind for her new *Feministing.* The first post on *Feministing,* cofounded by Jessica and Vanessa Valenti, went up on April 12, 2004. By 2004, others — *Feministe, Pandagon*[8] — were already visible in the blogosphere.

Valenti's group did not expect *Feministing* to take off like it did. One day they saw that "Katha Pollitt" had commented on the site, and they set off trying to find out if it was the "real" Katha Pollitt, the legendary feminist columnist from the *Nation* magazine (it was).

Web technology made them fast. One day the Labor Department in the Bush administration announced it was going to stop keeping track of women's wages. *Feministing* had a protest up the same day. Weeks later, NOW issued its press release protesting the move. The technology made them connected. Women out in the boonies with no feminist anything in their town found *Feministing* online, just like the legions of gay and lesbian youth connected over the internet from their isolated outposts.[9] They googled "feminism" or came upon *Feministing* through a random online inquiry. Once connected, women commented. The commentary section became a place where new feminist writers emerged. When a woman from Toronto wrote a post in *Feministing*'s open community blog, the *Toronto Star* called to ask her for an op-ed. Another community blogger wound up on NPR.

The legacy feminist organizations were so sensitive to the way the backlash had portrayed women as angry and sexually promiscuous they tried hard to avoid feeding the backlash beast. But Valenti's bloggers figured, "They're going to hate us anyway, so why don't we just say what we think?"[10] By 2007 *Feministing* had half a million readers a month. That would be six million a year.

Almost from the beginning, *Feministing* focused on sex discrimination in the realm of sex. "We watched the church groups," Valenti said. "They were obsessed with female sexuality. They said it was us hypersexualizing everything, but they were really the ones who were talking about it all the time. We had a message: women have sex and women like sex, and that's normal." That insight came, Valenti reflects, because "it was my story. I was being called promiscuous in high school and college, and my male friends were high-fiving each other and I had a bad reputation. They thought certain girls were dirty, and I was thinking, well, you're the one who put your penis in them, why would that make them dirty?" It was lonely for Jessica, feeling like she was the only one who saw through the illogical and bigoted treatment of women's sexuality.

And then she took a women's studies class in college. For the first time, someone told her she was not the problem; it was society that was the problem. In every movement that reshuffles the relationships of power, that realization is powerful.

And so Jessica Valenti unknowingly reenacted the process Catharine MacKinnon had gone through twenty years earlier, focusing like a laser on workplace sexual harassment as just another way of keeping women down. Society is the problem. Franklin Kameny, one of the founders of the modern gay-rights movement, had had a similar epiphany in 1957 when he understood that it was unconstitutional to fire him from his government job because he was gay. You're not the problem, it's society that's the problem.

The realization came slowly to one of *Salon's* Broadsheet founding editors Rebecca Traister. Her story is emblematic. Traister didn't come from nowhere. Her mother, an English professor, had long earned more than her father, a rare-books librarian. Being the only (half) Jewish kid in her grammar school, Traister says, "We didn't observe anything religious, not a thing, and still I was so exotic."[11] As one of only a handful of Democratic families at the polling place in her hometown every election, she was clear about her outsider status. When she went to the pro-abortion March for Women's Lives in DC in 1989, at the tender age of fifteen, she sensed that she was in the middle of a gathering of people whose politics were the same as hers.

Despite feminism being part of her upbringing, Traister didn't emerge from childhood with her politics fully formed. "Katie Roiphe made me a feminist," she confesses laughingly. Traister was a college freshman in 1993 when date-rape denialist Katie Roiphe turned her two *New York Times* pieces into a book, *The Morning After: Sex, Fear and Feminism.* Traister was living in the only all-girl floor of a dorm smack in the middle of a ring of frat houses with nonstop partying at heavily Greek-oriented Northwestern University. Drunken men, she says, would stream through the area all night long. Not only had she had been pressured for sex in what would now be recognized as perilously close to rape, but the girls she knew had similar experiences all along the spectrum. None of them reported it, because they were being told it was just bad sex. Traister remembers seeing Roiphe's book around the fraternity houses that year.

After Northwestern, Rebecca came to New York, and in her mid-twenties had become an entry-level journalist. Even at her first journalism job at the *New York Observer,* writing about movies, she included some stories about women in film. Armed with all the "data points" of abortion marches, bad sex, and unequal treatment at work, she still didn't make the crucial step to feminist politics. Because what did feminism offer in 1997? The third wave. "The third wave was the first stage of feminism coming back from the backlash years," she says. "I never responded to the third wave. It seemed so futile, it did not inspire you, you had no sense it was catching any kind of wave." As we saw in Susan Faludi's *Backlash,* the culture kept pushing the accommodating third wave when it was weak, framing it as so uncool. "And," Traister observed, "they kept weakening themselves more and more in a futile effort to accommodate. The sex-positive manifestos of the third wave might have been truly radical," Traister speculates, but they weren't. "Instead they were all about women's freedom to wear high-heeled shoes."

Traister moved to the new web technology in 2003, taking a job at *Salon,* working with female editors Lori Leibovich and editor in chief Joan Walsh. With the explosive online appearance of Howard Dean's presidential campaign in 2004, young people in Dean's campaign were finally using the internet for political activism. In an echo of the birth of second-wave feminism out of the often wildly chauvinistic student movements of the 1960s, the women of the left started noticing that their lefty male colleagues online were engaging in oblivious sexism. Jiggle ads for *Gilligan's Island* on the liberal websites?[12]

Over at *Salon,* a robust woman-centered conversation was already on the rise. At the outset called, unexpectedly, Mothers Who Think, two women, married to the founders of *Salon,* had started a feature whose smarts belied its retrograde origins and (ironic?) name. Leibovich's and Traister's women-oriented online writings in *Salon* were attracting attention. They made an effort to make feminism appealing, by diluting the politics with pop culture, but the conversation was broadening out to politics. The liberal men on the internet probably spurred it, just like making the coffee at the Students for a Democratic Society radicalized the women in the 1960s.

Following the uptick in interest, Traister, Walsh, and Leibovitch decided to pitch the feminist feature at a conference call. "We were always encouraged at *Salon* to come up with new features," Traister remembers fondly. Traister was inspired to suggest naming the site "Know Your Misogyny," but after a chilling moment of silence from the mostly male editors the deed was done: Broadsheet. Five years later, the prestigious web publication *Slate* opened DoubleX, which its founders later described as having a particular focus on womanhood.[13] Like Traister's abortive suggestion, *Slate* almost called it . . . Moxie.

Like *Feministing,* Broadsheet was a team effort. At first they tried assigning each woman a day of the week to post all day. "There were days when you had nothing," Traister remembers. Journalists were not reporting stories of rape, for instance, and so there was not yet any of the "mutually reinforcing indignation that later surfaced."

As usual, activists of color came to the insight early. They were, Traister says, "doing that work before us in places that had been invisible to me." Traister now views her journey at *Salon* as one "from a white world, unnoticed and unexamined, but gradually enlightened by challenges from women of color, readers at *Salon,* and especially Melissa Harris-Perry, Tami Winfrey-Harris, Pam Spaulding, Pamela Merritt, and Patricia Williams."

Pam Spaulding, black, gay, and activist out of Durham, North Carolina, had started the now iconic *Pam's House Blend* in 2004.[14] Meanwhile, in St. Louis, Missouri, Pamela Merritt was working at the local LGBTQ newspaper the *Vital Voice.*[15]

Merritt was more than something of a phenom. Placed by her parents in St. Louis into a mostly white school district, because they had fought so hard to get school integration, she endured a nightmare of racial abuse throughout her younger years. But Merritt knew where the road out lay. She channeled her anger and her sadness into a life-altering impressive record of grades and scores. At sixteen, she entered Bard College at Simon's Rock, an "early college" for highly motivated students. It was the first place she really felt good. Graduating, after transfer, from Brandeis, she went to work in the ad business in Dallas. "It was *Mad Men*," she reported. Talk about intersectionality of oppressions; one day at a party, a white boss pulled her and another black woman, a client, no less, onto his lap and announced he'd always wanted to have sex with a black woman. And both women looked at each other and both knew they would get away and they would say nothing.

When 9/11 happened, she had asked herself what her life would mean if she died, and she decided to do something more meaningful than selling TV ads in Texas. She settled in to her old hometown and went to work. One of her best friends, also her boss, was a blogger. They had breakfast every day, and she would go off on whatever was on the morning news. And one day he said, you need to blog. She had a lot of feminist opinions — she had joined a woman's group to meet friends and they volunteered at a woman's shelter for women who have just given birth or were pregnant.

He set her up, and they gave it a name, *Angry Black Bitch*. Starting February 10, 2005, Merritt began by just saying whatever she thought each morning, two cups of coffee and a cigarette in hand. She thought she was just talking to herself and maybe some local friends. She never looked at the statistics, but one day Michel Martin called from NPR to ask to interview the St. Louis blogger. After Merritt posted about the movie *King Kong*, she woke up and saw four hundred comments, and she realized someone was reading her besides her friends. She started contributing to *Feministing*, in addition to her own blog.

She concluded in her public role that you need to be unapologetically who you are. She was a black woman, a fusion, not an intersection. On the one hand, black bloggers criticizing her for writing for *Feministing* deprived her entirely of agency. "And I shall not be used . . . or schooled on a history I live every fucking day and know all too well," she blogged, "or judged to be a sell out by people who don't even have the decency to call me by name."[16] On the other, she found herself deeply alienated by white feminist Gloria Steinem's op-ed supporting Hillary Clinton against the rising threat from Barack Obama, and she was an early voice of black women pushing back: "After reading Steinem's Op-Ed I felt invisible . . . as if black and woman can't exist in the same body. I felt undocumented . . . as if the history of blacks and the history of women have nothing to do with the history of black women."[17]

But she thinks she contributed to the expectation that black women are necessary for feminism and that it is possible and actually critical to center black women in feminism. Having the ability to publish without an editor gave unfiltered access for her voice, the single most powerful experience of her life. A black woman, the descendant of slaves, being able to say what she wanted. She built a career, got a job at Planned Parenthood, and got writing assignments, because she could write and publish freely.

When things came up, like the Duke lacrosse case or Hurricane Katrina, mainstream feminist bloggers were focused on the classic feminist issues, and black women bloggers could see things the white bloggers could not. She saw Hurricane Katrina as a black women's reproductive issue, and she focused on the fate of the black neighborhoods. At the end, she was proudest of the range of topics she covered. She wanted to cast a feminist web over all of her writing, regardless of subject matter and to encourage every diverse black female voice to come in, even when she disagreed with them. At that specific time, 2003–10, it was, Merritt thinks, like "Dorothy Parker and the Vicious Circle. It was an amazing time to be alive."

Also, she finally got to feel and say how angry she was about having to gag down the white guys' fantasy of sex with a black woman.

Laboring away at the now looks-and-sex-obsessed *Glamour* magazine in 2002, twentysomething Anna Holmes also remembered *Sassy*.[18] Holmes was an unusual combination — a political idealist who understood the value of earning an income. Her white mother, working in New York for a gender and racial activist, and her African American father met at a party of civil rights workers in a Southern town in the 1960s. They moved to Davis, California, hoping a liberal college town would be more welcoming. There were copies of the *New Yorker, Ebony,* and *Jet* lying around Holmes's house, and her mother took her to Take Back the Night marches and abortion rights rallies in San Francisco. In the evenings, her parents would watch TV and yell at the news. Although she found it painful to witness their anger, the message somehow sank in.

Holmes got that she was different. Her schoolmates were well-off white children, and she felt keenly her parents' anxiety about money. As she describes it, her parents saw to it that she and her sister always had enough to wear and eat and even an occasional road trip vacation. But at Davis High School, there were BMWs in the school parking lot while her parents agonized over whether their ancient Chevy would last another minute, and how they were going to send their daughters to college at all. Her mother, possessed of two graduate degrees, spent much of her life teaching snotty high school kids how to type to support her family.[19] So Holmes conceived the idea that she would grow up and make a lot of money. Nursing the ancient Chevy, Anna's father dreamed California dreams of having a big Chevrolet Suburban and, she says, "I was going to grow up and buy him a Suburban."

Holmes left California as soon as she could to go to college at New York University. At NYU, Holmes's frustration with her female colleagues boiled over into a first venture into feminist writing, an article in *Manhattan South,* the NYU journalism magazine. Where had she seen writing about feminism at NYU? On the wall of a college bathroom.

Despite her feminism and her fond memories of *Sassy,* and although she dreamed of writing serious nonfiction, Holmes couldn't afford to take the jobs reserved for the East Coast elite, unpaid internships and the like. So she went to work for *Entertainment Weekly* and at women's magazines, ultimately at Bonnie Fuller's *Glamour.* Anna, tall and blessed with beautiful olive skin, nonetheless dressed in jeans and sneakers as a silent rebellion against the *Devil Wears Prada* skinny dressed-up environment at Condé Nast.

And she got really pissed off at the state of women's media, comparing the current *Glamour* to the old, politically relevant *Glamour* she remembered and listening to her friends' reports of feminism from the middle of the third wave. Holmes eventually landed at another women's magazine, *InStyle*. *InStyle* was okay; it was materialistic and shallow, but it didn't tell women how to act.

When she left it was because she got an offer to launch a blog for up-and-coming Gawker media — *Jezebel* ("Celebrity, Sex, Fashion for Women. Without Airbrushing"). She thought it would be perilous to categorize what she was about to do as compared to the not-for-profit and openly political *Feministing*. *Jezebel* was going to be commercial, and Holmes was going to be properly paid. Celebrity magazines were at their height and there was a real focus on celebrity and consumerism. Well, she thought, if that's what they want to read about, that's fine.

But still Anna Holmes had an agenda. She was pissed off at the women's magazines, with their disempowering messages for women. She would transform *Jezebel,* the commercial website she'd been asked to run, into a Trojan horse, she thought. Each of the Gawker sites had their eyes trained on the mainstream businesses in its wheelhouse. The sports site was constantly going after ESPN, and Gizmodo, the tech site, was all over Apple. It just made sense that the women's site would go after women's media, the regressive other outlets responsible for sending harmful messages to women. And that's what Anna Holmes set out to do.

The first thing *Jezebel,* the site without airbrushing, took on was, as announced, the airbrushing. In July 2007 *Jezebel* ran the "before" cover photo of Faith Hill from *Redbook* before the magazine airbrushed pounds from her neck, shoulder, back, and arm, and took her eyes where the crows don't fly.[20] *Redbook* had transformed the thirty-nine-year-old mother of three into an anorectic twenty-five-year-old. Whew, in a couple of days the brand-new site had 11,500 Google hits. The story, ABC News reported, "will make you gasp."

Feministing, for one, gave its commercial sister a shout-out.

Anna Holmes was going to talk about things that had not been discussed openly. "Abortion. Sexual assault up to and including rape. Saying you were a feminist was a dirty word. If we were going to be addressing a wide swath of feminism we had to use the words and not use euphemisms. Sexual assault has been a fact of life for most women in some point in their life." *Jezebel* was going to address those issues without airbrushing and with a certain amount of anger too. Holmes was angry about living in a culture that was backtracking about women's roles in the culture. She was angry at consumerism and at her participation in it at *Glamour*. But, being Anna Holmes, she also wanted to talk joyfully about superficial things. There was an article about designer Marc Jacobs and whether the covered-up dresses in his current show were actually "polygamist fashion," as in the breakaway branches of the Mormon church.[21] Complete with luscious pictures of the garb.

Within two months, the site had attracted a spontaneous following of women, who called themselves Jezzies, or Jezebelles, a vibrant ecosystem of commentary. Four months after the site launched, Holmes began to push to do electoral coverage, and the readers wrote in to say they loved it, especially the coverage of the 2008 female candidate for the presidency, Hillary Clinton. Turns out, there was a need. After a decade or more of "I'm not a feminist," "lipstick feminism," "do-me feminism," and sex parties intended to equalize the female gaze, attracting the very creepiest men,[22] the need Holmes had felt to call out retrograde attitudes toward women was everywhere. In those days, the site updated once every five or ten minutes, so people kept refreshing it all day. It created a brand.

In 2008 *Jezebel* announced it had hired "our very own 35-inch hipped, gel-schellacked, battle-weary, jealous boyfriend–having human clothes hanger!" to give the inside dope on New York Fashion Week.[23] Pretty soon "Tatiana" had gotten beyond whether models eat food and/or do coke to the obvious possibilities of abuse in a business of powerful men and powerless, beautiful young women.[24] Within a year, Tatiana had cropped her hair, quit the business, and outed herself as former New Zealand model Jenna Sauers. On March 16, 2010, Sauers published "Meet Terry Richardson, the

Worlds Most F—ked Up Fashion Photographer," reporting that Richardson pressed and cajoled his young models into doing nude shoots, demanded they jack him off, and said of breaking into modeling, "It's not who you know, it's who you blow. I don't have a hole in my jeans for nothing." "Frankly," Sauers wrote, "'creep' seems inadequate to the task of describing Richardson's behavior . . . Given the power differential that exists between Richardson, who is old, wealthy, regarded as an artist, and vastly influential, and most of his model subjects, can the consent of these women even be said to be freely given?"[25]

Within days, Sauers posted again: "Following the publication of [the] allegations, other stories of Richardson's questionable behavior at work poured forth. I heard from modeling agency bookers and former bookers, photographers . . . fashion writers, magazine editors, models of all descriptions, stylists, and others in the industry. Because of Terry Richardson's extraordinary position of power, all of these people spoke to me anonymously, for fear of losing their own jobs or being blacklisted in an industry that hates to endure any overt challenge to its power structure."[26] Anybody else got stories? Sauers asked. Email me. *Jezebel* was relentless in following the story in the ensuing months.

Another *Jezebel* reporter, Sauers reported, contributed to the follow-up on Richardson. Her name was Irin Carmon. Seven years later, in 2017, Carmon, then at the *Washington Post,* would turn her attention to television legend Charlie Rose. She cowrote the article about his decades of sexual harassment at work that brought the rich and famous media icon and mogul down. "Everybody at *Jezebel* knew about Charlie back then," Holmes says. "But you couldn't prove a thing, without the kind of time and institutional power the legacy media had." Maybe not, but *Jezebel* is where Irin Carmon got her start.

The explosion of investigatory journalism that fueled the #MeToo movement starting in 2016 is dotted with other scribbling women from the feminist internet revival. In addition to Carmon, Rebecca Traister at *New York,* who gave the movement its narrative of anger, the blockbuster *Good and Mad: The Revolutionary Power of Women's Anger;*[27] *Feministing's* Jessica Valenti, demanding equality in sex; and Jodi Kantor, who broke the Harvey Weinstein story, came, not from *Slate's* women-oriented site DoubleX, but still from *Slate.* A universe of commentators who migrated from the internet to write in a range of traditional media like the *New Yorker* and the *New York Times* — Michelle Goldberg, who started at *Salon,* Jill Filipovic from *Feministe,* Amanda Marcotte from *Pandagon, Jezebel* alum Jia Tolentino — have enriched the understanding and power of the revelations immeasurably.

Almost all social movements surge on a wave of technological change in the means of communication. The Protestant Reformation sold its vernacular Bibles, so everyone could read and understand the Bible for themselves, rather than as the Catholic Church told them to understand it, through the invention of movable type. Thanks, Gutenberg! For the first time in human history, words could be printed and shared other than through the painfully slow interaction of feather, ink, vellum. Less famously, the newspaper- and pamphlet-driven movement to abolish slavery came about in the early nineteenth century just as the not so United States acquired steam-driven printing presses and cheap paper made, ironically, of cotton. William Lloyd Garrison's abolitionist engine, the *Liberator,* started out on a hand press, not unlike Gutenberg's, but soon cheap copies of inflammatory abolitionist rhetoric were flooding the country. The Southern states forbade the post office to deliver them.

And so, after many backlash years in feminism, the internet. And women who wanted to offer feminist activism and occasionally to make some money. Holmes bought her dad an Audi.

End Rape on Campus

What a good idea. When current and former University of North Carolina students Annie E. Clark and Andrea Pino founded the organization End Rape on Campus (EROC) in 2013, the movement against campus sexual violence was forty years old. Indeed just two years before Clark and Pino's effort, in 2011, Yale undergrad Alexandra Brodsky and sixteen students and young alumni filed a complaint against Yale with the United States Department of Education's Office of Civil Rights, charging the university with "failing to eliminate a hostile sexual environment." The following year, a mutual friend put Brodsky in touch with Amherst student Dana Bolger, who was working to raise awareness about her college's mishandling of sexual assault. They were ignited upon encountering each other. They'd been heartened to learn that federal law required their colleges to do something more than tell them, as a dean at Amherst told Bolger, to take a leave and get a job at Starbucks until her stalker graduated. Clark and Pino and Brodsky and Bolger were determined to change things. But it had been forty years, and rape and other sexual assault on campus was still an issue.

The consciousness around date rape[28] surfaced as part of feminist efforts to reform the antiquated rape laws in the United States after the publication of Susan Brownmiller's book *Against Our Will* in 1975.[29] The term "date rape," meaning rape by someone the victim knows, may have first appeared in print in an article on rape law reform in Indiana in 1973.[30] Rape too often went unpunished, an Indiana criminal court judge told the reporter in a situation where a woman put herself in harm's way. As Brownmiller chronicled two years after the Indiana law reform proposal, courts were reluctant to recognize coercion like social pressure and threat outside of the physical, and when a person made a charge of rape against someone they may have been with willingly prior to the offense (hanging out in a dorm room, for example, or in a bar, or on a date), the victims' behavior almost always "looks bad . . . in court."[31] Since prosecutors and juries seem reluctant to punish date rape as harshly as rape perpetrated by a stranger, the answer, the Indiana judge proposed, was in part to set out levels of wrongdoing, distinguishing date rape from stranger rape to give law enforcement some milder sentencing options.[32] Even if downgrading date rape, which is not inherently less serious than stranger rape, was not the best solution to the underenforcement of rape law, at least, like sexual harassment at Cornell at the same point in time, the behavior was now named: date rape. And naming the offense, as we have seen, can be the first step to social change.

The first documented campus rape-crisis center, at the University of Maryland, actually dates back even earlier — to 1972. The Maryland activism, initiated by a group of resident advisers, older students responsible for supervising college dorms, was a response to a series of gang rapes on campus.[33] In 1973 the University of Pennsylvania experienced six campus rapes in quick succession, and the gang rape of a pair of student nurses. The first Take Back the Night marches were held in Philadelphia in 1975 and Brussels in 1976, as candlelight processions protesting violence against women, but the marches soon became a staple of campus antirape activism.

In 1980, with Catharine MacKinnon again providing the theory, the federal courts recognized that sexual harassment on campus could violate Title IX, which prohibits sex discrimination in federally funded educational institutions.[34] *Ms.* magazine commissioned a prominent psychologist, Mary Koss, to do a study; Koss reported her findings in 1985 in the article "Date Rape: The Story of an Epidemic and Those Who Deny It."[35] Koss reported that one in four college women were victims of rape or attempted rape. (The statistics on campus rape are among the most contested data in social science, but no one argues seriously that there is no problem.)[36]

In the next decades, Congress, federal and state courts, and the United States Department of Education created a universe of theory, decisions, and administrative orders, all directed to compel educational institutions to protect their students against sexual abuse. In 1990 Congress passed another law, the Clery Act, to require universities with federal funding to track and report the instances of sexual abuse on their campuses. A few years later the Supreme Court ruled that students could sue schools under Title IX if the professors harassed them[37] or their fellow students did the same.[38] In 2011 the Obama Department of Education sent out a "Dear Colleague Letter" to remind institutions receiving federal assistance of their legal obligations, including proactive steps to stop campus harassment and abuse.[39]

Andrea Pino, a voluble intellectual, the daughter of Cuban immigrants, and Annie Clark, the self-possessed child of a white middle-class family, both came to the University of North Carolina with liberal activist inclinations.[40] In 2007, while in school, although off campus, Clark was raped. Turning to the university for support, she was told to examine her own behavior for what she should have done differently. In response to the university's lack of support, Clark started a system of complaint-card boxes by which students could report sexual assault, and placed them all over campus. In response to Pino's own encounter with sexual violence four years later, she tracked down Clark, whom she had known in passing, and in 2012 the two women connected over Skype. What could they do? Luckily for them, Pino was taking courses in political theory and gender studies, and what should she find in her assigned reading but the work of Catharine MacKinnon?

The two were not comforted by the decades-long history of campus antirape movements. They realized that the school wasn't in compliance with the requirements of the Department of Education's "Dear Colleagues" letter sent out in 2011. They weren't even doing what MacKinnon asked for in the seventies! Pino and Clark thought. NYU's Stephen Schulhofer, a renowned criminal law professor who would later take up the fraught task of revising the criminal law of sexual assault, observes that the Department of Education's letter of guidance got little attention when it was first issued. "A lot of universities did not act on it for years," he remembers.[41]

Why wasn't someone enforcing the rights that had been laid down in the previous forty years, culminating in the demands of the 2011 Obama administration letter? Pino and Clark asked each other. "I had moved across the country and I found the students at Oregon were having the same experience I had. We've got to do something," Clark remembers thinking. She and Pino began discussing Title IX to see what the law might offer regarding resistance to sexual violence on campus. "I woke up in the night," Clark says, thinking about the Clery Act. This may have been the first time in the history of human dreaming that a young woman woke up thinking about the 1990 law requiring universities to keep a log of and report incidents of sexual violence.

Pino, first in her Cuban American family to attend college and still pursuing her undergraduate degree, joined the ranks of Catharine MacKinnon and Susan Brownmiller and Kimberlé Crenshaw. She took the experience she had and was hearing about and began theorizing. Campus rape, she noticed, was being framed episodically. Reports were of individual women, and victims were reduced to their story, or they were presented as anonymous Jane Does. There was no larger, or political, story. Pino decided she and Clark would train themselves to talk about sexual violence thematically, look for political actors who had addressed the issue, and focus on political action. Clark and Pino were going to make a *movement*. This was not just about them.

They began by reaching out to victims of campus assault, as Annie Clark had through her complaint-card boxes. How did they find those who'd been affected? "Social media of course," the women said. "We used Facebook, Twitter." Since they used their real names in their online profiles, it was easy for others to find them. "Someone from Swarthmore even came in through LinkedIn," Clark said, chuckling. "What student uses LinkedIn?" The many rape victims Annie had met at Oregon and the ones they were hearing about at UNC convinced them they were looking at an epidemic. As the students began to contact them with their stories, the two young women, unemployed and with no resources, decided to make a map situating student complaints. They divided the United States according to time zones, and between them tracked complaints in the various zones. They would share their political approach with the student victims. The targets were the schools, their systems of responding to rape charges, and their compliance with federal regulations.

And then there was the network of feminist online media, especially, no surprise, *Jezebel*. Clark aggressively went after the attention of *Jezebel* reporter Katie J. M. Baker, who had written a harrowing piece about rape at the University of Montana, in Missoula, in May 2012.[42] (Missoula was a particularly ripe target, because the feds had started a civil rights investigation into the handling of rape cases by law enforcement and the university authorities there.) In the next two years, Baker would write dozens of posts on rape: at Amherst, Northeastern, and EROC's own University of North Carolina. As usual, the feminist internet of the mid-aughts led the way.

Clark and Pino were not focused only on the heady connectivity of the internet. They had a bet about when they would score *Time* magazine. But, Pino says, it was the *New York Times* they really cared about. Richard Pérez-Peña covered higher education at the *Times*, and they had been trying to get hold of him for a long time. "You're covering the rapes one at a time," they tried to tell him. "Why aren't you putting them all together?"

One day while Pino was in Oregon visiting Clark for spring break, they got a phone call from the reporter "Hi!!" the caller said, "Is there a movement happening?" Yeah, there's a movement happening, the women answered, have you read your own stories? And we have a map.

On March 19, 2013, Clark and Pino appeared in the *New York Times*, "College Groups Connect to Fight Sexual Assault."[43] The photograph accompanying the article shows them sitting together in front of their map. "This is actually happening," they realized.

A month after the *Times* article appeared, Columbia University junior Emma Sulkowicz filed a complaint against a fellow student, charging him with rape.[44] When the university cleared him, Sulkowicz protested the decision by carrying a fifty-pound mattress on her back everywhere she went on campus her senior year, 2014–15. "Carry That Weight," representing the male student's continuing presence at Columbia despite the charge, was a work of performance art in every sense of the word.[45] For Sulkowicz, a visual arts major, it was her senior thesis.[46] As art and often only art can do, Emma Sulkowicz's performance piece, enacted at a college in the media capital of America, captured the public eye. "Carry That

Weight" recalled a tactic used by the AIDS activist organization
ACT UP from a generation before, when, impatient with the pace
of new drug testing while gay men were dying, ACT UP demonstra-
tors carried cardboard tombstones to the lawn of the FDA.[47] "Carry
That Weight" was the subject of numerous articles in the *New York
Times* and a host of other publications. In 2014 New York senator
Kirsten Gillibrand took Sulkowicz with her when she announced
legislation aimed at combating campus sexual assault, and Sulkowicz accompanied Gillibrand to the 2015 state of the union address.
(Sulkowicz, then described with female pronouns, now identifies as
gender nonconforming and uses they/them.)[48]

By 2013 the team of Brodsky, by then a writer at *Feministing*, and
Bolger had made good progress in enabling students to learn their
rights other than through the accident of being in a law school class,
as Brodsky did. Brodsky and Bolger worked with other survivors
to launch of website full of legal "know your rights" information
and strategy for campus activists under the banner "Know Your
IX."[49] The organization grew, training students across the country
to advocate on their campuses and bringing those student voices
to policymakers to advocate for better state and federal laws. In the
summer of 2013, the group launched a protest in front of the Department of Education demanding better enforcement of Title IX,
which spooked agency and White House officials into inviting the
group to meet and discuss, eventually leading to adoption of some
of the group's policies. By 2015 they had enough money to hire an
executive director.

The pieces began to fall into place. Students with the experience
of rape on campus; young feminists who grew up not with *Sassy*
but surrounded by the feminist blogosphere—*Jezebel, Feministing;*
and Title IX, the gilt-edged inheritance from the second wave of
feminist activism. The last piece was Hollywood. Right after Know
Your IX went up, Smart Girls, the activist organization founded by
award-winning television comic and actress Amy Poehler and the
producer Meredith Walker, partnered with the group on an educa-

tional video for You Tube. In 2012 filmmakers Kirby Dick and Amy Ziering came to UNC, where Pino was working as a resident adviser in a dorm while she finished college. Dick and Ziering were touring with their film *The Invisible War* about sexual assault in the military. Pino had a poster for *The Invisible War* in her dorm room, and during the filmmakers' Q and A one of Pino's students told Dick he should meet the RA in her dorm, that Pino was dealing with many of the same issues Dick was.

A few months later Clark and Pino moved to LA. They had no jobs, no money, and nowhere to live. But Dick was making a documentary about campus rape—*The Hunting Ground*. He was going to—and did—make them stars. They worked on the movie for nothing until one of the producers, Paul Blevin, found out and got up a little funding at the end of 2014. *The Hunting Ground*, about Pino and Clark and the women their movement had supported, debuted at the Sundance Film Festival in 2015 and then appeared on CNN. Meanwhile, Joe Biden, of the Hill/Thomas hearings fame, had sent his adviser on Violence Against Women, Lynn Rosenthal, to represent the White House on the National Advisory Committee on Violence Against Women.[50] The Know Your IX activists protests outside the Department of Education had gotten the administration's attention, and after many meetings with them Rosenthal reached out to Pino and Clark.

On April 29, 2014, years after the passage of Title IX, President Obama's Department of Education issued a document in the form of a Q&A on Title IX and sexual violence.[51] The information and examples in the document were designed to guide the schools in their existing duties, for instance, to adopt procedures to address sexual misconduct on campus, rather than leaving the issue to the criminal justice system. The guidelines described what constituted notice to a school of sexual violence, the elements of an investigation, and, most controversially, what was allowed if the school held hearings on the charges. And, most controversial of the hearings procedures, the guidelines imposed a standard of preponderance of the evidence (that the charges were more likely than not true) in the hearings. In a separate measure, the department released a list of the universities they were investigating for violation of Title IX by not having adequate sexual-violence procedures.

There was resistance, mostly from the faculties. In a fair article summing up the faculty disputes,[52] well-regarded Michigan law professor Samuel Bagenstos suggested that the controversy arose because many universities responded to the 2014 guidelines by setting up systems that went well beyond what the government required. "The fair-process problems with . . . the policies don't arise so much from the adoption of the preponderance standard," Bagenstos said, "as from the lack of other protections for those named in a complaint." For example, in one college system, "respondents are not entitled to lawyers or 'meaningful sharing of information' regarding the basis for the claims against them. Respondents receive 'one week to respond' to written accusations, and they are not entitled to a hearing. Instead, facts are found through interviews conducted by an 'investigative team' appointed by the university's Title IX office, with any appeal to the Title IX officer who has supervised the team throughout. And neither respondents nor their counsel are entitled to cross-examine witnesses to test their stories."

Although the federal guidelines did not require it, some colleges and universities began adopting the formulation of affirmative consent in sex—a legal doctrine that dates all the way back to a New Jersey judicial decision in 1992.[53] In recent years, the rape reform movement had achieved the enactment of affirmative consent in, one professor counts, the law of rape in Montana, New Jersey, Vermont, and Wisconsin.[54] Where no such law applied, some colleges adopted the requirement of affirmative consent to each sexual act. New York and California enacted legislation imposing the affirmative consent standard on the colleges in their jurisdictions.[55]

Once the universities started paying—or, as Bagenstos argues, overpaying—attention to the Obama administration demands for serious systems to process complaints of sexual wrongdoing, law professors led the resistance to the protections. Especially, in an un-canny replay of the liberal rally around Bill Clinton, law professors of the liberal persuasion.

Honestly, sometimes you don't know whether to kiss or kill all the lawyers. After all, starting with the Supreme Court decision in 1963 that accused criminals are entitled to be represented by a law-yer,[56] liberal law professors, especially professors of criminal law, had been devoting themselves to the unimpeachable liberal cause of getting constitutional protections for people accused of committing crimes. Kiss the lawyers. Now, the universities were taking acts that looked like criminal behavior (although they had long been covered by laws like Title IX, as we have seen) and trying and punishing them with steps including expulsion. Not being criminal tribunals, the colleges were proposing or instituting procedures that little re-sembled the protective systems the liberal law professors had fought so hard to establish and defend—the right to a lawyer, the right to confront and cross-examine your accuser, the right to see the evi-dence against you. The objectors were especially incensed that the accuser only had to prove sexual wrongdoing by a preponderance of the evidence: 50% + 1. In criminal law, of course, guilt must be proven beyond a reasonable doubt.

On October 15, 2014, twenty-eight members of the Harvard Law School faculty issued a statement to the *Boston Globe*, decrying their university's procedures.[57] The Harvard process, the protesting faculty asserted, lodged all fact finding and decision making in one office; the procedures for the accused to defend himself were wholly inadequate; the code included a broad definition of sexual wrong-doing, and also of what constituted drunken impairment.[58] Law school dean Martha Minow launched an initiative intended to sep-arate the law school's treatment of sexual offenses from the proce-dures of the whole university. The Harvard initiative coming from the law school was often acknowledged to be the brainchild of Pro-fessor Janet Halley,[59] who is mostly known for being a prominent voice in the queer, sex-positive school of legal thought and who had already criticized feminism harshly as a way to understand and deal with the subject of sex.[60] Four months later, Penn Law School issued a similar statement.[61] At both Harvard and Penn, the resistance to university guidelines attracted a wide range of faculty support, including from some very traditional feminist professors.

The faculties then turned their fire on the universities' voluntary adoption of the standard of affirmative consent. A month after the Harvard letter, Yale law professor Jed Rubenfeld took on the consent standard in the *New York Times*. "The redefinition of consent," he wrote, "encourages people to think of themselves as sexual assault victims when there was no assault. People can and frequently do have fully voluntary sex without communicating unambiguously; under the new consent standards, that can be deemed rape *if one party later feels aggrieved*. [emphasis added]."[62]

Rubenfeld had written a scholarly article suggesting that the concept of consent did not belong in the law of rape at all.[63] Rape should go back to being a crime of force, an argument that would turn the clock back on twenty years of rape-law reform in many jurisdictions. Rape originally was defined as having sex with a woman with force and against her will. Long before the modern campus rape movement, rape reformers had campaigned hard to get courts and legislatures to remove the element of force from the crime. Requiring women to resist sexual attacks such that force had to be used against them exposed them to terrible danger and made it almost impossible to prosecute rape, particularly among acquaintances. By the time Rubenfeld wrote, no more than sixteen states required force as an element of rape.[64] The remaining disagreement focused on what constituted consent, or, put another way, who bears the burden of silence? Existing laws ranged from requiring the complainant to say no, with silence meaning consent, all the way to requiring the initiating party to obtain affirmative consent, which equates silence with nonconsent.

Under a hailstorm of criticism, Rubenfeld defended his liberal credentials, asserting that his definition of force would include even the threat of force. Women would not have to risk their lives by provoking the rapist to use force to bring a claim of rape. All the remaining failures of consent — sex after ignoring protestations of no, or sex while having power like a prison guard has — should be covered by lesser offenses, like assault.

The concept of a graded scheme of sexual assault is not obviously wrong. In most proposals, including what emerged shortly from the prestigious lawyers' group, the American Law Institute, force triggers the most severe legal response. Rape involving other failures of consent, like threat or unequal social power, would trigger lesser penalties. In his op-ed, though, Rubenfeld reveals that, whatever the offense would be called, his concept of consent would fall to the pro-defendant side. Ambiguity, the hot potato of the rape debate, would be the burden of the accuser. "After all," he wrote, "people can and frequently do have fully voluntary sex without communicating unambiguously." Similarly, for alcohol. Unless the complainant was incapacitated to the extent of being unable to stand up, Rubenfeld wrote, the burden of sex while drunk would fall on the complainant. The complainant could not claim that anything short of falling-down drunk tainted their implied consent. Unsurprisingly, Rubenfeld's proposal elicited a robust body of criticism on the merits.[65]

In addition, since last summer, Yale Law School has been investigating allegations of sexual wrongdoing against Rubenfeld himself, including charges of inappropriate, creepy, flirtatious, and line-crossing[66] conduct by present and former female students. Much of the faculty protest throughout had centered on the implications of the new rules for not only student sexual behavior, but constraints on faculty/student sexual relations.[67] The news had been buzzing around the alumni community for some time, and in September 2018 the story surfaced in the *Guardian*.[68] The law school maintained a strict no-comment position.

Amid the firestorm of criticism about the proposed or pending campus rules, perhaps inevitably someone screwed up royally. On November 19, 2014, *Rolling Stone* published "A Rape on Campus." The "rape" supposedly involved a victim, identified only as Jackie, and a gang of fraternity brothers from Phi Kappa Psi. The campus was the University of Virginia at Charlottesville. Almost from the beginning, the fraternity and later the university denied the truth of the story, and a phalanx of other journalists descended on Charlottesville to check on the accuracy of their fellow reporter. By April, six months later, the magazine had taken it all back. *Rolling Stone* could no longer stand by the reporting it had published. Erik Wemple of the *Washington Post* called the piece "a complete crock." The story won the booby prize of journalism, when the prestigious Poynter Institute named it as the "Error of the Year."[69] A dean at the school won a $3 million dollar verdict against *Rolling Stone*, which ultimately settled suits with the fraternity and its members.

The outcome of the first real effort to rein in harassment and abuse in the anarchic world of sex among the young was not at all clear.

The ALI: America's Legal Deep State and the Law of Sexual Assault

Then, on the eve of the debate in the academy, the American Law Institute decided in 2012 that it was time for a new model law for rape and related offenses.[70] After all, the Model Penal Code the institute had produced dated back to the 1950s. And even though it helped usher in the sexual revolution a half century ago, one of the most outmoded sections of the code was the law of sexual assault.

If the legal profession has a deep state, it has to be the American Law Institute. The ALI was founded in 1923 on the initiative of the dean of the University of Pennsylvania Law School.[71] Its incorporators included chief justice and former president William Howard Taft, future chief justice Charles Evans Hughes, and former secretary of state Elihu Root.[72] Today, the ALI includes all the justices of the US Supreme Court, the chief judges of the US Court of Appeals and of the highest state courts, deans of almost all law schools, and a limited number of law professors and distinguished private practitioners. Members are elected, and the elected membership is limited to three thousand. The process of getting the required nomination and recommendations to get in ensures that membership, as it has been from the beginning, is limited to the elite of the legal elite. Few groups with such outsize influence are so little known.

The original reason for the existence of the ALI was to try to bring some uniformity and order to the sprawling, diverse system of American law. Not only are there fifty states and a national government, each with its own body of law, but American law by nature is crafted by judges largely on a case-by-case basis, rather than written by a legislature in a broad sweep to cover a whole social matter. Thousands of judges, in scores of states, deciding cases in successive minuscule decisions, was, to put it mildly, messy. So when people with a dispute, or lawyers or judges wanted to know what the law was, they had a big research problem. The ALI decided to try to set forth the basic principles in each legal area, restating the law as it had developed. So from a thousand decisions about different kinds of threats, for example, the ALI would distill a grand principle of the civil action, or tort, of assault. Then it would set forth all the principles in a restatement of the Law of Torts. Almost from the beginning, the ALI committees responsible for these restatements gave in to the irresistible temptation to combine their restatements of the world as it is with opinions about what the best rules should be. The ability to shoehorn one's beliefs about the correct regime of civil rights and wrongs into a supposedly factual tool was pretty heady stuff.

Then the ALI got even bigger ideas. It would admit it was dreaming of an ideal world, and produce "model" codes to inspire judges and legislatures around the country to change their law to the best of all possible worlds. Most famously, the ALI approved a Model Penal Code in 1962, in an effort to encourage reform and change in the criminal law. Courts cite the Model Penal Code, and at least thirty-seven states adopted it in, with various modifications; several states actually adopted most of its provisions. The ALI rightly brags that this "seminal work played an important part in the widespread revision and codification of the substantive criminal law of the United States."[73] It was the Model Penal Code, drafted at the ALI in the oppressive 1950s, for instance, that first suggested the decriminalization of homosexual sodomy.[74] But now in 2012, what looked progressive in 1962 was long overdue for a rehab. Little did the solons of the ALI know that their entry into the fraught arguments over sexual assault in 2012 might actually bring down the whole ALI. Just shy of its hundredth birthday.

In 2012 Columbia law professor Lance Liebman, who ran the ALI, called his old law school classmate Stephen Schulhofer to take up the cause of proposing a new code of rape and related offenses for the ALI. Schulhofer anticipated controversy, but not a firestorm of public polemic, although he probably should have. Way back in the early 1980s, as the younger coauthor on a law school casebook on criminal law, he had insisted that the new edition include a chapter on rape (and cases on the issues in rape), which had been, bizarrely, missing from every criminal law book used to teach generations of American lawyers. His senior coauthor, Sanford Kadish, resisted. People won't use a casebook with a rape section in it, Kadish said. It's too controversial to try to teach it. Schulhofer found an appropriate case, *State v. Rusk,* which involved the hardest issue, the meaning of force, and decided to test teach it. "It was the worst class I ever had," Schulhofer remembers. "No one would say anything. I could not get a discussion going no matter what I tried." When he later queried his trusted research assistant about what went wrong, the student shared with their teacher that *State v. Rusk* had been the talk of the law school all week. The students were silent because they were uncomfortable airing their feelings on such explosive issues in that large public setting. Kadish was essentially right; the next competitive book put rape at the end to give teachers a chance to avoid it, but after Kadish and Schulhofer, the ice was broken. Criminal law teachers have been struggling with how to teach rape material, trying to navigate between too muted and too tense.[75]

In 2000 Schulhofer, apparently undaunted, wrote a book on the subject, *Unwanted Sex: The Culture of Intimidation and the Failure of Law.* He included an appendix, "Model Criminal Statute for Sexual Offenses." "Piece of cake," the late Danny Meltzer of Harvard Law School, a rising star at the ALI, had told Liebman in 2014 when contemplating the ALI's new code. Since Schulhofer had already done much of the work, the project, Liebman said, should only take a couple of years! Schulhofer invited his colleague Erin Murphy to work as associate reporter on the new code.

The ALI has a process: first, proposals are reviewed by two advisory bodies, then go to the governing council, and then, if passed, they may be presented to the whole membership at its annual meeting. It tells you something about the state of liberal politics and sexual behavior that, from May 2013 to the present day, the rape proposals have gone through numerous advisory committee discussions, eight council meetings, five meetings of the whole membership, and limitless negotiation between the director of the ALI, Richard Revesz, and the most vociferous members.

Schulhofer and Murphy presented their original proposal that sexual intercourse or penetration without consent should be a felony. The proposal is not substantively different from Schulhofer's book, consent being defined as "a person's positive agreement, communicated by either words or actions, to engage in a specific act of sexual penetration or sexual contact."[76] Note that this proposal is a very traditional criminal law formulation, requiring objective, verbal, or behavioral evidence of a disputed fact, in this case whether there is permission.

A number of critical council members objected immediately. A well-respected criminal defense lawyer argued that such consent is unrealistic in the way sexual relations unfold, defendants will be exposed to false accusations, and it will be very difficult to defend against such lies. A second objector, a voice from academic life, translated the argument into the campus setting. Basically repeating the arguments that had been emerging from various law faculties in the rape on campus disputes, the academic asserted that the movement against rape had gone haywire, with miscommunications, hypersensitive complainants, and morning-after regrets being translated into a "death sentence" for the accused.

The opponents were almost entirely focused on whether Schulhofer and Murphy's proposal of objective evidence of consent would require the dreaded "only yes means yes." In life, often people are silent. Underneath all the talk, who must bear the burden of the hot potato of silence during sex is the most pressing question in the formulation of the rules. In the first of a dozen compromises, Reporters Schulhofer and Murphy agreed to work with members of the council to make clear that consent could be communicated by action and not just words and that in some circumstances, even inaction could be consent.

As of the early years at the ALI, not among conservatives, not among liberals, nowhere was there a reliable political constituency for equalizing women's status when it comes to sex. Traditional liberals like Clinton judicial appointee José A. Cabranes lined up with Ronald Reagan's solicitor general, the conservative legal scholar Charles Fried, to argue against Schulhofer and Murphy's proposal.

Remember, Schulhofer and Murphy were basically proposing a standard for consent drawn from a person's observable words and actions, what lawyers call "objective" evidence. Weirdly, the opponents of toughening the standard for consent lined up behind the opposite concept — a *subjective* standard of consent. What was the accuser thinking at the time? Even a moment's thought reveals that this could really hurt the accused! All the rape victim would have to say is that in her head she was not agreeing: yes means no. Given the current state of sexual power and the history of rape convictions, it's unlikely that a court would believe a female accuser without more, but that is the logical outcome of the highly unconventional position the opponents to Schulhofer and Murphy took. At the other extreme, if all that matters is the victim's state of mind, even saying no wouldn't save her. Since the dawn of time accused rapists have been saying that "no means yes."[77] Although, unbelievably, there were a handful of ALI members who were okay with the antediluvian notion that No could mean Yes, most did not want to open the door to that scenario again. Nonetheless, the weird alliance of liberals and conservatives had produced a proposal that would make things worse for both victim and accused in the law of rape, as judges and juries tried to read the accuser's mind.

While the ALI debated about the criminal protections, journalists kept inveighing against the strengthening of the legal protections against campus sexual offenses. In June 2015, Emily Yoffe, then at *Slate*, took on *The Hunting Ground*, with a very different version of the Harvard Law School rape story, one of the offenses it portrayed.[78] The incident involved a man and a woman from Harvard and an unnamed friend of hers, with the Harvard woman accusing the man of sexual assault after a long alcohol filled night. The documentary highlighted her dissatisfaction with the university's response. The story as Yoffe sees it, "is not an illustration of a sexual predator allowed to run loose by self-interested administrators. The record shows that what happened that night was precisely the kind of spontaneous, drunken encounter that administrators who deal with campus sexual assault accusations say is typical. Nor is [the student's] story an example of official indifference. Harvard did not ignore her complaints; the school thoroughly investigated them. And because of her allegations, the law school education of her alleged assailant has been halted for the past four years." Worse, the alleged assailant was an African American man, a group with a long history of bearing the brunt of false white American rape accusations.

The same month as Yoffe's article, a conservative DC magazine, the *Washington Examiner*,[79] attacked Schulhofer and Murphy with the pointed question, "Has the federal government ever had sex?"[80] Although it's unclear what the feds have to do with the ALI, which has no governmental power, or with rape law, which is almost entirely enforced by the states, it's catchy. And the article was scathing. "A push to bring authoritarianism into the bedroom," the article announced in boldface type.

In a similar piece a few months later, Harvard Law School professor Jeannie Suk Gersen weighed in at the *New Yorker* to warn that the ALI proposal to raise the standard for consent in the criminal law risked all the injustices the faculty had worried about on campus but with the much graver consequence of prison sentences.[81] She chose, for impenetrable reasons, to make her stand behind the case of Owen Labrie, the eighteen-year-old senior at tony St. Paul's prep school, who had lured an underage fifteen-year-old girl into a laundry closet for sex.[82] Labrie was acquitted of felony sexual assault. New Hampshire law did not require affirmative consent, and the jury did not interpret the girl's frozen silence as a no, even though she testified she had told him no as well. Labrie was, however, convicted of sexual assault because the girl was only fifteen, below the statutory age for consent. The young man was fulfilling St. Paul's "so-called Senior Salute," Suk Gersen wrote, "the campus tradition of graduating boys inviting younger girls to a romantic encounter." Like her sweet description of luring freshman girls to a laundry closet as a "campus tradition" and frozen sex as a "romantic encounter," Suk Gersen characterizes Labrie as a "scapegoat" for a sexual culture "that we increasingly reject."

By 2016, at the end of the four-year journey, the members of the ALI had agreed on a model standard for consent. Not surprisingly, their language looks like nothing more than word salad. "Consent," the approved draft read, "means a person's willingness to engage in a specific act of sexual penetration or sexual contact." Taken by itself, this is the stunningly foolish subjective standard, but the draft tried to explain what it meant. "Consent may be expressed or it may be inferred from behavior, including words and conduct — both action and inaction — in the context of all the circumstances." The standard then addresses the fraught question of physical and verbal "resistance." And the ALI has it every which way. Resistance is not required, which seems to put the hot potato of silence on the accused, but then they say also the lack of resistance may be considered, which puts the hot potato right back on the accuser. Realizing they had walked right into the "no means yes" trap, the barristers then add out of the blue that "a clear verbal refusal" — such as "No" — "suffices to establish the lack of consent."

MacKinnon is not surprised that the ALI draft is incoherent. She rejects the way that consent is defined in law altogether. Given the structural inequality of the sexes in society, consent, meaning acquiescence to power, simply gives power what it wants.[83] MacKinnon suggests instead a standard of "welcomeness." This is not pie in the sky: sexual harassment law, as we saw in the decision in *Meritor v. Vinson*, has used that standard for decades. As the Supreme Court said in that case: "The fact that sex-related conduct was "voluntary," in the sense that the complainant was not forced to participate against her will, is not a defense to a sexual harassment suit brought under Title VII . . . The correct inquiry is whether respondent by her conduct indicated that the alleged sexual advances were unwelcome, not whether her actual participation in sexual intercourse was voluntary."[84]

As MacKinnon explains it, "When a sexual interaction is equal, consent is not needed and does not occur because there is no transgression to be redeemed. Call it sex. And when a sexual incursion is not equal, no amount of consent makes it equal, hence redeems it from being violative. Call it sexual assault. This statement does not end here. If sex is equal between partners who socially are not, it is mutuality, reciprocity, respect, trust, desire — as well as sometimes fly-to-the-moon hope and a shared determination to slip the bonds of convention and swim upstream together — not one-sided acquiescence or ritualized obeisance or an exchange of sex for other treasure that makes it intimate, interactive, moving, communicative, warm, personal, loving."[85]

The progress made by the ALI efforts, MacKinnon concedes, are "minimal, although not nonexistent."[86] But at the end of the day, then, Schulhofer and Murphy spent years much devoted to get to word salad just on the crucial task of defining consent. (To be clear, the years of work also included struggles over other very important and controversial issues like the definition of force, aggravation, penalty levels, and a host of other issues.[87]) There's a reason the battle over consent is epic and has taken fifty years since the last Model Penal Code. "You may wonder," Schulhofer says wryly, "why am I still doing this [working on the rest of the revisions of the Model Penal Code sex provisions]. Well, many jurisdictions still don't make penetration without consent a crime at all unless there is force, and many others a minor offense not a felony. The ALI process should speed the trend to eliminate these anachronisms. Several Scandinavian countries just changed their law."

At day's end, the lawyers aren't going to be the leaders in changing the way women navigate the world of sexual abuse, whether on campus or on the street. Unlike the second wave of feminism, no Ruth Bader Ginsburg in a quiet office at the ACLU is going to change the world for women. She had conservative resistance, to be sure. But the movement to change the law of rape, like most reckoning with the politics of sex, attracts liberal resistance, and that potently divides the liberal defense lawyers from feminist lawyers, and reshuffles the normal alliances. Not the lawyers then.

But "meanwhile," as Schulhofer said in our interview in 2018, "the movement in society is changing."

9

Roger Ailes and Donald Trump
Republicans Corner the Market on Sex Abuse
2015–16

Candidate Trump Treats Women Like Animals

As many conventional liberals in academia and the ALI were lining up to fight against strengthening protections for victims of sexual abuse, an ally for women surfaced in the form of a commentator at the conservative television network Fox News. And not just any commentator, but the second-highest-rated star of Fox News, the host Megyn Kelly, who worked for Fox but had her own show with real control over its content. Kelly, one of several unambiguously beautiful blonde women at Fox, was, as the *Times* later put it, an "unlikely feminist heroine."[1] As part of a brilliant career as a harsh interviewer, she had inveighed against many feminist positions. For instance, she once ranted about the new federal guidelines on college sexual-assault adjudication: "Once you are accused, you're *done,* you can't have a lawyer in there representing you, and the rules say, 'Don't allow the accused to cross-examine the accuser, because it could be intimidating and threatening for her.' Well—she might be *a liar!* She might *deserve* a little intimidation!"[2]

But in August 2015, sitting in the powerful moderator's seat at the first Republican primary debate, she leveled a shot at candidate Donald Trump. After all, conservatives were still ostensibly the party of family virtue and upright sexual behavior. "You've called women you don't like 'fat pigs,' 'dogs,' 'slobs,' and 'disgusting animals,'" she asked. "Does that sound to you like the temperament of a man we should elect as president?"[3]

In that moment, Donald Trump revealed the secret of his improbable election as president of the United States. He knew women weren't powerful enough to call him to account for his long practice of judging them by their looks like cattle at a sexual auction. Thrice married and unfaithful to all his wives, he had probably known it his entire adult life. Without missing a beat, he revealed that he'd brought a gun to what Kelly, and probably everyone watching, thought was a knife fight. Instead of waffling, apologizing, defending, or reframing his insults as humor, he blamed the people he had defamed. For taking offense. His temperament was not the problem. "I think," the Republican primary candidate said, "the big problem this country has is being politically correct."[4] Looking back on the exchange a few years later, Kelly remembered it with impressive shrewdness. "His response to me was, 'What I say is what I say, and we've gotten too PC in this country,'" the conservative host told a FOX roundtable. "And that resonated with many people."[5]

In a heartbeat, he opened the door to the frank abuse of women in a world of unbridled sexuality to conservatives, who had always cloaked their hostility to women's rights in a mantle of virtue and paternalistic tradition. This was not a complete surprise. As Kelly's earlier remarks about rape victims on campus reflected, the conservative movement was never very sympathetic with women's efforts to get some traction for themselves. But the conservative hostility to college women organizing was always coupled with a kind of chivalric deference to women in their place as proper wives and mothers, not open season on treating women like animals.

The then-candidate continued with what Kelly reasonably heard as a personal threat. "I've been very nice to you, although I could probably maybe not be, based on the way you have treated me. But I wouldn't do that to you." And, as she anticipated, Donald Trump soon stopped being "nice" and began pounding on her in the crudest and most sexual terms. "You could see there was blood coming out of her eyes," Trump told CNN's Don Lemon in an interview the following night. "Blood coming out of her wherever."[6] It was the first of an unending shitstorm of tweets and attacks.

From that first question at the first debate, the issue was framed. It would be Donald Trump, and, gradually, the Republican Party he was taking over, versus the female pigs and dogs bleeding from their wherevers, as he had called them over the years and as recently as the day after the debate. Slowly, too slowly, women moved away. August 6, 2015, the day Megyn Kelly made a political question out of Donald Trump's treatment of women, was a landmark in the movement against sexual harassment and abuse. She later said she was just doing her duty as a journalist.

Not unreasonably, she might have expected Roger Ailes, the chairman and CEO of Fox News, a man with unreviewable control over every aspect of the operation, to back her up. Certainly her husband, the novelist Douglas Brunt, did. But, as she quickly enlightened her spouse, no one at Fox News was going to defend her. Ailes was busy trying to calm Trump down.[7] Top-ranked colleague Bill O'Reilly just kept putting Trump on his show.[8] Finally, realizing that no one at Fox was going to rescue her from Trump and his minions, she decided to rescue herself by going to Trump Tower and making peace. She describes herself at the meeting as feeling like a hostage who thinks her captor just might let her go. Showing her belly pretty much stopped the Trump assault. Kelly kept her perch at Fox News, but her relations with Ailes only got worse.[9]

Shooting at the King

Why would Ailes take Megyn Kelly's side? With all the conservatives' public presentation of family values—using the prospect of marriage equality as a scare tactic in the election of 2004, and passing ever more aggressive laws against abortion, the conservative movement and the Republican Party were not immune from the impact of the "Naughty Nineties." Even before Trump publicly embraced the weighing and measuring of women for their sexual value like enslaved females on sale before the Civil War, Ailes's news network was full-on picking and displaying their women employees for their physical traits. Everyone at Fox knew that their female news anchors were expected to wear short skirts and display their legs whenever they took the stage. Seventy-something Ailes had been making his anchor Gretchen Carlson's life a living hell for years, starting with his widely discussed demands that she twirl around, show her legs, and wear tight-fitting clothes. Trump fan O'Reilly had settled a huge claim against him from a longtime employee, Andrea Mackris, as long ago as 2004.

At the same time he was hanging Kelly out to dry in face of Trump's attacks, Ailes offered Gretchen Carlson a novel solution to her complaints about her sexist treatment at the network: "I think you and I should have had a sexual relationship a long time ago, and then you'd be good and better and I'd be good and better. Sometimes problems are easier to solve" that way, he said. It's not clear how the fifty-year-old married former Miss America Carlson would have been made good or better by having sex with Ailes, but Ailes definitely did not get good or better from his proposed solution. She was recording him on her phone.[10] (Steve Jobs has probably liberated more women than Susan B. Anthony.)

Carlson started recording her conversations with Ailes in 2014. She had complained about her sexist treatment by fellow *Fox & Friends* host Steve Doocy, and when he got word of it Ailes mocked Carlson and told her to stop being so easily offended.[11] After complaining, she was demoted from the high-ranking morning show. At that moment, armed only with her cell phone, Gretchen Carlson, Stanford educated and with years of experience in journalism, began a secret, one-woman campaign against Roger Ailes, and, through him, Fox News itself. Ailes kept guns in his office, he had people followed, and there were security cameras all over the office.

The culture at Fox was such a cult of personality and such a culture of fear that, like pronouncing the true name of the Old Testament God, no one felt comfortable even saying Ailes's name.[12] Carlson knew taping him was like going into the lion's den.[13]

Every social movement, however incremental, passes inflection points. Rosa Parks on the bus. *The Feminine Mystique.* Stonewall. Gretchen Carlson turned on her iPhone. She was certainly a less likely change agent than Betty Friedan or Rosa Parks. But in retrospect there were signs that she was not Fox News arm candy. She had taken time off from Stanford to make a winning run for Miss America, deploying her musical skills as a competitive violinist for the 35 percent of points that in those days rested on talent. There was an incident in 2012 where she walked off the set after her co-host made a sexist comment. "You read the headlines since men are so great," she said laughingly, leaving him alone on the couch.[14] She even gave warning about sexual harassment. In 2015 she wrote a long article about being sexually harassed at Miss America and several times in the ensuing years.[15]

Not being stupid, Carlson had also started looking for a lawyer. She found Nancy Erika Smith, a founding partner of the New Jersey employment law firm Smith Mullin. Smith, a rangy woman with a big smile and an energetic manner (her husband and partner, Neil Mullin, calls her the "blonde blur"), had been skiing between all the poles in her run to super employment lawyer, representing plaintiffs in every possible discrimination action — age, disability, race, sex.[16] By the time Carlson got to Smith, the firm had an established reputation for big wins, often fueled by imaginative legal theories.

Smith came by her principles honestly. She grew up in Keyport, New Jersey, daughter of an Irish bartender who also owned a liquor store. When her father died, her mom, Madeline Parry, took over. Since the liquor store was next to a butcher shop, Nancy's mother soon found out who in their town could or could not afford a Thanksgiving turkey. Those who could not afford a turkey received a turkey from Parry, who remained anonymous.[17] Smith came from an integrated town, and went to integrated public schools — including college and Rutgers Law School. One day, when she was in law school, she went to an event in Washington, DC, and heard feminist lawyer Catharine MacKinnon speak. "Amazing," she still remembers. One of the benefits of a public education, she had little debt when she got out, so she could afford to represent the powerless and wait years to start turning a profit from her practice.

Representing plaintiffs with employment disputes, Smith had long been fighting the system of contracts that forced her clients into private arbitration, rather than allowing them into the ordinary public, civil courts. She calls it "corporate arbitration," since the arbitrators are often retired judges who have little sympathy for the lowly outsider civil rights plaintiffs she represents. And, indeed, arbitration is something of a Hobbesian state of nature, where there is no law. "No rules of evidence, no rules of procedure, no public record, no appeal," Smith laments. She had been plotting for years to get a case that would allow her to start to cut back on the power of the arbitration clauses.

When Gretchen Carlson walked into her office, she knew she had her case. Fox had structured the arbitration clause in Carlson's contract without including Ailes: he was not a signatory and was not identified. Smith and Carlson laid elaborate and careful plans for her suit against Ailes, based on the argument that he was not covered by the arbitration requirement. They hired a public relations firm, they hired social media experts to separate Carlson's Facebook page from Fox so they had a record of all her followers, they beefed up their online security in anticipation of an attack. Roger Ailes was no minor adversary.

For Smith's larger strategy to work, however, Carlson had to agree to go public and file the suit in court. The minute Ailes got wind she was going to sue, he would strike first and file an arbitration, arguing for coverage. No matter how good Smith's arguments were, it's much harder to get out of an arbitration once it has started than to beat back arbitration demands once you have already gotten into court. Generally in the suits before Carlson's, the women complain, the harassers invoke arbitration, then settle in secret. That's why there are no court records for journalists to find, no matter how hard they try. On June 23, 2016, Fox let Carlson know they would not be renewing her contract. She was only fifty, but in show business that meant her career was essentially over. She had made enough money, and her husband was a successful sports agent. She was ready to shoot at the king. She and Smith had an inkling — although no one could have foreseen the magnitude — that accusing Ailes in public would set off a storm.

On July 6, 2016, just under the limitations period from his invitation to get good and better with him, Gretchen Carlson sued Roger Ailes. He had said he thought "we should have had a sexual relationship a long time ago," Carlson's complaint recited.[18] Boom.

Being a victim of sexual harassment in New York City, Carlson was better off than if she'd been harassed in most other places. In 2005 New York City changed its local law to part company with the federal scheme. Does the behavior amount to inferior terms of employment, the New York law asks? A few years later, a landmark New York court decision confirmed that in New York plaintiffs don't have to meet the unhelpful federal standard of severe and pervasive misconduct. Gretchen Carlson wanted nothing to do with the mighty federal government. She framed her complaint as a suit under the New York City Human Rights Law.

The Murdoch family, which owned Fox News, did not take a lesson from Trump's scorched-earth response to accusations of sexism. Megyn Kelly says she told Lachlan Murdoch and the Fox general counsel right away. It was early days in the conservative embrace of open Trumpian sexism; after Kelly's revelations, the Murdoch family decided to hire an independent law firm, New York's Paul, Weiss, Rifkind, Wharton and Garrison, to look into the allegations. Meanwhile, the law offices of Smith Mullin were so swamped with calls from additional women accusing Ailes they could attend to nothing else. Smith knew who to send the new accusers to: *New York* magazine's Gabriel Sherman, who had written a scathing biography of Ailes a few years earlier.[19] Sherman had already unearthed the only on-the-record story of a young woman Ailes had harassed years before. Sherman knew the women were telling the truth, because he had heard so many stories off the record. Three days after Carlson went public, Sherman published his blockbuster article on the other accusers: "6 More Women Allege That Roger Ailes Sexually Harassed Them," the headline screamed.[20] Kellie Boyle, fifty-four, former Republican National Committee field adviser, Marsha Callahan, seventy-three, former model, and four others identified with pseudonyms. The most shocking part of the first of the Sherman revelations was the ages of the anonymous victims. Susan, sixteen, Diane, eighteen, Pat, twenty-four.

The investigators from Paul, Weiss asked to talk to Megyn Kelly. She didn't think Ailes should be pressing other Fox stars — Jeanine Pirro, Greta van Susteren — to endorse him as a good boss. In 2006, when she was newly divorced and appeared vulnerable he had harassed her. Kelly, the intrepid Sherman reported, personally approached other women at Fox to talk to the investigators at Paul, Weiss.

It must have been so sweet for Megyn Kelly. Ailes had hung her out to dry, as Trump rose. From the day he was appointed chairman of Fox News, Ailes understood that conventional conservatism — elite, intellectual, and East Coast–driven — would never take over the nation's politics. After 1996 Ailes made Fox into the voice of an increasingly large bloc of the Republican base, people who thought their country was disappearing. Donald Trump fit that model like a glove.[21] In the years before Trump's presidential run, Fox News repeated and legitimized his signature claim that President Obama was not a natural-born American citizen. Then when Trump actually ran, the signature Fox show *Fox and Friends* extended him an invaluable podium, allowing him, any morning, to phone in to the widely watched show and defend whatever controversial move he had made the night before.[22]

Faced with a viewing audience solidly loyal to the Trump he himself had created, Ailes had no choice but to buckle to Trump after Trump started attacking Kelly. Megyn Kelly couldn't bring down

Donald Trump. But mere months before Trump's general election campaign for the presidency, her testimony to investigators and leaks to reporter Gabriel Sherman had helped bring down Ailes, in many ways the man who had made Trump's candidacy possible. On July 21, Ailes accepted a forty-million-dollar severance from Fox, and Fox issued a formal apology to Gretchen Carlson. Fox reportedly paid Carlson 30 million dollars.

Carlson's suit and the Sherman revelations that followed clearly prophesied the accusations that would surface a year later to make the #MeToo revolution.[23] Like movie producer Harvey Weinstein, the offensive Roger Ailes had a long history of out-of-control sexual abuse. He had lost his job at CNBC for similar reasons and lost out on numerous other obvious opportunities from places not as toxic to women as Fox News. Like Weinstein, the rumors about Ailes's behavior were broad and deep. Gabriel Sherman had tried to wrestle the many complainers into going on the record for his critical biography of Ailes a few years before Carlson sued, but, with one exception, they were too scared. Abused women stepped away from Ailes, because he used a combination of threats of public scandal or legal action against them and offered those who posed the largest danger to the Fox media empire large sums of money. The people who ran his place of business were in it up to their necks.[24] He was in a rare moment of weakness when Gretchen Carlson took aim at him. Fox owner Rupert Murdoch had started sharing management with his two sons, who had long tussled with Ailes, and Murdoch was not entirely in the tank for Donald Trump.

Ailes still did not preview the full scope of the upsurge to come. He was a conservative, the committed political and then journalistic activist whose agenda was all about advancing the power of the Republican Party. Insofar as the GOP embraced a range of policies adverse to women's interests, like opposing abortion rights and laws addressing violence against women, Ailes was already the adversary. The devilish problem presented by the likes of Bill Clinton still remained unaddressed. What is a feminist to do when a liberal male ally is found to be abusing women in private?

A few blocks away from Fox News, however, at the offices of the *New York Times* in Times Square, an energetic and well-regarded political reporter, Jodi Kantor, was watching the events of summer 2016. Carlson had "brought down the boss," she noted. Not an easy job when the harasser is also the undisputed chief of the business you work at.[25]

What next? Jodi wondered.

Shooting at the King — and Missing

She did not have long to wait. For a brief time on Friday, October 7, 2016, the traffic on the *Washington Post* site caused the newspaper's server to crash.[26] A source had sent the *Post* a recording of presidential candidate Donald Trump sharing his opinion about how to treat women: "Grab 'em by the pussy."[27] And the *Post* put it up.

The tape originated at NBC. In 2005, the station had invited Trump to participate in its celebrity fluff show *Access Hollywood*. The *Access Hollywood* bus was taking Trump to the set of the soap opera *Days of Our Lives*, where Trump was making a cameo appearance. As he rode to the shoot in a tour bus with the show's host, Billy Bush, they spotted the attractive woman, actress Arianne Zucker, there to greet the guests when the bus stopped.

"Your girl's hot as shit. In the purple," says Bush, who was by then a cohost of NBC's *Today* show.

"Whoa!" Trump says. "Whoa!"

Then: "I better use some Tic Tacs just in case I start kissing her. You know I'm automatically attracted to beautiful — I just start kissing them. It's like a magnet. Just kiss. I don't even wait.

"And when you're a star, they let you do it. You can do anything."

"Whatever you want," Bush agrees.

"Grab 'em by the pussy," Trump says. "You can do anything."[28]

NBC News had known about the tape for some time. There are disputed claims about why the network had not broadcast it as news,[29] but, at 11:00 a.m. on October 7, someone phoned it in to

Post reporter David Fahrenthold. The choice of Fahrenthold is not a surprise; he had been doing Watergate-level investigative reporting on the candidate for months. Fahrenthold had started down the road that would eventually lead to a Pulitzer Prize for national reporting (2017) investigating Trump's somewhat elusive charitable record.[30] Trying to find out about Trump's philanthropic activity often caused him to hit a brick wall, so Fahrenthold brilliantly exploited a new method: linking his legacy medium to the new technology, he asked for help on Twitter. He even tweeted out pictures of his old-fashioned reporter's pad, with a list of the charities that weren't answering his questions. Tips poured in.

Still, the tip about the sex tape was a new turn of affairs. In a matter of hours the *Post* had vetted it, lawyered it, and called for comment from NBC and from the campaign. At 4:00 p.m. the *Post* put the tape online. Seven minutes after Fahrenthold posted, NBC took the story on air.

Trump's opponent, Senator Hillary Clinton, tweeted out the predictable indignant response, as did Planned Parenthood and myriad other Democratic and liberal voices. At first, it seemed, the anti–pussy grabbing movement might be bipartisan. Republican senator Kelly Ayotte (New Hampshire), who was running for reelection and had said she would vote for Trump, called his comments "totally inappropriate and offensive."[31] Republican National Committee chairman Reince Priebus, Trump supporter, asserted that "no woman should ever be described in these terms or talked about in this manner. Ever."[32] Former presidential candidate Mitt Romney, a Trump critic, said "Hitting on married women? Condoning assault? Such vile degradations demean our wives and daughters and corrupt America's face to the world."[33] Trump's campaign seemed to falter; Republicans, who had never been enthusiastic about the insurgent reality TV star, began eyeing the exits.

No exit. With the same uncanny sense for the weakness of women's power he displayed decrying "political correctness" to Megyn Kelly at the first debate, Trump made the pitch-perfect response.

"This was locker room banter, a private conversation that took place many years ago . . . I apologize if anyone was offended." He was sorry if women, those delicate snowflakes, and their wussy allies like Mitt Romney were offended, not sorry that he had said something offensive, much less done something offensive. And then he moved in for the kill: "Bill Clinton has said far worse to me on the golf course — not even close."[34] Gonzo journalist Gabriel Sherman says it was a knockout blow: Trump's fatal scandal fell right into the media whataboutism narrative. What about Hillary's husband?

Senate Majority Leader Mitch McConnell had said the *Access Hollywood* comments were "repugnant, and unacceptable in any circumstance" and made clear Trump's brief statement would not suffice. But Trump's statement did suffice. It more than sufficed. Tony Perkins of the Family Research Council told BuzzFeed's Rosie Gray: "My personal support for Donald Trump has never been based upon shared values."[35] His support, Perkins continued, was based on interests they shared, like ending abortion. As would become increasingly clear, however, restricting women's reproductive choices, like restricting their freedom by sexual assault, has the value of keeping women down. Would the Republican candidate's ownership of that issue cost him the election?

The second debate between the feminist candidate Hillary Clinton and the *Access Hollywood* candidate Donald Trump was, dramatically, scheduled for two days after the *Post* posted — Sunday, October 9, 2016. In those two days, *Trump's numbers basically did not move*. On Sunday morning, Fox News reported, "before the tape leaked, Morning Consult's polling had Hillary Clinton up 41 percent to 39 percent over Trump. In the first poll conducted after the tape came out Friday afternoon, conducted by Morning Consult for *Politico*, Clinton's lead expanded only slightly: It's now 42 to 38. GOP women don't appear to be reacting all that differently from GOP men: only 13 percent of Republican women thought Trump should drop out, which was totally in line with all Republican voters."[36] The women didn't seem upset.

When debate moderator Martha Raddatz asked Trump if the behavior on the tape was still ongoing, Trump immediately responded with an attack on Bill Clinton's actions toward women (and a speculative attack on Hillary, the actual candidate). "If you look at Bill Clinton, far worse: mine are words, his was action. His was what he has done to women. There's never been anybody in the history of politics in this nation that's been so abusive to women, so you can say any way you want to say it, but Bill Clinton was abusive to women. Hillary Clinton attacked those same women and attacked them viciously. Four of them are here tonight."[37] Sitting in the stands with Bill Clinton's other accusers, Paula Jones, who had declined to kiss the then-governor's penis and got told by the judge that what happened to her wasn't that bad, got a little revenge after all.

Instead of issuing a ringing call to action on behalf of every woman, Republican and Democrat, who had been grabbed and pawed by Donald Trump, Hillary Clinton was reduced to word salad: "So much of what he just said is not right, but he gets to run his campaign any way he chooses. He gets to decide what he gets to talk about, instead of answering people's questions, laying out the plans we have that make a better life and a better country. That's his choice." Clinton finished with a ringing invocation to political suicide, the converse of Trump bringing a gun to the knife fight with Megyn Kelly a few months earlier. "When I hear something like that, I am reminded of what my friend, Michelle Obama, advised us all: 'When they go low, you go high.'"[38] Go high against Donald Trump. Great plan. Of course, Bill Clinton's wife couldn't go low; her husband was already there. That was the problem.

Maybe it would not have mattered, but the race was so close, a sneeze might have mattered. And the Republican-dominated Senate had been holding open the Supreme Court seat vacated when Justice Antonin Scalia died in 2016, refusing to hold confirmation hearings for President Obama's nominee.[39] So two branches of government were in play in the presidential election of 2016. In the days after the *Access Hollywood* tape, women started coming out of the woodwork with hair-raising stories about Donald Trump.[40] Four days after the *Post* scoop, two women, one whose story dated to the early 1980s, the other's to 2005, went on the record: the first, who had been seated next to Trump on an airplane, called his action an "assault"; she described him as being "like an octopus . . . His hands were everywhere"; the other said he forced a kiss on her lips.[41] The women's stories inspired one Kristin Anderson to go public with her 1990s encounter with Trump. Sitting next to her on a couch at a New York nightclub, Anderson reported, the real estate tycoon did in fact reach under her skirt and grab her by the pussy.[42]

Days later, after additional accusations started to come out[43] (unwanted kissing, two breast grabs, three ass grabs, two complaints from beauty pageant contestants that he walked into their dressing rooms while they were naked), and when people, importantly for polling, got to discuss the matter among themselves, a reliable ABC/*Washington Post* poll showed that just one-third of respondents said the tape made them less likely to support Trump (*and they were the same voters already profiled as unlikely Trump supporters in the first place*).[44] The Republicans climbed on board as fast as rats swimming toward a rising ship. On Election Day, white women, more likely to be married, religious, and dependent upon their husbands' incomes, voted like married women, for the Republican.[45] Immediate exit polls showed that 53 percent of white women voters, or about twenty-five million females, voted for Donald Trump for president. Better, later polls calculate the percentage of white women for Trump at 47 percent (compared to 45 percent for Hillary and the rest scattered).[46] Maybe white women mostly didn't care about the president groping his airplane seatmate like an octopus, reducing an innocent young employee to tears, or harassing Miss Utah.

The *Washington Post* had fired at Donald Trump with the *Access Hollywood* tape, and the media had predictably mobilized an army of previously unknown female victims. On Tuesday, November 8,

2016, the country learned that these seemingly fatal blows had not killed Trump's candidacy. Donald Trump, accused by over a dozen female citizens of helping himself to various of their bodily parts without consent, was now the forty-fifth president of the United States. In his inaugural address, he expressed his belief that the nation he'd been elected to lead had fallen into a state of "carnage."[47]

10

Pink Pussies at the Women's March 2017

The Turnout Was Huge

One day after the boastful pussy grabber Donald Trump was inaugurated to the most powerful position in the world, women all over the United States took to the streets in protest. The Women's March, January 21, 2017, was likely the largest single demonstration in the history of counting demonstrations. The *Washington Post's* best guess at the number of women who poured into DC was a million, and at all the marches was over four million, or around 1 percent of the American population.[1] A record turnout.

Of course, for every person, mostly women, who marched in protest, five white women (and a few women of color) had voted for Trump for president, for a total, as we've seen, of twenty-four million voters, 47 percent of white female voters. White women matter. Not only did a lot of white women vote, they are, by biology and culture, scattered over places like Pennsylvania and Wisconsin, states that swung the election. For all anyone knew, the four million marchers against Trump all came from the sixty-five million people who had voted against him to no avail in the first place. Did four million marchers matter? Pundits and commentators have been discussing that ever since.

The Women's March started, legendarily, with a Facebook posting after the 2016 election by a retired lawyer in Hawaii. There should be a pro-woman march, she posted to the pro-Clinton private page Pantsuit Nation. Anyone else interested?[2] By the time she went to sleep that night a few dozen friends had signed up. Ten thousand were on board by the time she woke up. The new technology was again driving social change. With warp speed, DC activist Vanessa Wruble signed on as head of campaign operations, and brought in professional organizers Carmen Perez, Linda Sarsour, and Tamika Mallory, and Bob Bland joined in. With its board of Anglo, Latina, African American, and Palestinian American/Muslim leaders,[3] the Women's March did one thing successfully: it navigated, for the moment at least, the fraught territory of the intersection of race, ethnicity, and sex. Displaying astonishing efficiency, in two months the organizers planned routes, got permits, rented sound systems, and recruited speakers in cities from Walla Walla, Washington, to Washington, DC. People marched in 673 locations worldwide.[4] Their biggest problem on the day was that they succeeded too well. In Chicago, for instance, the rally was so big, the march after it had to be canceled for safety reasons. Cable channels, YouTube, and even broadcast networks devoted the day to covering the gatherings,[5] their size, their diversity, their signs: IF YOU TAKE AWAY MY BIRTH CONTROL, I'LL JUST MAKE MORE FEMINISTS; I'VE SEEN SMARTER CABINETS AT IKEA; SEX OFFENDERS CAN NOT LIVE IN GOVERNMENT HOUSING.[6] The images were everywhere, in stark contrast to the images of the sparse crowds at the inauguration the day before.

The DC Metro reported the second-largest number of trips in its history; twice the number as on Trump's inauguration day.[7] Gloria Steinem gave a speech. So did the head of Planned Parenthood, and many, many more. By all accounts the breakout star of the DC rally was, improbably, the actress Ashley Judd, who read a poem, "Nasty

Woman," written by a nineteen-year-old community college student, Nina Donovan, from Franklin, Tennessee, who was inspired to poetry when she saw Donald Trump call Hillary Clinton "nasty."[8]

Parades are nice, but, inaugurated the day before, President Donald F. Trump appointed a justice to fill the Supreme Court seat the Republicans had held open for a year. In a few weeks, the Senate confirmed Neil Gorsuch without a fight. With four conservatives and four liberals on the court, Anthony Kennedy was once again the critical swing vote.

Savvy political operatives knew the march was a serious opportunity. The pro-choice Democratic candidates' organization EMILY's List had the foresight to organize a candidate training program in DC for the day after the march. EMILY's List typically dedicated its time recruiting potential candidates for its programs. Not this time. The training program had sold out the week before. VoteRunLead, which trains women to run for office, was flooded with women wanting to take its online and real-time seminars. She Should Run, an organization providing support for women candidates, reported the same spike, inquiries rising from in the dozens to in the thousands. A little more than a year later, the Center for Women and Politics at Rutgers University reported that women were running for 277 of the 435 seats in Congress and 27 of 35 seats in the Senate. All but one of the open races for governor included a woman candidate.[9] The March organizers themselves started follow-up initiatives to inspire women candidates, organize voter registration, and increase turnout.

Indivisible, the chapter-based resistance movement that is one of the most prominent of the post-Trump grassroots activist groups, doesn't keep numbers on the members' genders, but from the names and pictures, the leaders believe that it, too, is heavily female.[10] Started by two female former congressional staffers and one of their husbands after the 2016 election, news of Indivisible spread by means of women's social networks. The bad news was that, like most social networks in segregated America, the very white movement was having to make a big effort to diversify. The good news is that Indivisible was empowering suburban networked women organizers and candidates who previously never thought they stood a chance. One woman marching in the substantial 2018 follow-up to the 2017 Women's March carried a sign: GRAB 'EM BY THE MIDTERMS.

Outing Fox Again?

While the activist women waited for the next political opening, the torch passed back to the investigative journalists. Looking back, it is clear that Gretchen Carlson's suit against Roger Ailes was the critical moment ushering in the current #MeToo.[11] The Pulitzer Prize–winning reporter Emily Steel tells the story.[12] In 2016, after Carlson brought down Ailes, "Gabe Sherman [at *New York* magazine] had been coming out with scoop after scoop after scoop," and the *New York Times* was racking its brain to figure out how to compete. Executive editor Dean Baquet, who was at the *Los Angeles Times* in 2004, remembered a 2004 item about Fox News's Bill O'Reilly settling with a female employee, Andrea Mackris. He called in his media reporter, Steel, and paired her with DC politics reporter Michael Schmidt. Why don't we go back and see if there's anything more about O'Reilly there? Baquet asked, taking Steel off most of her other stories. It took the reporters eight months, until April 2017. Not that it was difficult to find more dirt on O'Reilly; that emerged very quickly. But the women involved were locked into confidentiality agreements with onerous penalties if they said a word. They did not want to talk about the stories, they had told no one, they were afraid they would not be believed. Bill O'Reilly's lawyer came to the *New York Times* to tell them they were chasing a nonstory.

Steel and Schmidt looked for a pattern, and a pattern emerged. O'Reilly would spot attractive women as guests on his show, then he would offer them help with their careers, then he would demand sexual services from them. Then, if they were compliant, he would advance them. More importantly, if they were not amenable to his demands, he would not advance them. So the reporters started looking at all the women who had appeared as guests on

O'Reilly's show and then disappeared as commentators. And Emily Steel would call them. The first return call she got was from Wendy Walsh, a psychology professor. Walsh told Steel her story. She had been O'Reilly's guest as an expert on his show, a valuable gig. He took her to dinner in LA and invited her to his hotel room. He said he could get her a job as a contributor on the show, which can pay thousands of dollars. She turned him down and never got invited onto the show again. The reporter and the source went back and forth, and finally after Steel flew to LA and showed up at Walsh's pilates class, they went for coffee and Walsh agreed to go on the record. Steel went back to her hotel room and cried. She was so excited.

On April 1, 2017, the *Times* ran a story headlined "Bill O'Reilly Thrives at Fox News, Even as Harassment Settlements Add Up."[13] The *Times* had identified five women who had been paid off by either O'Reilly or Fox to settle their sexual harassment claims. Most damningly, two of the suits were settled after the network fired Roger Ailes and said it would not tolerate such behavior. There was an explosion on social media, with women tweeting #getridof O'Reilly. Fox fired its star. Six months later, in October 2017, Steel reported a sixth post-Ailes settlement, this one for an eye-popping $32 million. O'Reilly had paid it in January 2017, four months before the *Times* published its first article about his harassment and abuse of women.

After the O'Reilly story, newspaper and magazine editors decided to go after other powerful men who had left a trail of sexual harassment and abuse. The potent machine of investigative journalism was unleashed on the perpetrators of what had formerly been treated as private behavior, covered by the hidden law of adultery. Finally, the power of the press was turned on the subject of sex, and the result was seismic.

11

The Press Presses and the Dam Breaks
Harvey Weinstein
2017–18

The White Whale

And so, on October 5, 2017, just shy of forty years after he forced theater student Cynthia Burr to perform oral sex on him in an elevator in Buffalo, fate caught up with movie mogul Harvey Weinstein.

During those forty years, Weinstein had come to be, arguably, the most powerful man in the movie business. With his brother Bob, he'd founded Miramax in 1979; the company was known for quality, innovative films that could attract a commercial audience: *Shakespeare in Love*, *Pulp Fiction*, *Chicago*, *Good Will Hunting*. The Disney Company bought Miramax in 1993; after a few tumultuous years running Miramax under Disney ownership, Bob and Harvey left the company to form a new independent studio. Pictures in the Weinstein stable ultimately won eighty-one Academy Awards in all, for everything from best picture to best original score.[1]

The Harpoon Lands

"Harvey Weinstein Paid Off Sexual Harassment Accusers for Decades," the *New York Times* headline blasted on October 5, 2017.[2]
Five days later, the *New Yorker,* which had been chasing the same
story, published the results of a ten-month investigation by Ronan
Farrow, formerly of NBC.[3] By the time PBS's *Frontline* broadcast
its documentary "Weinstein,"[4] five months after the *Times* and *New
Yorker* stories, more than a hundred women had come forward
with accusations against him. His name became a proper noun for
abuser, like Kleenex is to tissue. He was the quintessential harasser:
powerful, older, gross, relentless. The charges ranged from requests
for massages to actual rape. As accusations against other perpetrators emerged, a common defense sprang up: Weinstein.

The Long Pursuit; or, Scribbling Women Part 3
(AND SOME SCRIBBLING MEN)

Why in the world did it take so long? Weinstein's behavior had been
an open secret for decades.[5] In the 1990s, journalist Kim Masters
was pursuing the rumor that Weinstein had assaulted the Oscar-
winning star of his picture *Shakespeare in Love,* Gwyneth Paltrow.
Paltrow had told her agent and her then-boyfriend, Brad Pitt, Masters heard. A few years later, actress Zoe Brock accepted a ride at
the Cannes Film Festival to a supposed party at Weinstein's remote
hotel. Finding no one there but Weinstein, who demanded she give
him a massage, she locked herself in the bathroom and screamed at
him until he let her go. Brock told her agent, she says, and numerous producers, casting agents, and so on. The response was always,
Oh, yeah, Harvey. At around the same time, he insisted his assistant in London, Zelda Perkins, come into the bathroom with him to
"take a memo," reeling off the names of all the actresses he said had
had relations with him.

Perkins tolerated Weinstein's behavior for a while, but that ended when she was at the Venice Film Festival with him in 1998, and a new assistant came to her, enormously upset and saying that Weinstein had tried to rape her. The two quit Miramax, left the festival, and went to lawyers in London for advice. In a sign of things to come, the female assistants demanded not only money but that Miramax reform its process for dealing with harassment claims and that Weinstein be referred for mandatory therapy. Still, the Miramax settlement required them to sign a nondisclosure agreement. Perkins was, by all reports, the first one to challenge Weinstein from a larger perspective. After turning him down for a naked bathroom memo-taking, she asked him the one question everyone would like to ask: "How do you look at yourself in the mirror?"

"I have no problem at all," Weinstein replied.

David Carr, the renowned *New York Times* media reporter,[6] came tantalizingly close to Weinstein's abuses in a story, "The Emperor Miramaximus," for *New York* magazine in 2001. Unable to get the documentation he sought from a sealed settlement, Carr had to satisfy himself with a hint: "Something in [Weinstein's] unalloyed nature brings out the storyteller in people, as long as no name is attached. It's all sex, lies, but no videotape."[7]

The *New Yorker*'s Ken Auletta, working on a profile of Weinstein the next year, found out about Zelda Perkins coming to the aid of the fellow Miramax employee. He could not reach the other employee, and when he called Zelda, she was adamant: "I can't talk to you." At his last interview with Weinstein, Auletta had confronted Weinstein with the name Zelda Perkins, and Weinstein had one of his signature explosions, screaming, "Ken, you're going to ruin my marriage and destroy my family."[8] Because the claims were anonymous, Auletta was stymied at getting enough evidence to satisfy his publication's editorial standards — as *New Yorker* editor David Remnick put it, "He didn't have a lot of usable stuff . . . that[s] publishable at a certain level of value." Auletta remembers his editor saying, "We're not the *National Enquirer*," and he agreed. Thwarted, Auletta resorted to coded language in the article he could publish, signaling that Weinstein was often a beast. (Indeed, the profile was entitled "Beauty and the Beast.") In the second paragraph of his profile, Auletta purported to puzzle over why people in Hollywood would find Weinstein coarse: "After all, abusive behavior — starting with the casting couch — became something of an art form in the early days of Hollywood."[9] Later he reported that one of Weinstein's partners, a studio head, complained about feeling "'raped' — a word often invoked by those dealing with him."[10] Get it?

Auletta remained angry that the wealth of knowledge about the ugly behavior remained hidden. His editor, Remnick, says they had "uncovered a well of ugliness and abuse and unfortunately the behavior would continue." Across town, Carr chased the story until his death in 2015.[11]

The pursuit intensified when Weinstein took on someone who was willing to go to the police. In 2015 he groped the Filipina-Italian model Ambra Battilana Gutierrez, whom he lured to his office on the prospect of business. She was horrified and resistant, and when she got home, her friend took her to the Ninth Precinct. Instead of landing in Harvey Weinstein's lawyer's office as so many of his other victims had, she wound up at the Special Victims Division.[12] At least as far as the NYPD was concerned, by 2015 grabbing someone's breasts was no longer considered business as usual, even for Hollywood bigwigs. Officers had Battilana Guttierez set up another meeting and wear a wire. When the police heard the recorded conversation between her and Weinstein, they brought the case to the New York district attorney, Cyrus Vance Jr. The case was all over the New York tabloids. Auletta, still madly frustrated by his inability to expose Weinstein in 2002, went to sources he had developed in the police department.[13] "We got him red-handed," the police source told the *New Yorker* writer.

Auletta called Weinstein, again. The district attorney, Weinstein said, had told him not to speak to the press. Would Auletta meet with his team? David Boies, the chairman at the New York law firm Boies Schiller Flexner, who, for his work representing Al Gore in the contested 2000 presidential election and later challenging California's Proposition 8, was one of the most renowned litigators in America; the corporate investigations expert and titan of the industry Jules Kroll; and Weinstein's (and Woody Allen's) criminal lawyer Elkan Abramowitz. They showed Auletta incriminating material intended to smear Gutierrez, suggesting she had been a kept woman in Italy and had been dismissed as a witness in the scandalous trial of former prime minister Berlusconi on credibility grounds. Vance's office declined to prosecute,[14] and the police weren't willing to defy the attorney general and leak the wire tape to Auletta. At the same time, Ashley Judd wrote an article in *Variety* about being harassed by an unnamed Hollywood producer. Everyone thought it was Weinstein,[15] but she wouldn't talk to Auletta either. Auletta gave his notes and records for his *New Yorker* pieces and his books to the New York Public Library. Anybody who wanted access to them had to get his okay first.

When the board of the Weinstein Company renewed Harvey's contract in 2015, it added prohibitions against sexual misconduct and a penalty for him if he violated the policy. But not only did the arrangement, "unusual" by most experts who later saw it, allow him to essentially buy himself out of any of his actions, but laying the onus on Weinstein would distance the company from taking any action itself.[16]

But by then the hunt was closing in. In early 2017 *New York Times* executive editor Dean Baquet turned his take-no-prisoners political reporter Jodi Kantor onto the story. After all, Weinstein's behavior had been an open secret for decades, including at the *Times*, where despite years of trying, David Carr had failed to crack it. The accusations against Weinstein, absolute boss at his company, had a similar quality to Gabe Sherman's blockbuster story about Roger Ailes that had so impressed Baquet the year before. And Weinstein was tight with Hillary Clinton, always a subject of interest at the *New York Times*. By 2017 Weinstein was deep in negotiations with Clinton to produce a documentary about her failed campaign. If they could finally bring him down, the dirt would inevitably splash her too.

Kantor recruited Megan Twohey, a new arrival at the paper.

Twohey had been a finalist for the Pulitzer Prize when she was at Reuters for reporting an underground market in getting rid of unwanted adopted children.[17] And so Kantor and Twohey, still relatively young fortysomethings, joined their tiny, self-described high-voiced colleague Emily Steel on the sex abuse beat.[18]

Like *Strange Justice* coauthor Jane Mayer did in the 1970s, Kantor dropped out of graduate school, in this case Harvard Law, to go into journalism. She once told the *Yale College Journal of Politics* that, as the daughter of immigrants growing up on Staten Island, she had no connections and no role models for a career in journalism. Kantor's background is not as modest as that sounds. Her immigrant parents — father a successful real estate developer, with a degree from the University of Haifa; mother also a Haifa graduate, a real estate agent — were hardly peasants out of *Fiddler on the Roof.*

When Kantor decided to bail on Harvard, she immediately got a place as an editorial assistant at the newly launched online magazine *Slate* in 1997. By 2000 Kantor was running the New York office, while Jacob Weisberg was in the same office, as political editor.[19] Though he does not recall Kantor being particularly interested in feminist issues, he knew he was dealing with an unstoppable force of nature when it came to getting a story. Weisberg wasn't surprised when the *New York Times* hired Kantor away in 2003 to revamp the Gray Lady's tired culture section at the ripe age of twenty-seven. In 2007 Kantor came to the attention of Jill Abramson, author of *Strange Justice,* and by then managing editor of the *Times.* Abramson plucked Kantor from the culture beat and assigned her to the politics team, focusing on Obama.[20]

After the 2012 election, Abramson encouraged Kantor to focus on gender. It had been twenty years since Abramson's iconic reporting of the Clarence Thomas sexual harassment story. In that moment the line from the first wave of Scribbling Women in 1991 to the second was directly drawn. Kantor wrote a major story about how the elite Harvard Business School was trying to address the problem of women falling behind at every level,[21] and stories about working conditions at Starbucks and Amazon.[22] And now Kantor would be part of the third scribble.

Kantor's partner at the *Times*, Megan Twohey, had the proverbial printer's ink in her veins. Her mother was a television news producer and later worked in public relations at Chicago's Northwestern University.[23] Her father was an editor at the *Chicago Tribune*,[24] and in 2008, ten years after graduating from Georgetown, she went to work at the *Tribune* herself. She was "drawn towards investigating cases of sex crimes and misconduct . . . not only were the underlying crimes so outrageous, but I was also repeatedly infuriated by the failure of institutions that were designed to protect women."[25] New reporters are often assigned to the suburban beat, and Megan immediately found a sex scoop there: the police departments in Chicago's outlying towns had two years of evidence kits from rape claims sitting untested on the shelves, the perpetrators long gone. The next year, Illinois became the first state to require all rape kits to be tested.[26] Two years later, she turned up a pattern of sexual abuse, shrugged off in the most maddening way, at the huge Buddhist temple in southwestern Chicago, and then in other Buddhist temples across the community.[27] Legendary Chicago journalist Mary Schmich says of her former *Tribune* colleague, "when the moment in the culture came for this movement to explode, Megan was there with a longstanding journalistic interest in it. She didn't have to study the problem, her sense of the problem was not merely personal, she had explored it journalistically."[28]

The two started down the settlement trail, tracing the legal and financial records of the agreements Weinstein had used to silence women who came forward.[29] Looks like someone or multiple some-ones at the Weinstein Company was leaking like an old earthen dam, and the two got paperwork of the most damning sort.[30] They "reverse-engineered" the documents as evidence that something had happened. They made a timeline.

One of the most important documents they got—a 2015 memo from twenty-eight year literary scout and production executive Lauren O'Connor—is also evidence that the cultural waters around

Weinstein were changing. When Weinstein started on O'Connor, only six years out of the University of Virginia, and O'Connor observed the harassment and the behaviors that enabled him, she did not think it was normal.[31] She wrote it all down and sent the memo to several Weinstein executives. They bought her off, too, with a nondisclosure agreement and all its accompanying silencing mechanisms. O'Connor wouldn't talk to the *Times*. But old memos never die. They just leak away. The *Times* even got the documents on the settlement with Zelda Perkins, the assistant who wouldn't talk to Ken Auletta (or the *Times*) and the settlement with actress Rose McGowan, one of the early heroes of the Weinstein revelations, who had only been willing to accuse Weinstein as an anonymous Hollywood executive.

Then they turned to the victims the documents identified and people surrounding Weinstein to talk and then talk on the record. They did not have an easy time. People they needed responded with cynicism and mistrust, as Weinstein had succeeded in killing the stories so many times in the past. As Twohey recalls, she and Kantor had to constantly assure people "that this is a story that has the support all the way up to the top of the *New York Times*, and we're going to work at this story as hard as we can around the clock until we get it, until we get at the truth. And we're going to publish the truth."[32] "A couple of sources," Kantor says, "said they spoke to us because we are women reporters with a long history of reporting on women."[33]

While Kantor and Twohey were chasing the paper trail on Weinstein, at NBC, newbie reporter Ronan Farrow had been pushing to do a series about the dark side of Hollywood."[34] Farrow had had an unsuccessful one-year run with his own show on MSNBC, *Ronan Farrow Daily*, and was then doing specials, "Undercover with Ronan Farrow" for NBC's morning program, *Today*.[35]

Farrow was weirdly part of the larger sex abuse story.[36] In the course of an angry breakup, Farrow's mother, the actress Mia Farrow, had accused his father, the legendary filmmaker Woody Allen, of molesting Ronan's sister, Dylan. By then the fifty-six-year-old Allen had taken up with (and eventually married) Mia Farrow's adopted daughter Soon-Yi Previn, thirty-four years his junior. NBC was not willing to go as far into the proposal on the dark side of Hollywood as pedophilia and race in Hollywood. But Farrow did retain a greenlight on a story about sexual harassment and casting-couch culture. So he started interviewing actresses about it, and that's when he began hearing stories about Weinstein.

Very early in the reporting, Farrow got a copy of the wire tape Ambra Battilana Gutierrez had obtained, recording Weinstein at the behest of the New York police. And he began looking for women who would talk about Weinstein on the record. One obvious candidate was *Charmed* star Rose McGowan, who had published an online account of her sex abuse at the hands of an unnamed Hollywood powerhouse. By June of 2017 Farrow had enough material to approach Ken Auletta for access to his notes on the Weinstein sex scandal, and for an interview with the journalist on video.[37] Auletta did not know Farrow at the time, but after hearing about his extensive reporting on the Weinstein story, the experienced media reporter invited him out to his home in Bridgehampton, New York, where Auletta was writing a book. Farrow arrived with a full camera crew. "He told me he had eight women, three on the record and five shielded, and he also had the audiotape of Ambra," Auletta reports. Farrow shared with Auletta that his next step was to meet with the president of NBC news, Noah Oppenheim.

When Farrow finished his interview with Auletta, Auletta told him to turn the camera back on. Turning to the lens, Auletta said slowly, "If NBC doesn't run this it's a scandal." Auletta explains, "I did that, because I wanted him to show his bosses that a media reporter thought he had the story." A few weeks later Auletta followed up to see what had happened, and Farrow told him NBC had in fact turned the story down. "Who would want this?" Farrow asked the older man. Hold my beer, Auletta essentially replied. He called *New Yorker* editor David Remnick and said, "This guy has the goods, and he's judicious." Have him call me, Remnick said.

NBC says Farrow did not have any women on camera.[38] Auletta says, "Ronan clearly convinced me this was false."[39]

The *New Yorker* may have enabled Farrow to further develop his article, but no one outside of NBC supports the network's account that the Weinstein story was unverifiable just two months before.

Landing the Fish

The race between the *New York Times* and the *New Yorker* seems like something out of newspaper lore, harking back to the *Times* scooping the *Washington Post* in 1971 by getting the *Pentagon Papers* story of the lying behind American involvement in Vietnam. Or the *Post* returning the favor in spades the following year with the story of the Nixon campaign breaking into Democratic National Committee headquarters at the Watergate in DC.[40] Kantor says she was at first only "dimly" aware that Ronan Farrow was working on something. *New Yorker* editor David Remnick says, "Of course we knew" about Kantor and Twohey, with an air of revealing the obvious. "Sources talk."[41] Indeed. As the stories were about to publish, *New York Times* editor Dean Baquet, who served on the Livingston Journalism Prize Board with *New Yorker* writer Ken Auletta, tried without success to winkle the *New Yorker*'s pub date out of his pal.[42]

The *Times* published first.

"HARVEY WEINSTEIN PAID OFF SEXUAL HARASSMENT AC-CUSERS FOR DECADES" was the top story on the front page, with a picture of a smiling Harvey Weinstein, surrounded by fans.[43]

The story opened with an incident from twenty years before and one from 2014. "Two decades ago," the article begins, "the Hollywood producer Harvey Weinstein invited Ashley Judd to the Peninsula Beverly Hills hotel for what the young actress expected to be a business breakfast meeting. Instead, he had her sent up to his room, where he appeared in a bathrobe and asked if he could give her a massage or she could watch him shower . . . 'How do I get out of the room as fast as possible without alienating Harvey Weinstein?' Ms. Judd said she remembers thinking." Not alienating Weinstein of course is why readers were first learning of this twenty years later. Fast-forward: "In 2014, Mr. Weinstein invited Emily Nestor, who had worked just one day as a temporary employee, to the same hotel and made another offer: If she accepted his sexual advances, he would boost her career." She complained to colleagues, "who sent [the objections] to Weinstein Company executives."

Making masterful use of the documents — legal records, emails, and internal documents from the Weinstein businesses — Kantor and Twohey told the story of "three decades" of misconduct. The stories are weirdly similar. Weinstein would lure actresses or employees to an isolated spot, usually a hotel room, present himself in a bathrobe or naked, and make escalating demands for massages, watching him shower, groping them, demanding sex. Executives and others, like the young Lauren O'Connor, whose memo played a central role in the story, found themselves conscripted to present the victims for his abuse. If they complained, Weinstein deployed an armory of legal and economic weapons against the victims. There were legal threats, payoffs, and robust confidentiality clauses. The *Times* even reported on the criminal complaint by Ambra Battilanna Guttierez. Other than Ashley Judd and Rose McGowan, most of the women named in the first article were not the rich and famous actresses who later came forward.

How did he get away with it? Kantor and Twohey explained. The allegations piled up even as Mr. Weinstein helped define popular culture. His movies won record numbers of Oscars, and the sweet spot he had seen between high and low won him a unique role in defining the culture. When crossed he could be vengeful and volcanic. The women talked among themselves for thirty years, but, as Lauren O'Connor put it in 2015, "I'm at the beginning of my career. So it's Harvey 1, Me 0."[44] Weinstein and the company responded in the *Times* article with a mixture of denial, carefully cabined remorse, and paeans to corporate tranquility.

It was a bombshell. But in some ways, Kantor and Twohey buried the lede. Deep in the text (but, at least online, cannily placed above and below the predictable picture of Hillary Clinton grinning at and caressing Harvey Weinstein), the *Times* reported, "In public, he presents himself as a liberal lion, a champion of women and a winner of not just artistic but humanitarian awards. In 2015, the year Ms. O'Connor wrote her memo, his company distributed 'The Hunting Ground,' a documentary about campus sexual assault. A longtime Democratic donor, he hosted a fund-raiser for Hillary Clinton in his Manhattan home last year. He employed Malia Obama, the oldest daughter of former President Barack Obama, as an intern this year, and *recently helped endow a faculty chair at Rutgers University in Gloria Steinem's name* [emphasis added]. During the Sundance Film Festival in January, when Park City, Utah, held its version of the nationwide women's marches, Mr. Weinstein joined the parade." Weinstein is not Clarence Thomas, Donald Trump, or Roger Ailes. We have met the enemy, the *Times'* story revealed, and if it is not, as Pogo said, us, it is certainly our ally. A skeptic told Kantor and Twohey as they labored away that nothing would change.

Five days later, on October 10, 2017, Ronan Farrow landed the second harpoon. "From Aggressive Overtures to Sexual Assault: Harvey Weinstein's Accusers Tell Their Stories."[45]

Farrow not only had documents but a lineup of actresses that could fill the entire red carpet at the Academy Awards. Like Kantor and Twohey, with their opening of the searing portrait of Ashley Judd, Farrow's first big anecdote is the most wrenching example: Lucia Evans, who said Weinstein forced her to perform oral sex on him in 2004 right after her junior year at Middlebury College: "As she objected, Weinstein took his penis out of his pants and pulled her head down onto it. 'I said, over and over, "I don't want to do this, stop, don't," she recalled. 'I tried to get away, but maybe I didn't try hard enough. I didn't want to kick him or fight him.' In the end, she said, 'he's a big guy. He overpowered me.'"[46] (Evans's story would fuel the first of the criminal rape charges brought against Weinstein.)

Farrow unleashed the boldfaced names. The Italian actress Asia Argento (unwanted oral sex), Mira Sorvino, who had won an Oscar for *Mighty Aphrodite* (Harvey chased her around and, when she resisted, harmed her career), Ambra Battilana Gutierrez (grabbed her breast and stuck his hand up her skirt), the French actress Emma de Caunes (lured her to his hotel room, where he presented himself naked and with an erection; she resisted), Rosanna Arquette (Harvey in a bathrobe demanding a massage; she said no, harmed her career). There's no music on the *New Yorker* website, but the article reads like the servant Leporello's catalog aria detailing his master's conquests in Mozart's *Don Giovanni*.[47]

My dear lady, this is a list
Of the beauties my master has loved;
a list which I have compiled;
Observe, read along with me.

In Italy six hundred and forty;
In Germany two hundred and thirty-one;
One hundred in France, in Turkey ninety-one;
But in Spain already one thousand and three.

Save the Whales

Farrow's first article and then a subsequent article, "Harvey Weinstein's Army of Spies,"[48] about his lawyers' and private investigators' roles in intimidating and discouraging women from speaking out, revealed something more disturbing than the catalog of individual cases: Weinstein's behavior was made possible by a universe of institutional structures of harassment, in his company, in the film industry, and in American law and legal practices. Quite as if Catharine MacKinnon and Paulette Barnes and Mechelle Vinson had never walked the earth, Harvey Weinstein's entire adult life reveals a society organized to empower abusers.

How did this happen? From the outset, as Alyssa Milano described it,[49] "you can look at a lot of aspects of the underrepresented in that industry being sex workers, whether it got to sexual acts, the intention, the trophy wife, escort existence ripe for abuse. Naïveté or ambition that a young woman has, they set up the system to make women believe that this is what they had to do, this is part of their job."

Sex workers. With few jobs and little social safety net in the early twentieth century, women flocked to California, hoping for stardom.[50] They were making a perilous journey. Actresses had always been vulnerable. The notion that if you're onstage or on-screen, subject to the gaze of an audience or producers, then you are sexually available as well, dates back before motion pictures, to women's theatrical stage debuts in 1660.[51] Hollywood was like Restoration English theater on steroids.

Marilyn Monroe probably expressed it best. The men she knew saw Hollywood as "an overcrowded brothel, a merry-go-round with beds for horses."[52] So it had been from the earliest days. Mack Sennett, the Irish-Canadian émigré who created the Keystone Kops comedies, is credited with inventing the casting couch. And that was 1913![53] After the studios consolidated into the Big Eight in the 1920s and 1930s, there were kings and every one of the studio heads had a harem. Darryl Zanuck, Samuel Goldwyn, Harry Cohn at Columbia. The only part of the MGM in MetroGoldwyn-Mayer that didn't demand sex work from its female stars was the Metro.[54] Mayer was particularly loathsome, publically and repeatedly fondling the very young Judy Garland, herself a hotbed of insecurity, completely dependent upon his favor.[55] When the studio system unraveled, the behavior simply became the province of individual star directors and producers. Alfred Hitchcock's abuse of Tippi Hedren in the 1960s is only the most famous example.[56] Harvey Weinstein is only the icon. Marilyn Monroe was clear on two things. Having sex with the gatekeepers might be necessary, but it was not sufficient to become a bona fide movie star. And second "Most of the men are such horrors that they [the actresses] deserve all they can get out of them!"[57]

Like with Weinstein, the stories have a weird sameness to them.

The vulnerable and ambitious young woman is asked for sex in exchange for access. If the woman says no, she is penalized immediately and harshly, contracts disappear, parts evaporate, auditions come to nothing. Actresses came to anticipate the abuse as part of the price of doing business, and, often entirely isolated from any support structures, to try to figure out ways to minimize it. Unsurprisingly, even then, there was a Shitty Media Men network. Joan Collins was warned against Darryl Zanuck by none other than Marilyn Monroe.[58]

Why did it go on for so long? After the dust settled on the cases in the 1980s and '90s that established sexual harassment as a violation of the Civil Rights Act, we might have expected that employers would take the relatively easy steps the court laid out for them to try to rein in the offending behaviors. All they had to do to defend against responsibility for harassment at the workplace was prove they had exercised reasonable care to prevent and promptly address the behavior and that the complainer unreasonably failed to take advantage of the preventive or corrective opportunities the employer provided.[59]

And yet, as Gretchen Carlson's lawyer Nancy Erika Smith reports from her twenty years of practice representing plaintiffs, the well-trained people in human resources soon came to understand their job as being to protect the company and its powerful executives no matter what.[60] Several former Weinstein employees told *New Yorker* writer Ronan Farrow "that the company's human resources department was utterly ineffective; one female executive described it as 'a place where you went to when you didn't want anything to get done. That was common knowledge across the board. Because everything funnelled back to Harvey.'" She described the department's typical response to allegations of misconduct, "in perfect opposition to the Civil Rights Act, as being, 'This is his company. If you don't like it, you can leave.'"[61]

Sure enough, Farrow reported, when temp employee Emily Nestor, on the job for one day in 2014 when Weinstein propositioned her, had a conversation with company officials about the matter, the officials said that "Weinstein would be informed of any-thing she told them."[62] When the Weinstein scandal broke, some management-side lawyers contended that well-established public companies are better at administering the protections against sexual harassment. But recent events proved them to be seriously misplaced. Harvey Weinstein got away with constant harassment during the decade plus that Miramax was part of the giant Disney company. On June 21, 2018, Intel Corp, the seventh-largest global tech company with $24 billion in value, announced the departure of its CEO for violating the company's nonfraternization policy.[63] On July 20, giant Texas Instruments canned its misbehaving CEO.[64]

If the executives are extremely productive, they can pursue a course almost as extreme as Weinstein's for years. Rumors of wrong-doing at the giant publicly owned CBS network had been swirling for months when Ronan Farrow unleashed his harpoon on CEO Les Moonves in the August 6, 2018, issue of the *New Yorker*.[65] "Six women who had professional dealings with him told me that, be-tween the nineteen-eighties and the late aughts, Moonves sexually harassed them," Farrow reported, complete with four names and various dates. So valuable was Moonves to the CBS board that for a few weeks the company resisted even Farrow's revelations (rarely a good idea). When talk of one hundred million dollars in "sever-ance" payoffs to the abusive executive surfaced, however, Farrow struck again with six more accusations. From the 1980s to the early 2000s, the several-hundred-million-dollar man at CBS had been jumping everyone from female producers to female massage ther-apists.[66] Like Weinstein, Farrow reminded his readers, "Moonves was a great friend to women, helping to found the Commission on Eliminating Sexual Harassment and Advancing Equality in the Workplace, which is chaired by Anita Hill." This founding father of the Commission on Eliminating Sexual Harassment was not some single good guy looking for dates; this was a married man acting out so badly that most masseuses told the hotels they would not go to his room.

And so it seems that after the Supreme Court issued its mealy-mouthed "guidance" for companies seeking to avoid strict liability for sexual harassment of their workforce, resourceful harassers assembled their protective systems. Those who could negotiated for big-ticket employment contracts that provided them with huge separation bonuses without regard to fault. Looking at a multimillion-dollar payout for an exec, companies had a lot of money to "settle" with the complaining employees. Similarly, the harassers in the entertainment industry directly affected the success of the same agents the victimized artists had. Kantor and Twohey and Farrow all reported countless cases where the artists complained to the agents who are supposed to represent them, with no results.

Discrimination law builds in a radical imbalance of legal firepower to begin with. The federal civil rights law gives accusers a very short time to file after the offense, and the nature of sexual harassment makes it very hard to aggregate the claims into a class action. So there's little money for plaintiffs' lawyers, except in the rare case of a highly paid accuser like Gretchen Carlson at Fox News. The accused perpetrators have lots of money for lawyers—for lawyers to threaten defamation suits against the accusers, to claim libel if the whistle blowers get to the media, and to negotiate airtight nondisclosure agreements with extortionate penalties. In the aftermath of Weinstein, after scuba instructor Melanie Kohler posted on Facebook accusing Hollywood producer Brett Ratner of rape, he filed a defamation suit against her.[67] Andrew B. Brettler of the Los Angeles firm Lavely and Singer, described as the "pit bull" of Hollywood lawyers, represented Ratner in his suit against Kohler, and also had the brief for Bryan Singer, a producer accused of raping a seventeen-year-old boy in 2003.[68]

The defendants often have money to hire private investigators, to dig into their accusers' pasts and threaten to out them, often in the tabloid press. Harvey Weinstein is the most famous employer of this tactic, using both his legendary lawyer David Boies to aggressively represent him and private intel firms like Black Cube and Jules Kroll's K2 Intelligence to gather information about his pursuers. When Amber Battilana Gutierrez went to the police, stories of her involvement with much older men and complaints about other sexual affronts she'd made surfaced in the New York tabloids instantly. Ken Auletta says that Kroll and Boies brought that very material to their meeting with him to keep Auletta's Weinstein story out of the *New Yorker* in 2015. Weinstein kept the hammer on youthful low-level employee Emily Nestor after he harassed her, showing her negative news items about another individual who had crossed him that very day.[69] The clear message was that he would not hesitate to do the same to her.

Investigative journalists hunted him for decades, and they finally brought him in. Would Weinstein be the beginning of a trend?

12

#MeToo
2017–18

In October 2017, five days after the *New Yorker* published Ronan Farrow's first article on Harvey Weinstein, the actress and activist Alyssa Milano was lying in bed with her daughter when her phone buzzed;[1] her friend Charles, now Charlotte, Clymer, an activist in Washington, DC, had sent her a screenshot. It read: "Suggested by a friend: if all the women who have been sexually harassed or assaulted wrote 'Me too' as a status, we might give people a sense of the magnitude of the problem." Milano added a sentence to her friend's message and posted it on Twitter: "If you've been sexually harassed or assaulted, write 'me too' as a reply to this tweet."[2]

Social Media and Social Change

When Milano woke up the next day, #MeToo was trending number one on Twitter. It had been retweeted fifty-five thousand times. In the next six weeks, the hashtag appeared on Facebook eighty-five million times. Milano didn't know it at the time, but the actual #MeToo hashtag was started in 2006 by the African American activist Tarana Burke and had a long history online as a grassroots movement against sexual abuse of women of color.[3] This was a happy coincidence, Milano says, giving the #MeToo movement a way to stand with women of color and to recognize the pioneering role of women of color in resisting sexual abuse.[4]

But hashtag activism is not a slam dunk.[5] For years critics have referred to social media protests, particularly on Twitter, as "slactivism"[6] — participation that is limited to a few computer clicks amplifying a message via likes or retweets. Such action may give people the sense that they're contributing to a cause, but it does not produce social change. One example is the economic-inequality protest movement #OccupyWallStreet.[7] In 2011 a crowd of mostly white college-educated young people took up residence in a park near Wall Street to protest corporate influence on government and income inequality and student loan debt.[8] A social media frenzy — Occupy pages on Facebook, a deafening level of Twitter chatter — ensued.[9] After a couple of months, the police removed the occupiers. The protest rightly deserves credit for raising awareness of inequality in political discourse. Since Occupy Wall Street, however, inequality in America has continued to rise.[10] Any social change that depends on the electoral realm will eventually have to manifest itself not just online but in the polling booth, and, reasoning backwards, to get-out-the-vote movements, registration drives, town hall meetings, demonstrations, and so on.

By good fortune, the #MeToo movement is in a sweet spot for social media social change. #MeToo involves two elements where social media is disproportionately useful: legitimation and storytelling. "It is not a coincidence that hashtag activism has been especially notable in recent struggles for racial justice and gender equality," sociologist Guobin Yang notes in his critical study of #BlackLivesMatter.[11] Why do groups turn to hashtag activism? Because they are marginalized, disparaged, and misrepresented in the media.[12]

Absent recordings, like Gretchen Carlson's taping of Roger Ailes and the police wire on Harvey Weinstein, disbelief and denial are the first responses to female claims of sexual abuse, which often takes place in secret settings, with no witnesses. The viral nature of the hashtag is particularly potent for legitimating victims whose stories are not believed. One woman may be lying about her sexual abuse, but a hundred million others? It strains credulity. It is not a coincidence that #MeToo is related to the 2014 hashtag #YesAll-Women. #YesAllWomen was born after the mass shootings in Isla Vista, California. The shooter, Elliot Rodger, who killed himself after his rampage, had left a video castigating all the women who had rejected him.[13] When men took to social media to say that not all men are like Rodgers, #YesAllWomen shared stories of how widespread sexual abuse and harassment actually is, even if it does not always end in killing. #YesAllWomen showed that mass hashtag testimony offsets the traditional disbelief of women's experiences.

Hashtag activism is particularly useful for storytelling. The hashtaggers are literally inventors of their own empowerment. They "link past and present," and "connect the psyche, society, and world, the forms of feeling that encapsulate moments in time," as the rhetorical criticism scholar Karlyn Kohrs Campbell has noted.[14] One particularly powerful method of effecting your own empowerment is by sharing personal stories. The #MeToo movement started with a lawsuit and some media coverage. But the media can't cover thousands of stories the way hashtag activism does. It was the multiplicity of stories of abuse that moved readers to compassion.

And, rightly or wrongly, the retailing of sexual stories often humiliates the abuser in a uniquely potent way. When wrongful, such public revelation of sexual behavior is often called "revenge porn," sexually explicit material posted on the internet to cause the subject distress or embarrassment. The wire tape of Weinstein in the Battilana Gutierrez case, which shows his pathetic begging and wheedling, is an emblem of humiliation. Or consider the gripping stories of comedian Louis C.K. cornering hapless women to watch as he masturbated.[15] C.K. used his sexual hangups as the subject matter of comedy, but it's one thing to use masturbation as your comedic material, another to have it described as part of your offstage behavior by unwilling witnesses to the act. Even the *New Yorker*'s fearless editor David Remnick ("Investigative reporting is what we do") makes a distinction: "It would be a disaster to accuse somebody of these things and have it be false. If you accuse somebody of a sexual crime as opposed to breaking and entering, [the sexual crime] would be worse," he admits reluctantly.[16]

The humiliation experienced by the outed abuser is not about sex, per se. The repeated public tales of revulsion and rejection at the core of #MeToo portray the abusers as so repulsive, they can't get what they want — sex — without forcing it on a terrified subordinate. If the forcing and compelling are part of the sexual abuser's concept of desire, that makes the behavior all the worse. Somehow, someone reduced to breaking and entering, to use Remnick's comparison, does not seem as culpable as Harvey Weinstein, pressing and begging Ambra Battilana Gutierrez to come into his hotel room. It's hard to imagine assistant Emily Nestor saying to a burglar, "How do you look in the mirror?" Storytelling through hashtag activism works on all these levels.

In the December 2017 issue of *Time* magazine, the impact of the stories empowering marginalized victims and humiliating the abusers was clear. *Time* named the women who came forward, including Milano and Tarana Burke, as its People of the Year. The Silence Breakers, *Time* called them.

The Mind Reels

Unlike Donald Trump's presidential campaign, some American commercial enterprises are vulnerable to the humiliation power of social media campaigns. In the first few weeks after Milano tweeted, seventy-one men, mostly from media but also from other sectors, fell from power.[17] After Weinstein: Andy Signore, senior vice president of content at Defy Media; Roy Price, head of Amazon Studios; Chris Savino, creator and showrunner of Nickelodeon's *The Loud House*; Robert Scoble, tech blogger; Lockhart Steele, editorial director of Vox Media; John Besh, restaurateur; Terry Richardson, fashion photographer; Leon Wieseltier, former editor at the

New Republic; Steve Jurvetson, venture capitalist; Knight Landesman, publisher of *Artforum*; Rick Najera, director of CBS's Diversity Showcase; Mark Halperin, NBC News and MSNBC contributor and coauthor of *Game Change*; Kirt Webster, music publisher; Kevin Spacey, actor; Hamilton Fish, president and publisher of the *New Republic*; Andy Dick, actor. And that was just the first month.[18]

The hits just kept on coming: the next rounds of departures included NBC's Matt Lauer; the head of the New York City Ballet; Richard Meier, the superprominent American architect; longtime Metropolitan Opera music director James Levine; wheelchair-user radio host John Hockenberry; rappers; Morgan Freeman, who sounded just like God; cartoonists; a children's book author; congressmen of both parties and all parts of the country, including one accused of soliciting sex with a staffer to produce a baby for his existing marriage; avid women's rights advocate New York Attorney General Eric Schneiderman. The accusations against Schneiderman were so awful he didn't last three hours after the story appeared. Garrison Keillor, the *Prairie Home Companion*, for crissake.

As of June 25, 2018, ALI reporter Stephen Schulhofer had identified 222 very public individuals who have been sanctioned for sexually inappropriate behavior in or related to work. Of these, there were 53 in media, 7 in business or nonprofit, 36 politicians (some involving their private lives), 89 in entertainment, 12 academics, 4 in sports, and 21 others.[19] In a different tally going back to the Bill Cosby trial, the crisis management firm Temin & Co. toted up 417 major offenders (407 men), 348 with sanctions.[20]

The Bill Clinton Moment, Again

Aside from Fox News moguls Ailes and O'Reilly, a lot of the first offenders came from liberal media. Starting in 2016, the Republicans had rallied around their own political abusers and harassers, beginning with Donald Trump. Thanks to Trump, the family values party finally stood with the libertines. When a similar case arose in the other party, would feminists confront their liberal allies? Or would feminists once again be left with no place to go?

Early in the process, one month after Weinstein, November 16, 2017, the question was presented squarely when the spotlight landed on a liberal icon, Senator Al Franken. Franken, the gifted comedian who had turned his razor-edged tongue on the Republicans in a best-selling 2003 book, *Lies and the Lying Liars Who Tell Them,* ran for the Senate in 2008 and won, proving himself to be a powerful fundraiser and smart legislator. Al Franken was that rare Democrat, a natural performer.[21] His questioning of Republicans from his place on the Senate Judiciary Committee was masterful. His accuser, Leeann Tweeden, a radio host and model, was a professed conservative, and news of her accusations had leaked to the conservative talk show *The Daily Caller* before she went public. While on tour entertaining the troops, the then-comedian, Tweeden contended, had forced a full-tongue kiss on her in the guise of rehearsing their show. Then he put his hands over her breasts while she slept on the military plane taking them to their next gig. She didn't have a picture of the tongue kiss, but she had a picture of the breast episode, with Franken grinning into the camera. Someone had circulated it to the tour before she woke up. Franken was a little remorseful. The photo was clearly a bad joke, he said, but he didn't remember forcing his tongue into Tweeden's mouth.[22]

The Democrats were looking at a Bill Clinton moment. Here was an effective, telegenic, smart liberal politician, who maybe couldn't keep his hands to himself. Some started tiptoeing away from Franken at once.[23] Others were not so sure. How maddening that the admitted serial harasser Donald Trump was snugly ensconced in the White House, while Al Franken was being brought down by a Republican woman who had posed in *Playboy.* Why did Democratic men have to stop harassing women, when Republicans could do whatever they wanted to? Franken had agreed to cooperate with an Ethics Committee investigation to judge Tweeden's accusations against him; why not see it through?[24]

The Democrats were in a tough spot. It had just been revealed that senior congressman John Conyers, an African American from Detroit, had paid to settle a harassment case with a female employee and was facing multiple other accusations from over the previous two decades.[25] As the accusations against Conyers mounted, Minority Leader Nancy Pelosi risked the ire of the Congressional Black Caucus and forced Conyers to resign.[26] Women, albeit with agonizing slowness among the white cohort, were sorting themselves into the Democratic Party, a part of the overall sorting that had produced the heavily white and male Republican Party in 2016. The handful of elections since that watershed indicated that women, led as usual by black women but with the operative sliver of white women too, might actually finally be enough to offset the massive male partisanship on the right. Maybe Democrats could no longer get away with treating women's concerns about sexual assault and harassment with as little care as Republicans did. The plot thickened when, one week before Tweeden went public about Franken, *Washington Post* reporters routinely covering the Senate special election race in Alabama turned up allegations of child sexual abuse against the Republican candidate, Judge Roy Moore.[27] In a now familiar pattern, within days, seven accusers, most from their tender years, came forward against Judge Moore.[28] The Republicans stood by their man. The polls tightened. And the Alabama election was only a week away.

Meanwhile, six more women came forward with stories about Franken.[29] Senator Franken grabbed a butt when posing for a photo op at the Minnesota state fair; two anonymous women reported being butt-grabbed by Franken at Democratic campaign events; an army veteran told of Franken grabbing her breast at a photo op on his USO tour; a congressional aide and an elected New England official each said he tried to force a kiss on them during taping of his radio show. Unlike the Senate when Anita Hill came forward in 1991, in 2017 the legislative body included several women. Senator Kirsten Gillibrand, who had been the point person fighting sexual harassment in the military for years, was now alarmed. While the Senate was waiting to see what Franken would do,[30] on December

6, a writer for the prestigious *Atlantic* magazine came forward to say that Franken had "copped a feel" when posing for a picture with her.[31]

Gillibrand, followed immediately by dozens of her male and female colleagues, including Minority Leader Chuck Schumer, called on Franken to resign. On December 7, 2017, he did so.

Liberal pundits, some of whom were Franken's social friends, were not pleased.[32] "Heady times for women at last being heard," *Daily Beast* columnist Margaret Carlson wrote. "But questions abound. There is also value in finding out if any of Franken's accusers told someone in real time about the conduct, as victims usually do, and if they happened in the work setting or were a professional power play." Apparently Carlson had missed the report in *Politico*, published just two days before her column, that at least one victim had done just that: "Two former colleagues of the woman [accuser] independently corroborated her version of events, including Franken telling her he had the right to try to kiss her because he was 'an entertainer.' The first former colleague interviewed by *Politico* said she was told of the incident in 2006, shortly after it happened. The second former coworker said she was made aware of the encounter sometime in 2009 or 2010."[33]

Franken defenders moved to the next argument. So maybe Franken's seven accusers were telling the truth, but forcing Franken out was a political calculation, *Daily Beast* columnist and pundit Michael Tomasky wrote. Worse, it was a mistaken calculation: "It's a contrast, and maybe it will impress some female swing voters in Alabama. But it seems more likely that the Republican way of handling these things is going to win." Barack Obama's former campaign manager David Axelrod, a man with some knowledge of campaigning against a candidate implicated in sexual scandal, was more circumspect: "Part of the wager here was to try to force Franken out before Tuesday [the day of the Alabama special election], to draw a bright line around Moore's alleged transgressions. Tuesday will be the test."[34]

With a little more than 1 percent of the votes to spare, Democrat

Doug Jones beat Roy Moore on December 12, becoming the first Democrat elected from Alabama since 1992. White women with college degrees supported Jones by 45 percent, driving a doubling in white support for Jones over prior votes for Obama.[35] Minority leader Chuck Schumer chose Cory Booker and the experienced prosecutor Kamala Harris for the open seats on the Judiciary Committee. As we will soon see, just under a year after the Democrats replaced Franken with Kamala Harris, the Judiciary Committee undertook to examine the qualifications of Supreme Court nominee Brett Kavanaugh.

Six months after Franken's resignation, *Vox* editor Laura McGann reported that "many progressive men didn't see the fall of Al Franken over sexual misconduct allegations as the loss of a Democratic senator. It was the loss of a progressive icon. And they haven't moved on."[36] *Daily Beast* special correspondent Michael Tomasky, McGann noted, certainly hadn't. Accusing Senator Gillibrand of acting like the Queen of Hearts, "Lewis Carroll's unhinged monarch" in *Alice in Wonderland*, Tomasky wrote a piece in January, on the day Franken would officially step down. He called for Franken to run again and for Schumer to restore the seniority Franken lost by resigning in an act of contrition.[37] Aged Democratic donors, rarely the most progressive force in the party, declared Senator Gillibrand untouchable; one even threatened to withhold all donations to any senators who supported Franken's ouster.[38]

Who should ride to the women's rescue but, of all people, Bill Clinton. On June 4, 2018, Clinton launched the book tour for his debut novel, *The President Is Missing,* with an appearance on NBC's *Today.*[39] After the predictable fluff about what it was like for Clinton and his coauthor, best-selling thriller writer James Patterson, to work together, host Craig Melvin asked the former president how he would approach the Lewinsky matter differently in this moment of "reckoning." First Clinton said he thought he did the right thing and that the new attention to him was because people couldn't get at Trump.

Melvin pressed harder. "[Monica Lewinsky] wrote that #MeToo

had made her change her mind about sexual harassment. Quote: 'He was my boss, he was the most powerful man on the planet, he was 27 years my senior, with enough experience to know better. He was at the time in the pinnacle of his career while I was in my first job out of college.' Looking back on what happened then through the lens of MeToo now do you feel differently or feel more responsibility?"

"No," Clinton answered. "I felt terrible then. And I came to grips with it."

"Did you ever apologize to her?"

"No, yes," he stuttered. Then he went on the offensive: "And nobody believes I got out of that for free. I left the White House $16 million in debt . . . 2/3 of the American people sided with me." Plus he was a liberal ally: "I had a sexual harassment policy when I was governor in the eighties and I had two women chiefs of staff when I was governor, no one had as many women as I did . . . I apologized to everybody in the world."

Melvin: "But you didn't apologize to her."

Clinton: "I have not talked to her . . . but I did say publicly on more than one occasion that I was sorry."

At that point, in an obvious effort to help, Patterson intervened. "I think this thing has been — it was 20 years ago. Let's talk about JFK, let's talk about LBJ, stop it already."

Apparently not realizing that the whole issue was whether American men should stop imitating JFK already, Clinton lit up and went on the attack: "That's also interesting. I don't think — do you think President Kennedy should have resigned? Do you believe President Johnson should have resigned?"

That day, Clinton started trending, and not in a good way.[40] In the ensuing days, he made several appearances seeming to blame his public blunder on the interviewer, the editing, the passage of time. And of course the more Clinton blamed the press, the more the press rallied around NBC's well-liked reporter.[41] Republican strategist Steve Schmidt drove in the stake: "What you saw there, I

think, is the end of Bill Clinton's life as a public figure in this country," Schmidt said. "Because of that interview, I don't think he's campaigning anywhere ever again unless he can clean it up and fix it
pretty quickly."[42]

Bill Clinton is unlikely to reappear on the campaign trail. What
mattered was the glimpse the encounter with NBC provided into
why Al Franken would be ill-advised to try to reclaim his Senate seat, as Tomasky suggested. Or, more to the point, what would
be asked of Joe Biden, finally, should he reappear on the political
scene. For starters, an enterprising reporter is sure to ask the former
vice president why there is no mention in his several-hundred-page
memoir, *Promises to Keep*, of anyone named Anita Hill.

Yes All Women

Social change wasn't going to come from one accusation after another, even mounting into the hundreds. Hashtag activism might be
necessary, but it was never sufficient.

In January 2018, a group of Hollywood women launched an activism initiative, Time's Up.[43] Time's Up first sponsored a symbolic
action in the form of actresses wearing black to the Golden Globes,
the Hollywood Foreign Press Association awards ceremony. The
event was pretty successful for its purpose — showing how many A-
list players were committed to changing the way Hollywood treated
its female workers. Predictably, the prospective success had a thousand mothers. One Hollywood media reported that star actor and
producer Reese Witherspoon and her wide circle of friends had
birthed the movement through their email exchanges.[44] More cynical commentators speculated that megalith talent agencies like William Morris Endeavor and CAA were supporting Time's Up in an
effort to make up for their complicity in the structure of abuse.[45]
Four female agents at CAA had been at the center of the organizing since it went public, if not before.[46] Simultaneously other activists started a commission on Hollywood practices, to try to address

the casting-couch culture that dated all the way back to the studio years of the 1920s and 1930s. The commission hired Anita Hill to chair the effort.

At the same time, Tina Tchen, Michelle Obama's former chief of staff, just happened to be in Los Angeles, working with the United State of Women, another effort on women's and girls' issues that started out of the White House. Very early on it became clear to her as a lawyer that the only way to address sexual abuse and harassment, especially with the legal bullying, was to get lawyers for people in need.[47] Then Tchen got wind that Melanie Kohler, the scuba instructor who had accused producer Brett Ratner of rape, had been sued for defamation. Kohler could hardly afford to defend herself against the most aggressive lawyers in Hollywood.

As longtime movement lawyer Robbie Kaplan tells it,[48] she got a call from Tchen and CAA powerhouse Michelle Kydd Lee saying that there was this woman who had put up a Facebook post about Brett Ratner raping her and that Hollywood lawyer Marty Singer was threatening her with a defamation lawsuit and "would I be willing to represent her." Kaplan, who had risen to national fame as the lawyer in *United States v. Windsor*, the 2013 marriage equality case, had just left her big Wall Street firm and started her own shop. She said yes to Tchen and Lee, but adds that "I did say, look, I have a brand-new firm and we can take on cases like this, but it is difficult given the costs, who is on the other side, and especially since Melanie Kohler lives in Hawaii. We have to figure out a way to help pay for the costs of cases like this that are unlikely to get pro bono support."

The eruption of #MeToo had Kaplan thinking about the increasing roadblocks that had been put in the way of women bringing discrimination claims in the last thirty years. In 2011, in a case called *Wal-Mart v. Dukes*,[49] the conservative Supreme Court had shut down any incentive lawyers had to represent women in discrimination cases by making it much harder for them to consolidate their claims into one class action under the civil rights laws. Such class actions can bring huge damages, and the lawyers can receive large fee awards. Once the court decided *Wal-Mart* (by a majority vote of all five Republican-appointed justices), there was little incentive for lawyers to represent women plaintiffs in most employment cases. So, for the vast number of women who experience harassment, there are no legal services. "We need to re-incentivize the market," Robbie thought. "Big firms can't take plaintiffs' discrimination cases because they're conflicted. Most of them represent corporate clients who are vulnerable to claims of discrimination. We need to change the landscape to make it desirable for lawyers to bring these cases."

Kaplan, an icon of the gay legal movement, had been thinking about the model the gay rights activists had used in 2008 in challenging California's anti–gay marriage initiative, Prop 8. In confronting Prop 8, Chad Griffin, now head of the major LGBTQ organization the Human Rights Campaign, and his Hollywood partners like producer Rob Reiner, had started a not-for-profit and raised money to pay A-list lawyers Ted Olson and David Boies (the same David Boies who now represented Harvey Weinstein) to bring the lawsuit. Movements stand on the shoulders of the ones that went before. The Prop 8 campaign is where the idea for Time's Up Legal Defense Fund, to represent women like Melanie Kohler in sexual harassment lawsuits, came from.

Time's Up Legal Defense Fund was the most successful Go Fund Me campaign ever. By the time the fund launched, it was sitting on $13 million. As of this writing, the fund is north of $20 million. Kaplan had been a longtime member of the board of one of the feminist organizations going back to the golden age of the early 1970s —the National Women's Law Center in Washington. She called up Fatima Goss Graves, the CEO of the Women's Law Center, and asked her if she'd like to have $20 million to spend on lawyers for women's rights.

Technicolor Funders and Disputes of Color

The new fund was particularly tasked not with taking cases for rich white actresses from the Technicolored world of movie sets, but with the vastly larger number of cases where the plaintiffs could not afford lawyers. That meant a lot of color: blue collars, black and brown skin tones. And, as it turned out, golden, as in Golden Arches.

On May 22, 2018, the National Women's Law Center announced its first big Time's Up case. Ten McDonald's employees were bringing sex harassment charges with the federal Equal Employment Opportunity Commission. They charged McDonald's, the franchisees who owned the stores they worked in, and a company-owned store with violating the Civil Rights Act and various state laws. Since the law does not allow true class-action cases, the ten plaintiffs were asking the EEOC to consolidate its investigation, at least.

A year or so earlier,[50] Tanya Harrell had been minding her own business working at the counter and as a cashier at a McDonald's in Gretna, Louisiana, outside New Orleans. A new employee, to whom she had been friendly, came up behind her and grabbed her private area. She pushed him away: "What are you doing?" Undaunted, he came up behind her again and grabbed her breasts. Grabbing, grabbing, asking her to touch him. Finally she complained to her shift manager. The manager "suggested that [he] and I were romantically involved and that the touching was consensual." The other manager thought she was "childish to complain about it."[51]

She felt helpless and exposed, as if there was nothing she could do to protect herself from his touch. She needed the $8.15 McDonald's was paying her to survive. Three years before, she had quit high school because her grandmother, who she lived with, was sick, and she had to have money for medicine and doctors. She gave up her dreams and started working at $7.45 an hour at her first McDonald's job. She left that one and went to work for a different McDonald's, because the first job didn't schedule her to work long enough to make the money she needed. Now she made more, and the outlet was closer to home. But right after the first incident of harassment, a second coworker forced her into the men's bathroom, pinned her against the wall, took out his penis, and tried to have sex with her. All she could do was cry and cry until he finally stopped because he heard the manager calling for him. She knew not to expect help, but she told the manager, who treated it like nothing. "Where were you," the manager said. "I was looking for you." "Where else could I be," Harrell asked. "This dude had me in the bathroom, trapped, choking me, harassing me." Harrell started having a terrible time coming to work. The manager kept threatening to fire her.

Perhaps the most harrowing of the dozen complaints in the Time's Up case came from a fifteen-year-old in a McDonald's in St. Louis who complained that an older male employee had said to her: "You have a nice body; have you ever had white chocolate inside you?" When she reported the remark to her manager, she said, she was told, "You will never win that battle." Unsurprisingly, nothing was done.[52]

Having to deal with rubbing, touching, choking, grabbing, with coworkers exposing themselves, all the way to assault — the charges against McDonald's make for an unhappy repast. Sexual harassment at McDonald's had been cooking along for years. In 2016 three women's organizations,[53] the National Partnership for Women & Families, the Ms. Foundation for Women, and Futures Without Violence, commissioned the well-respected Hart Research firm to survey fast-food workers about their experience with sexual harassment and abuse.[54] A staggering 42 percent of women in fast-food businesses reported being harassed at work. Twenty-one percent experienced harrowing retaliation — schedules messed up, hours reduced — for resisting or complaining. African American workers (33 percent) and Latinas (32 percent) are more likely to face these types of work disruptions than are white women (25 percent).

The offenses ranged across the fast-food industry, but since 2012 the iconic McDonald's — the second-largest private employer in the world — has had the bad fortune to be in the sights of the formidable labor union Service Employees International Union. Ideally, SEIU wants the company to agree — and contract with its franchisees to agree — to let the union try to organize employees, not to wage a campaign against the union when it comes in, and to recognize the union as the employees' bargaining representative when a majority of workers sign up. The SEIU has its work cut out for it, because the employees are scattered, low wage, and doubtless often undocumented. "The union has spent its members' dues money in the past two years attacking the McDonald's brand . . . in an unsuccessful attempt to unionize workers," the company said in a statement in 2015.[55]

The union, facing dizzying odds against a conventional organizing campaign in that environment, has tried a number of bank shots to get the giant company's attention. Several regional groups, called "Fight for $15" from the campaign to raise the minimum wage, are now joined in the National Fast Food Workers' Union, an affiliate of SEIU.[56] Fight for $15 committees used walkouts and demonstrations to campaign for minimum-wage hikes in cities and states around the country.[57] Starting in 2012 the fast-food movement launched a growing series of one-day strikes for higher wages and union representation. Initially in single digits, by 2015 the one-day strikes had spread to scores of cities around the country and closed down many fast-food outlets.[58] The campaign has succeeded in a lot of places — New York, Los Angeles, San Francisco, Seattle. The movement has started suing for wage theft, alleging that the employers were not crediting the workers for the hours they worked or the minimum wage they earned.[59]

A few months after she quit high school to work for $7.50 at McDonald's, Tanya Harrell's friend David, who worked at another McDonald's, told her about Fight for $15. She started talking to the other workers at her McDonald's, doing education work and passing out fliers.

In 2016 the union organized a handful of sexual harassment complaints against McDonald's, filing with the EEOC and starting the slow process of getting them to court. McDonald's responded with a unified defense, organized by Jones Day, then the largest law firm in the United States. "Zero tolerance for any form of sexual harassment," McDonald's intoned.[60]

The plaintiffs say there is zero enforcement of the zero tolerance policy. There is no training. McDonald's sends a packet to the franchisees to hand the employees, with boxes to check. Even a help line for employee complaints just gets turned back to the franchisee. And the union had a devilish time finding attorneys to defend the female plaintiffs they unearthed in 2016. The individual claims of low-wage employees are not worth much, under the tight-fisted federal law.[61]

But, after the Weinstein fall, the organizers thought there was a better possibility of successfully pursuing the sex harassment claims.[62] Working on organizing since 2012, the union movement had compiled huge lists of workers in these stores, active on whatever issues are important to them. When the union decided to take another run at the sex harassment problem, all those networks were activated around this particular issue. They reached out person to person and one on one. They identified workers who could file a claim, were willing, and were willing to use their names.

The organizers were hoping to bring a lot of cases and use the EEOC process for consolidating the investigation. As we saw, in *Wal-Mart v. Dukes,* in 2011, the Supreme Court had ruled that scattered employees with individual complaints could not bring class actions against an employer, but the fast-food organizers would get as close as they could. It might be more than just vindicating one woman's abuse; it might be larger-scale social change. Although each client must always make a decision in her own case, their clients were really interested in systemic change. They work at McDonald's and they want the sexual harassment to stop.[63] Organizers alerted the well-regarded union-side law firm Altshuler, Berzon of San Francisco to prepare a battle plan for representing individual plaintiffs in a collective way. Would the Time's Up Legal Defense Fund like to fund the case? One of the lawyers, Eve Cervantes, says it would have been almost impossible for Altshuler, Berzon to do the work without the support of the Time's Up fund. (Time's Up is also funding the Outen Golden firm from New York and DC for the McDonald's case.)

On May 21, 2018, the plaintiffs gathered in Chicago for the big Fight for $15 demonstration at the McDonald's shareholders meeting. In the car from Springfield to Chicago, four of the women workers shared their stories with each other for the first time. Tanya heard about #MeToo and how people like her had gotten strength from sharing their stories.[64]

The organizers arranged for the rest of the women complaining to meet each other. They gathered in a cold and sterile conference room at a hotel in Chicago. When Tanya walked in, she met the women from St. Louis, and Chicago, and Kansas City, and Florida, sitting in a circle. As they tried to tell each other their stories, the temperature in the room rose. A little at a time these people, previously strangers, shared experiences that many of them had not even been able to talk about with their own families. Many were doing it for their mothers, who had been abused, they shared. "How can I ask my mother to tell her story, if I won't even tell mine?" one of the complainants said. And for their daughters. And their sons, to learn what they must never do, or tolerate. They even shared strategies for coming out as survivors of sexual harassment to the most important people in their lives. And as they talked, they wept. Sad. Hurt. Upset. Angry. And then they couldn't speak; it was so emotional, there was so much crying.

The feeling shifted when they left the hotel to march in front of the shareholders meeting, though, to excitement and empowerment. When Tanya took the microphone to speak at the rally, there was not a dry eye in the audience. Not even the TV cameramen. At the end, the others from the hotel room gathered around her and held her up.

On May 22, Time's Up announced the litigation. It's going to be a long journey, but, Harrell says, whatever it takes, she's up for it. "I do half of it knowing that God is always good," she says. "I hold my truth and I feel a lot of empowering from him. And I have two younger sisters and I want to be their role model and make change in the world.

"It's the union that we need," she says. "We really need the union. This is wrong what McDonald's seeks to do. They want to have everything, half the wages we need, no training for sexual harassment, no training for the managers."

As she goes forward, Harrell says, she doesn't feel so alone. She got a lot of peoples' numbers after the meeting in the hotel conference room, and they stay in touch. Now she has the group behind her and she loves them more than anything. At the march to the McDonald's headquarters, the women held the banner, but the men at the end of the line chanted: "We've got your back. We've got your back."

Oh, and on August 13, 2018, Tanya Harrell went back to school. It had always been her dream. With agonizing slowness, the EEOC was "investigating" the cases.

Who Will Press the Presses?

What is it with the agencies of law enforcement? Although most people date the #MeToo movement to the publication of the *New York Times* and *New Yorker* revelations in October of 2017, the modern movement really has its roots in Gretchen Carlson's lawsuit against Roger Ailes, the year before.[65] Since the revelations, the Manhattan District Attorney's Office has finally brought rape charges against Harvey Weinstein. After decades of complaints from women charging that Bill Cosby drugged and raped them, and a 2017 trial that ended in a hung jury, the actor and comedian was tried a second time in 2018, convicted, and sentenced to three to ten years in jail. The revelations of the #MeToo movement are shot through with legal wrongdoing — rape, assault and battery, extortion, blackmail, and civil violations of the Civil Rights Act. Yet it was not the agencies of law enforcement or the EEOC that drove the accelerated reckoning. It was the press.

"Finding the truth is our mission," Margaret Sullivan, *Washington Post* columnist and former public editor of the *New York Times,* explains. "You may not get it all, but you can get damn close. No other institution, not law enforcement, has that mission. And," she continued, "with top quality diggers backed by powerful, deep-pocketed institutions that are committed to the mission of doing this kind of work, a great deal can be accomplished."[66]

Journalism is one of the few good jobs left that can be done without formal training or twenty years of practice. "It's a craft," Sullivan says. Ronan Farrow was a policy wonk and a diplomat before turning to journalism. Jodi Kantor, on the other hand, was a trained, experienced *New York Times* veteran, who had worked many beats and played many journalistic roles. What they had in common was the hunger. "How hungry are you?" Sullivan asks. "Are you willing to work night and day and make personal sacrifices and put it above all things? Are you willing to put all your energy into it, maybe even to fight with your editors or whoever is standing in the way?" That hunger, that single-mindedness, is something that editors may have to rein in at times, but, she said, echoing Kantor's early colleague, *Slate*'s Jacob Weisberg, "an editor is better off with a reporter you have to rein in a little bit."

Then, she explains, "Hungry reporters learn on the job. A newsroom is a breeding ground for learning investigative journalism. One young politics reporter at the *Post* sits next to David Fahrenthold [the *Post*'s Pulitzer Prize winner for the Trump investigations] and Carol Leonig [Pulitzer Prize winner for national security reporting in 2014], superstars and really good people. She's listening to them and learning how to do it." That's the team.

So a lead surfaces, like the rumors about Harvey Weinstein or Bill O'Reilly, and the reporter starts to try to build a relationship of trust with the source. "You're talking to people tirelessly, applying a lot of skepticism along the way. There's also a magic to it, the serendipity that so often rewards reporters who are hard-working and well-prepared. Then the stories start to come together as people with no connections to each other tell the same basic story. But you need more to truly nail it down. You're hoping for documents, recordings, video, some highly credible person who is willing to lend their name."

The reporters matter. But in often unseen ways, the institutions matter as well. Sullivan calls out both "the Sulzberger family" and her editor, Marty Baron, at the *Post* as institutional leaders indispensable to the expensive, risky work investigative journalism has turned in in recent years. Less obviously, the papers have great lawyers. Sullivan noted the *Times*'s newsroom lawyer David E. Mc-Craw, whose incomparable response to candidate Trump's threat of suit over the paper's reporting on the accusations against him, drew the singular honor of publication in his own client's paper. "If Mr. Trump," McCraw wrote, "believes that American citizens had no right to hear what these women had to say and that the law of this country forces us and those who would dare to criticize him to stand silent or be punished, we welcome the opportunity to have a court set him straight." Lawyers like David McCraw are interested in enabling the news to be published, not in stopping it and playing it safe.[67]

When, in July 2018, the anonymous tip line at the *Washington Post* got a call from a woman accusing a man nominated for the Supreme Court of the United States of sexual abuse, all the machinery of investigative journalism was turned on, from a sensitive female reporter who could build a relationship of trust to the deep pockets and news-oriented lawyering of the paper's newsroom counsel. As the institutions of politics refused or failed to pursue any approximation of the truth, other reporters, including the *New Yorker*'s new investigative journalist Ronan Farrow and the original scribbling woman, Jane Mayer, joined in the search for an approximation of the truth. On October 5, 2018, as the Senate prepared to confirm the nominee, Farrow told an audience at the New Yorker Festival that journalism was not done yet.

13

The Year of Reckoning
2018

War on Three Fronts

In the half century since Edward Kennedy drove Mary Jo Kopechne into the pond on Chappaquiddick, ending her life and sinking his presidential aspirations, the arc of history has not always bent toward justice. In any social justice movement in America — abolition, racial civil rights, feminism, gay rights — the battle always seems to involve the same three campaigns, although not always in the same order. First, the movement must appeal to the judiciary and the rule of law, so central to American democracy. Yet the court does ultimately follow the election returns, so the second field of battle is popular politics. Finally, to achieve the first two goals of legal and political change, a movement must, at day's end, win the air war and change the culture.[1] For fifty years, the epic battle against sexual harassment and abuse has been waged on all those fronts: the legal, the electoral, and the cultural. In 2018 it seemed to all come to a head.

Part One: The Legal

The first of the many confrontations occurred on June 27, 2018, when the critical swing justice on the Supreme Court of the United States, Anthony Kennedy, announced he was stepping down. On July 9, 2018, Republican President Donald Trump nominated movement conservative and US Appeals Court judge Brett Kavanaugh to take his place. If confirmed by the Republican Senate, it was widely understood, Kavanaugh would change the court definitively and for the foreseeable future. He was expected to be the swing vote to overrule *Roe v. Wade*, which would strip women of the reproductive rights they had won almost a half century earlier. The conservative movement had been aiming to capture the Supreme Court since the liberal Warren Court put the power of the Constitution behind the civil rights movement in the 1950s. In 1982, conservatives founded an official organization for this purpose, the Federalist Society, which would train law students in conservative beliefs and establish a conservative judicial pipeline.

The die was really cast in favor of the conservative takeover of the court on election day, November 8, 2016, when the Republicans won the White House and kept control of the Senate. Women in the ensuing resistance mostly focused on the insulting selection of an admitted harasser as president that day, but in the American system, the most significant reality was that the White House plus the Senate equaled the court. During his campaign, President Trump had asked the Federalist Society[2] for a list of reliably conservative anti-abortion candidates for potential appointment to the Supreme Court. Thanks to the Republican Senate majority leader's previous decision to refuse Democratic president Barack Obama a Supreme Court appointment after Justice Scalia died in 2016, the Trump administration got a Federalist Society–approved appointment right away: Neil Gorsuch. Conservative Gorsuch replacing conservative Scalia did not immediately change the court. Conservatives waited: Justice Kennedy, eighty-one, comfortable with his conservative origins, and never a fan of women's rights, announced his retirement, and President Trump nominated Judge Kavanaugh.[3]

Kavanaugh was a classic twenty-first-century Republican appointment. Son of a lobbyist and the product of elite private schools, Kavanaugh graduated from Yale and Yale Law School, where in 1988, he joined the Federalist Society.[4] After his clerkship, Kavanaugh went to work in markedly partisan positions, first for independent counsel Ken Starr in the scorched-earth pursuit of President Bill Clinton in 1998 that ultimately exposed the Clinton/Lewinsky affair. He represented candidate George W. Bush in the contested 2000 presidential election and worked at the Bush White House. In 2006, President Bush appointed him to the Court of Appeals for the DC Circuit.

Now, with the Kavanaugh nomination to the Supreme Court moving smoothly through the Republican-controlled Senate, the Democratic opposition centered on conventional, though dire, issues: the right to abortion, whether a sitting president could be subject to criminal prosecution while in office, why the senators weren't getting much of a look at the candidate's long paper trail.[5] His appointment would hurt women, especially in the fate of abortion rights, but no one could have known the confirmation battle would turn out to be Armageddon, the gathering of armies in the epic battle against sexual harassment and abuse.

Until, in an eerie reenactment of Anita Hill's testimony against Clarence Thomas, a fifty-one-year-old psychology professor in Northern California, Christine Blasey Ford, became increasingly uneasy with the prospect of the Georgetown Prep graduate ascending to the highest court in the land. Also raised in DC, she had gone to a nearby girls' school, and she had a harrowing story to tell about the would-be Supreme Court justice. She had not gone public with the story as he rose through the ranks of the federal judiciary, echoing Anita Hill's early reaction to Clarence Thomas's trajectory to the court. But the possibility of Kavanaugh being elevated to the nation's high court was eating away at her. The *Washington Post* had been her newspaper growing up; in early July she contacted its anonymous tip line. She made it clear that she did not want to be identified.

As she saw Kavanaugh's prospects rising, her uneasiness grew. Through the office of her congresswoman, she sent a letter to her senator, Dianne Feinstein, the ranking Democratic member of the Judiciary Committee, which would be hearing Kavanaugh's confirmation. On July 11, he was nominated. Ford continued to ask for confidentiality. Someone recommended she get a lawyer.

While silence reigned on the surface, once again the agencies of investigative journalism intervened. The resourceful and energetic Ryan Grim, of the *Intercept*, a web-based journal that bills itself as adversary journalism, got wind of her existence. On September 12, Grim published the story of the existence of an as-yet-unnamed accuser, no other details.[6] On September 13,[7] still without revealing Ford's identity, Feinstein referred the matter to the FBI. Judiciary Committee chairman Chuck Grassley was unconcerned. The vote on Kavanaugh's nomination was scheduled for September 20.

When other journalists began to show up at Ford's home and workplace, she knew her cover was blown; three days later, on September 16, she went back to the *Washington Post* to tell her story.[8] She had established a relationship of trust with the *Post's* Emma Brown, and Brown told the story:

> Ford said that one summer in the early 1980s, Kavanaugh and a friend—both "stumbling drunk," Ford alleges—corralled her into a bedroom during a gathering of teenagers at a house in Montgomery County.
>
> While his friend watched, she said, Kavanaugh pinned her to a bed on her back and groped her over her clothes, grinding his body against hers and clumsily attempting to pull off her one-piece bathing suit and the clothing she wore over it. When she tried to scream, she said, he put his hand over her mouth.
>
> "I thought he might inadvertently kill me," said Ford, now a 51-year-old research psychologist in northern California. "He was trying to attack me and remove my clothing."

Ford said she was able to escape when Kavanaugh's friend and classmate at Georgetown Preparatory School, Mark Judge, jumped on top of them, sending all three tumbling. She said she ran from the room, briefly locked herself in a bathroom and then fled the house.

It's never just one. In a week, the *New Yorker*'s sexual abuse reporting team of Ronan Farrow and Jane Mayer had uncovered another accuser, Deborah Ramirez, who said that Kavanaugh, again drunk, had forced his penis on her at a dormitory party.[9]

It was a critical confrontation for the movement against sexual abuse. The judiciary — and ultimately the United States Supreme Court — represents one of the essential paths to social change. We have seen how the epic battle against sexual harassment and abuse started with a legal theory — that sexual harassment at work violates the Civil Rights Act — and how the courts played and would play a crucial role in actualizing, and limiting, that claim up to the very moment Tanya Harrell filed her charges. The 2018 battle over Kavanaugh's confirmation could not have mattered more.

Pressed and reluctant, like Senator Biden had been all those years ago, Senator Grassley scheduled another Judiciary Committee hearing for Thursday, September 27. Ford and Kavanaugh — and no one else — would, in a classic she said/he said, come before the committee and tell their stories. From the day the story appeared in the *Washington Post* to the day the Senate voted to confirm Judge Kavanaugh on October 6, the Democrats begged, pleaded, demanded, and inveighed against the mano a mano format the Republicans had set up. There was other evidence against Kavanaugh, they asserted, echoing the journalists' description of how to investigate a charge of sexual abuse. But Grassley and the Republicans seemed determined to confine the evidence to the most conventional and unforgiving format for abused women: her word against his.

As we have now seen, in the half century before the Kavanaugh confirmation, the epic movement against sexual harassment and abuse had created a legal action for sexual abuse at work and on campus. Then, movement activists had taken back the high ground against the backlash and finally a generation of investigative journalists arose who took sexual abuse seriously. People were joking that the scariest three words any powerful man could hear after 2017 were "Ronan is calling." And yet. Just like when the first brave women of color went to the lowest trial courts to challenge their harassment in the early 1970s, sex would be treated by the Senate Judiciary Committee as a private dispute. Again. On national television. As long as Grassley held his eleven-member majority against the ten Democratic senators, the movement was helpless.

Unlike Anita Hill, single, black, without an identifiable political champion, Ford, making her first public appearance, was revealed to be a married, white, middle-aged suburban woman.[10] "Comprehensible," as feminist commentator Rebecca Traister put it, "as female within a white capitalist patriarchy."[11] In contrast to the stunningly disciplined Professor Hill, Ford allowed herself to admit she was "terrified."[12] She didn't need a better microphone, she agreed right away when the senators had trouble hearing her soft voice; she'd just sit closer. "I'm a consensus builder," she told the senators. For four hours, in her low-voiced, articulate way, Ford told her story, which turned out to be pretty much the same as what she'd told the *Washington Post*. She did add powerfully that she was "100 percent" sure it was Brett Kavanaugh who assaulted her. And that the thing she remembers best is "the uproarious laughter between the two and their having fun at my expense." After she finished her testimony, the Republican senators filed out of the hearing ashen-faced, and all the media commentators had it that the nomination was dead. She had been so moving, so believable, and so familiar.

Then Judge Kavanaugh took the witness seat. He'd been advised to express his feelings, and so he did,[13] delivering a blistering defense, denying he had ever sexually assaulted someone and denouncing a "frenzy" bent on destroying his nomination.

"This confirmation process has become a national disgrace. The Constitution gives the Senate an important role in the confirmation process, but you have replaced 'advise and consent' with 'search and destroy,'" Kavanaugh raged, red-faced and occasionally reduced to tears as he proclaimed his innocence and decried the damage the accusations had done to his family and his exemplary life. But the biggest takeaway from his time in the limelight was his stunningly arrogant treatment of the Democratic senators asking him questions. After questioning about his excessive drinking as a high school and college student, the confrontation culminated with his demanding to know if Senator Amy Klobuchar, who had just shared that her father had been an alcoholic, had ever been blackout drunk herself.

The Republicans ditched the female prosecutor from Arizona they'd hired to do their questioning for them and immediately took up the "questioning" themselves. Republican senators turned their time into a spontaneous operatic competition, delivering ever more melodramatic arias of male rage.[14] The biggest hit had to be South Carolina's Lindsey Graham, a man increasingly renowned for his performance pieces in the Senate. "Boy, you all want power," he said, rising in his seat, his face reddening and his voice booming. "God, I hope you never get it." The Democrats were executing a cynical political ploy to deny Mr. Trump a Supreme Court seat — "the most unethical sham since I've been in politics."[15] (Not a trivial standard.) By the evening news, the conventional wisdom had shifted 180 degrees. Kavanaugh would be confirmed.

President Trump, who had been uncharacteristically silent in face of another Republican man being accused of sexual abuse, saw his opportunity. After all, he had changed the climate of American politics the day he looked at Megyn Kelly in the primary debate and told the country that people were too concerned about hurting women's feelings. At a rally in Mississippi a few days later, he indulged in a classic attack on Ford — mimicking her testimony, ridiculing her for what he claimed were holes in her story, rousing the angry crowd: "Lock her up!"[16] Lock up the shy, middle-aged, achingly polite teller of a tale of teenage sexual trauma. The Trump GOP certainly now fully owned the abuse and harassment of women.

Majority Leader McConnell scheduled a full Senate vote for Friday, October 5. All eyes turned to two female Republican senators with mildly prochoice records, Maine's Susan Collins and Alaska's Lisa Murkowski. Murkowski announced she would be a no. On Friday afternoon, October 5, Susan Collins approached the microphone at the front of the Senate. Against all convention, two of the few female Republican senators, Shelley Moore Capito of West Virginia and Cindy Hyde-Smith of Mississippi,[17] sat behind Collins in the presiding chairs, forming a deliberately female backdrop to the crucial senator's announcement, white women again supporting the patriarchy. Collins opened her explanation with an attack on the "special interest groups" who "raced to oppose [Kavanaugh]." Like Lindsey Graham, she was furious that the Democrats had tried to fight her party's nominee. Like the majority of white women since the feminist movement began, and like the women who put Donald Trump in the White House, Susan Collins had other interests than the well-being of women. She would be voting to confirm Brett Kavanaugh. All the rest was commentary. The final vote was 50 to 49, as one Democrat, the embattled red-state senator Joe Manchin, cast a meaningless vote for Kavanaugh.[18]

And the beer flowed. The hashtag "Beers for Brett" started showing up on Twitter.[19] Republican candidates who had been notably hands-off during the fight started alluding to stories about a supposed left-wing "mob" phenomenon.[20] Predictably, Fox News thought the fight would motivate conservatives.[21] But in addition the New York Times's Jeremy W. Peters also reported that "anger over Justice Kavanaugh remains a potent motivating factor from now until Election Day," a task that "many Republicans believe" would unify their fractured and anxious party.[22] Cas Mudde of the Guardian was even more confident: "[The Kavanaugh nomination] will do more for conservative rage than liberal outrage. This means that the Kavanaugh nomination not only created a conservative majority in the Supreme Court, for several decades, but could also put an end to the Democratic dream of taking the

House and Senate."[23] Oh, those pesky women with their tales of sexual trauma.

Part Two: The Political

The first round of polling confirmed that the white male pundits were dead wrong.[24] It was a month to the 2018 midterms. The polls hinted that maybe, instead of conservative rage, the nation would see, as feminist revivalist Rebecca Traister put it in the subtitle to her book *Good and Mad*, "the revolutionary power of women's anger." Traister's well-timed book surged to the best-seller list as the nation waited for the midterms. People remembered 1992, when angry women voters put four (count them, four) females into the Senate, and doubled the number of women representatives. While more Americans did not initially believe Anita Hill,[25] a majority of people polled immediately after Christine Blasey Ford's testimony believed her.[26]

Seeing the prospect of a long-term electoral trend—the House in 2018, and the rest of the government in 2020—liberal pundits started speculating about how they could use their newfound political power to undo the conservative takeover of the Supreme Court. One popular suggestion was the impeachment of Justice Kavanaugh, the constitutionally prescribed method for removing federal judges.[27] The sexual attacks would certainly be grounds, if proven. A more realistic proposal involved the Democrats expanding the size of the Supreme Court from nine to, say, eleven justices, adding two liberals.[28]

This completely constitutional strategy of adding justices is known by the pejorative phrase "court packing," from the resistance to the last campaign to expand the court in 1937, when President Franklin Roosevelt proposed to add additional justices to save the New Deal. (Life-tenured right-wing justices had been striking down the emergency legislation the Democratic Congress had passed.) Support for FDR's plan declined after the formerly conservative court upheld the popular National Labor Relations Act and the staunchest of FDR's opponents on the court announced his retirement.[29] But if the newly conservative Roberts court started striking down economic legislation produced by newly elected liberal representatives after 2020, like the 1930s court did with the New Deal, court packing would have a certain satisfying consistency. More likely, however, the court will seek to gut women's reproductive rights. In which case, why not threaten justices with impeachment or seat additional liberal justices? The Constitution allows it. Why should the judiciary be immune from politics?

As it happens, the revived women's movement had very recently gotten a taste of what it was like to mobilize to call judges to account for their sexist behavior. On June 6, 2018, more than 60 percent of the several hundred thousand voters of Santa Clara County, California, removed criminal trial Judge Aaron Persky from his post.[30] No judge had been recalled in California in almost a hundred years.[31] Two years before the recall, on June 2, 2016, Judge Persky had sentenced defendant Brock Turner to six months — with good behavior, in California, three months in jail.[32] A jury had found Turner guilty of three counts of sexual assault for his attack on the victim, one "Emily Doe," passed out drunk outside a Stanford fraternity house. Two male graduate students who were biking by witnessed the attack and grabbed Turner, then called the police. Doe was so drunk she didn't wake up until the next morning.

Before Judge Persky announced the sentence, Doe asked to read her victim's statement aloud. The statement is so compelling because it gives fleshy reality to the harm of what are often portrayed as harmless, drunken, youthful indiscretions:

> [Turner] has done irreversible damage to me and my family during the trial and we have sat silently, listening to him shape the evening. But in the end, his unsupported statements and his attorney's twisted logic fooled no one. The truth won, the truth spoke for itself.

You are guilty . . . Your damage was concrete; stripped of titles, degrees, enrollment. My damage was internal, unseen, I carry it with me. You took away my worth, my privacy, my energy, my time, my safety, my intimacy, my confidence, my own voice, until today.[33]

After the victim read her long and anguished statement, Judge Persky gave Brock Turner six months. It was Judge Persky's misfortune that the victim was a family friend of feminist Stanford law professor Michele Dauber. Professor Dauber was sitting in the Palo Alto courtroom when the judge announced his decision. Dauber called her friend Catharine MacKinnon, stunned by the minimal sentence Turner had received. MacKinnon thought there might be some ethical procedure to penalize the judge for the sentencing decision.[34] "Judges in California are elected," Dauber responded. She started phoning around for a journalist to tell. The victim's statement went as viral as the flu epidemic of 1918. In the four days after BuzzFeed published Doe's statement on June 3, it was viewed eleven million times. Television newscaster Ashleigh Banfield read most of it aloud on national TV. *Glamour* honored Doe at the magazine's Women of the Year ceremony, where three great actresses recited her essay to the assembled multitudes.[35] She got an open letter from Vice President Joe Biden.

Four days after the victim statement went viral, Michele Dauber announced the "Recall Persky" campaign.[36] Dauber's executive committee was diverse and drew on the explosion of talent that surfaced after the 2016 election — volunteers from the Women's March, alums of the Hillary Clinton fundraising effort. The long-established national Feminist Majority Foundation signed on. The National Organization for Women pledged its support. One day, shortly after the effort began, Dauber was on the train to Hyde Park, New York, to give a speech. When word spread that she was on board, young women from nearby Vassar College began to come to meet her. They often were crying so hard they could not finish what they wanted to say. "When they started thrusting wet twenty dollar bills at me," Dauber says, "I knew we could pull this off." Hillary had lost, but many in her network of women supporters were still rich and now they were mad. Politically savvy and rich enough to fund a recall election, and mad. The campaign was a model of what women can do when united in the use of their electoral power.

Trying to take down a judge in the middle of his term, even using the entirely lawful means the state has provided, is almost unheard of. The bar and legal community stood up for Judge Persky.[37] The agency charged with reviewing the propriety of judicial behavior uniformly exonerated him.[38] Even the prosecutor, District Attorney Jeffrey Rosen, opposed recalling the judge.[39] Eighty-nine California law professors, mostly known as liberal or radical, and including about a third of Dauber's colleagues at Stanford, protested the recall in a letter as "naked political pressure."[40] The signers ranged across the landscape of the legal profession — conservatives, establishment stalwarts of the law school, men and women, young and old.

Surprisingly, much of the letter came from Professor Robert Gordon. Gordon had been a leader of the modern movement to treat judges as political actors, known as the Conference for Critical Legal Studies, or CLS.[41] This school of legal theory, the heir to the movement that produced the original court-packing plan in 1937, maintains that laws are used and judges are apt to use them to maintain the political status quo. The women's groups and their allies undertook political action. Nonetheless, despite his skepticism about the independence of legal decision-making, Gordon took the position against the Persky recall because he was opposed to the way elected California judges have been subject to political pressure for years.[42] He is a deeply radical "Crit," he says, but also an old-fashioned due process liberal. Interestingly, his other example of where his old-fashioned beliefs would dominate over his CLS political principles is again about women resisting sexual abuse. "I don't want campus harassers to get off without penalty," he volunteered spontaneously in an interview, "but you also have to be careful about witch hunts and excesses and going after people who don't really have an adequate chance to defend themselves."[43]

And so even the legal radicals enthusiastically defended the concept of judicial-process-as-usual when confronted with women trying to defend against sexual harassment and abuse ("witch hunt"). Feminists, who had finally stopped indulging their erstwhile liberal allies in the Democratic Party and on the left in general, found no comfort further left either. No matter. The ballot box is one of the rare places where women can connect directly without liberal or radical allies. Advance polling revealed that men supported the judge by anywhere from three to seven points and women wanted him recalled by point margins of twenty to thirty.[44] On June 6, 2018, two years after Judge Persky handed down the Turner sentence, the women got their wish.

"One morning Aaron Persky was on the bench," Michele Dauber recalls with satisfaction. "And that night he was not."

Part Two and a Half: The Year of the Woman

On the morning of Tuesday, November 6, 2018, the grab 'em by the pussy Republican Party was in control of every branch of the United States government and the legislatures or governorships of almost two-thirds of the states. And the night of November 6, 2018, they were not.

The 2018 election would not have taken its place in the epic battle we have described were it not for the redistribution of the issue of women's rights against sexual abuse and harassment into the Democratic Party. For that to happen, Democrats had to, at long last, give up their death grip on the defense of their harassment and abuse in the interest of the joy of sex. The Hot Manhattan Babes of the Clinton era and the one woman's pornography is another woman's ecstasy advocates from the pornography battles were headed for the metaphorical dustbin of history. Starting when most of the beneficiaries in the Democratic Party returned Harvey Weinstein's contributions after exposure of his sexual misdeeds, the party had confronted its sad legacy of defending abusers in the name of sexual freedom. In face of painful pushback, they rid themselves, as we have seen, of the albatross of Al Franken. Senator Kamala Harris was now sitting on the Judiciary Committee in Al Franken's seat. (Imagine if Franken had been sitting on the Judiciary Committee when Christine Blasey Ford sat down to testify.) In the 2018 midterms, no one wanted to campaign with Bill Clinton. The only question in the run-up to the 2018 midterms was whether the realignment would pay off right away or only in the long haul.

People could be forgiven for worrying. Referendums are rarely good for social change movements. The gains during the vaunted 1992 Year of the Woman had been largely debunked. Bill Clinton enjoyed a gender gap, but men as well as women voted for him over George H. W. Bush in 1992. So his election was hardly a feminist success story. Scholars taking time to do real research pointed to a host of factors that had been building long before Anita Hill took the stand. EMILY's List, the political organization prompting Democratic donors for women's campaigns, and similar organizations across party lines, had been organizing for years.[45] Worse, after some increase in women across politics, the rate of increase in female representation had flattened out.

The reduction of the women's wave to a trickle was not an accident: it was an early sign of the transformation of the GOP into the party of white men. In 1994 women's gains slowed almost to a halt two years after the Year of the Woman, when the Republicans swept Congress. A similar phenomenon happened in the red wave of 2010.[46] Three-quarters of the women in both houses of Congress in the run-up to the 2018 elections were Democrats. More tellingly, in the House of Representatives, where Republicans enjoyed an overwhelming majority, almost one-third of the Democratic minority were women, while only 10 percent of the Republican majority were women. The sorting of women's politics into the Democratic Party began long before Donald Trump told Megyn Kelly women could take their bleeding whatevers somewhere else. As the Republican Party rose, the growth in the numbers of women fell.

As the Trump administration continued on with its vulgar sexist ways, however, hopes rose for the long-awaited swing of educated suburban white women to the Democratic Party in numbers sufficient to take the House. We have seen that although women are the majority of the population and of the voting population, they are a widely dispersed and easily fractured majority. But the experience of sexual harassment and abuse is so widespread — hence the power of the #MeToo hashtag. Being sexually assaulted, abused, and harassed is so unequivocally obnoxious and traumatic, there can be no serious discussion of whether it's "just sex." And, finally, after Trump and #MeToo and the Kavanaugh hearings, there was a clear partisan home to which women could go.

Women poured into electoral politics, organizing the resistance and running for office. But the action was mostly on the Democratic side, and, as usual, women of color led the movement and provided an impressive number of the candidates. For a giant blue wave to break at the midterms, however, a slice of those faithful white Republican women voters would have to abandon their party. Winning was by no means a slam dunk even in the House. In many states, there are arrangements that interfere with a representative vote. Since the Democrats lost most state legislatures and governorships in the long wilderness years starting with the census election of 2010, Republican state legislatures have redrafted congressional districts to favor their party heavily; they have enacted voter registration and identification requirements tailor-made to repress the minority vote, and they have made voters invest more effort and wait in longer lines. The Senate is constitutionally set up to favor the old white populations of the empty western states, and in 2018 the Republicans did indeed increase their dominance of that unrepresentative body, unseating three leftover Democrats in deep red states.

With all its faults, the House of Representatives is as close as

America comes to a plebiscite. Now, with the votes finally counted, as of December 2018, the Democrats have won the House in a giant wave of blue, landing at 235 seats. They flipped 43 seats,[47] at least 22 flipped by women. As a result, a record eighty-nine of the Democrats in the House are female; 22 of them elected for the first time. Forty-two of the 89 women in the House are women of color. Five state governments also moved to the Democrats, raising their control from a pitiful eight states to a respectable thirteen (compared to Republicans' loss of four).[48]

Thanks to the magic of modern data gathering, we know a lot about how voters in 2018 felt about sexual abuse and harassment. "The hostile rhetoric toward women by Trump and Republican members of Congress is beginning to take their toll on the party's electoral fortunes," political science professor Brian Schaffner reported as part of the "What the Hell Happened Project" at the think tank Data for Progress. "In 2018, Republican House candidates were penalized by voters who don't hold sexist views in a way they were not in 2016. And this rhetoric does not appear to be winning the party any new supporters to make up for those losses."[49] The losses were real and they were massive: "In 2018, voters with the least sexist attitudes were about 15 points less likely to vote for the Republican House candidate compared to voters with the most sexist attitudes." There must have been a lot of those least sexist voters, because, Schaffner reports, "based on the graphic, this appears to have produced a penalty for Republican House candidates." Trump's sexist behavior now tainted the candidates of his party. The exit polls also revealed that people voting in 2018 had opinions about Brett Kavanaugh's confirmation; by 47 to 43 percent they were opposed to Kavanaugh. Over all, the gender gap in political support between men and women in the midterm elections reached a record-breaking 22 percent![50] Dauber's new organization, #Enough Is Enough Voter Project targeted a state rep in Washington who had been fired from his teaching job after a sex scandal. He resigned mid-campaign. Texas's representative Matt Rinaldi lost his election after an

Enough Is Enough campaign telling voters about his almost perfect record of opposition to protecting victims of sexual assault.[51]

Everywhere you look, women played an outsized role in the activism fueling the campaigns of many of the successful Democrats. Not only were a record number of women elected to Congress and governorships, but the presence of a woman on the ballot unequivocally made things better for the Democrats. As we have seen, twenty-two of the forty-three seats the Democrats flipped from red to blue were won by female candidates.[52] The blue wave also brought inspiring new female candidates of color to positions of governance. Michigan Democrat Rashida Tlaib and Ilhan Omar of the Minnesota Democratic-Farmer-Labor Party were elected as the first Muslim women in Congress. The election of Omar, a Somali-American refugee, is particularly gratifying in this anti-immigrant time. Two Native Americans, Sharice Davids and Deb Haaland (Davids also identifies as a lesbian), marked another milestone. Ayanna Pressley was the first African American representative elected from the supposedly liberal state of Massachusetts.

"Tuesday's results," *USA Today* opined, "offered evidence that Democrats had made some inroads with [white voters]. Twenty of the House districts that flipped were at least 60 percent white. That represents a break from current Democratic strongholds. Including the party's newly-won districts, only 87 Democratically-controlled House districts have a share of white voters higher than 60 percent."[53] The exit polls leave no doubt that most movement by white voters came from white women voters. It certainly wasn't white men, who, exit polls report, voted 59 percent for the Republicans on a national level.

The exit polls show white women breaking 49/49 red and blue nationally.[54] But the exit polls are notoriously unreliable. In 2016, exit polls reported 52 or 53 percent white female support for Donald Trump. When, two years later, the scientific and reliable Pew polling organization made the calculation using evidence with files from official voting records rather than conversations at the polling places, they found that white women had supported Trump by only 47 percent to 45 percent, a margin of 2 percent.[55] When the Brookings Institution looked beyond the most extreme Southern contests in 2018, it found white women favoring the Democratic candidate anywhere from around 20 percent (Ohio, with the popular Sherrod Brown, and Michigan) to 15 percent (Wisconsin) to just below even (Missouri).[56]

We have seen that the hardest organizational task in America is for a majority of white women to vote differently from the white men they live among. In 2008 white women voted 56 percent for the Republican presidential candidate; in 2012, 53 percent. Statistics from 2016 are debated, but in the unreliable exit polls, white women's support for the Grab 'em by the pussy candidate stayed steady at 53 percent. The unreliable 49/49 exit poll from 2018 is thus a big improvement over 2016 and 2012. A little math reveals that holding white women to an even split in a 60 percent white district plus even a small percentage of white men leaves the heroes and heroines of the Reckoning with 40 percent — voters of color and especially female voters of color — to carry the election. White women are slowly moving away from the Republican Party, not enough to give the demographic a medal for virtue, but getting women's support for the Republicans, the party of white male abuse, down to 49 percent may be a crucial landmark along the bend toward justice.

Postscript: Schaffner says the exit polls from 2018 are going to be way off. His numbers are showing that white women voted Democratic 54 percent, not 49/49 as CNN suggests.[57]

Part Three: The Hearts and Minds

In the 1800s, Harvard cultural historian Phyllis Thompson reports, suffragists were reluctant to talk about sex crimes of all kinds, in part because the topic was considered "indelicate." In addition, "to have a discussion of sex crimes in the workplace requires that one have an understanding that all genders legitimately belong in the workplace, and that was just simply not the case in the 19th century.

There was no sense of a right for women to have workplace treatment on a par with men."[58] Then, as throughout US history, African American women were the first and most potent agents of the message that harvesting women workers for sex was wrong. In 1833 the black female abolitionist Maria W. Stewart invoked women's rights to control their bodies as a foundational reason for abolition.[59] White women entering the workplace in numbers after publication of *The Feminine Mystique* coincided with the sexual revolution. It took a long time to separate out sexual abuse and harassment as too high a price to pay or ignore from the heady opportunities of revolution. Here again black women led the way. After the revival of feminism in the 1960s, while the white women at *Newsweek* worked at a company described as a "discreet orgy" and "screwing the researchers" was a perk of the male employees,[60] black women like Paulette Barnes and Sandra Bundy were looking for lawyers to sue their harassing bosses.

That the decades of successful litigation thereafter, culminating in the Supreme Court, in 1986, recognizing sexual harassment as a civil rights violation, did not put more of a dent in the behavior teaches a potent lesson in the limits of the first two avenues of social change, the courts and the elections. Even after the decision in *Meritor v. Vinson,* from the New Orleans McDonald's to the Four Seasons Beverly Hills,[61] the wrongdoing raged on, even reaching the Oval Office. The culture would have to change. There was one big problem: until 2017 the harassers were running the institutions of culture. They were making the movies and television shows. They were buying ink by the barrel, running the magazines, reviewing the books, writing the books. They were covering the politics.

NBC had the *Access Hollywood* tape in 2016. It never saw the light of day until someone leaked it to the *Post*. Ronan Farrow had to leave NBC, taking the Weinstein story with him. Since he broke the Weinstein story in October 2017, the media has been filled with speculation about why NBC did not pursue, much less air, Farrow's Pulitzer Prize–winning story about Harvey Weinstein. In August 2018 Farrow's coproducer at NBC, Rich McHugh, blew the whistle to the *Times*.[62] (I had found McHugh myself months before, but his interview with me was then off the record. His public story tracks what he told me in June.) NBC was "resistant" throughout the eight-month reporting process, McHugh told the *New York Times*. Then, in August, the network stopped supporting their efforts: "Three days before Ronan and I were going to head to L.A. to interview a woman with a credible rape allegation against Harvey Weinstein," McHugh said, "I was ordered to stop, not to interview this woman . . . And to stand down on the story altogether." Although McHugh would not name the names, *HuffPost* had already identified the decision makers as NBC chairman Andrew Lack and NBC News president Noah Oppenheim.[63] Farrow has promised to tell the story of being pressed not to pursue the story in his forthcoming book.

Writing in the *New Yorker* almost to the day that McHugh went public, Farrow revealed allegations of sexual misconduct against the chairman and CEO of the second of the four national networks, CBS.[64] The stories about CBS executive Les Moonves and others in his regime, like Jeff Fager, the executive producer of the gold-standard news program *60 Minutes*, had been circulating in media circles for a while. In June, two months before Farrow broke the story, journalist Irin Carmon accepted the Mirror Award for the Best Story on Sexual Misconduct in the Media Industry, which she won for outing CBS's Charlie Rose; in her speech she called out the people in the audience who were part of the system by which harassers and abusers continued to be protected. That story, she predicted, "will one day see the light of day."[65]

Farrow's first story about Moonves involved six women and accusations of forcible advances and forced kissing followed by career-ending retaliation. Echoing Carmon's language of systemic abuse, Farrow found not only accusations against Moonves but thirty reports that the behavior permeated the network — harassers promoted and complainants paid to go away.

For the first time since the Weinstein story, a major media outlet resisted the pressure. We'll just hire some lawyers to investigate, the CBS board announced, turning to a firm that normally did work for the network. Not that an investigation would help much anyway. As eighty-three-year-old board member Arnold Kopelson summed it up: "I don't care if 30 more women come forward and allege this kind of stuff. Les is our leader and it wouldn't change my opinion of him."[66] Word of a hundred-million-dollar severance package for Moonves began to circulate.

While CBS was debating how many women it would take to make them take the charges against Moonves seriously, on September 9 Farrow tested the limits. "Six additional women," he reported, "are now accusing Moonves of sexual harassment or assault in incidents that took place between the nineteen-eighties and the early two-thousands. They include claims that Moonves forced them to perform oral sex on him, that he exposed himself to them without their consent, and that he used physical violence and intimidation against them. A number of the women also said that Moonves retaliated after they rebuffed him, damaging their careers." Farrow's report immediately added an update: *Three hours after the publication of this story, CNN reported that Moonves would step down from his position at CBS. Later the same day, CBS announced that Moonves had left the company and would not receive any of his exit compensation, pending the results of the independent investigation into the allegations.*[67]

The stories were awful, and there was much relief expressed when CBS finally bit the bullet with Moonves. Even his hundred-million-dollar severance package proved to be at risk. But the most potent response to Moonves's toppling came from someone he had never touched. A few days after his firing, the legendary television producer of the long-ago megahit *Designing Women*, Linda Bloodworth-Thomason, told the *Hollywood Reporter* her Les Moonves story.[68] "I was never sexually harassed or attacked by Les Moonves. My encounters were much more subtle, engendering a different kind of destruction," she revealed.

In 1992 Bloodworth-Thomason had the largest writing and producing contract in the history of CBS. Three years later, the network hired Les Moonves. Bloodworth-Thomason had heard a rumor that Moonves had hated *Designing Women*, with its loud-mouthed female heroines. She was in the middle of a pilot for one of the contract series when Moonves took over. As soon as the filming stopped, he told her it would not be picked up. "I was at the pinna-cle of my career," she remembers. "I would not work again for seven years. People asked me for years, 'Where have you been? What hap-pened to you?' Les Moonves happened to me."

Moonves was not just a powerful employer, he was at the helm of one of a handful of institutions that create the culture, Blood-worth-Thomason reminded her readers. Moonves gave the tele-vision-watching public a quarter century of misogynistic garbage. Moonves, reputably credited with the casting standard "If I don't want to fuck her, why would I hire her?" at the same time "loaded up the network with highly profitable, male-dominated series," Blood-worth-Thomason. observed. Where once there had been Mary Ty-ler Moore and Murphy Brown, Moonves primarily "presided over a plethora of macho crime shows featuring a virtual genocide of dead naked hotties in morgue drawers, with sadistic female autopsy re-ports, ratcheted up each week."

When complicit media not only silence the stories of sexual ha-rassment and abuse, but offer sexist fiction to fill our leisure hours, they shape peoples' hearts and minds. And their politics. Rebecca Traister, who had written a serious book about Hillary Clinton's 2008 campaign, zeroed in on the later disgraced political pundit and author Mark Halperin: "Mark Halperin co-authored *Game Change* . . . which featured all kinds of history-making candidates who were not powerful white men. Halperin's view of Hillary Clin-ton in particular was two-dimensional: Through his lens, she was a grasping and scandal-plagued woman; her exaggerated misdeeds and the intense feelings she engendered were all part of propelling his profitable narrative forward."[69]

As Margaret Sullivan, the informal conscience of the media in these crucial Trump and #MeToo years, put it after Moonves, "It's impossible to know how different America would be if power-happy and misogynistic men hadn't been running the show in so many influential media organizations — certainly not just CBS ... A media figure doesn't have to show up for a business meeting in an open bathrobe to do harm, though that strange practice has turned out to be something of a leitmotif. He can help frame the coverage of a candidate's supposedly disqualifying flaws ... All these little moments add up, though we'll never know their full cost. Only that it's very, very high."[70]

Just as Farrow was finally driving the stake in the Moonves case, the *New York Review of Books*—poster child of oblivious and entitled male-run media[71]—took an ill-timed crack at rolling the culture back to the power-happy misogynistic days with an exculpatory essay in September 2018 by the disgraced Canadian media star Jian Ghomeshi. The powerful and wildly successful host of the arts and culture radio show "Q" on the Canadian Broadcasting Company, Ghomeshi lost his job when three old girlfriends accused him of serious physical misconduct in 2014. Although he was acquitted of the criminal charges (other than having to file a peace bond), by the end of the inquiry, more than twenty women, including a young producer at "Q," had accused him of a cornucopia of sexual wrongdoing at and away from work.[72] Ghomeshi, in his "Reflections from a Hashtag" essay for the *NYRB*, professed to speak for men "bewildered by gender relations." The essay consisted substantially of his rejection of most accusations against him and his protestations against the pain he had suffered as a result.[73]

The editor at *NYRB* behind the piece, Ian Buruma, had just replaced the founder and longtime editor Robert Silvers, whose tenure was replete with criticism of his abysmal record in reviewing or commissioning work by women.[74] As the protests against the Ghomeshi essay exploded, Buruma, a sixty-six-year-old academic who had written for the *New York Review* for years, agreed to an interview with *Slate*'s devilishly even-toned killer interviewer Isaac Chotiner.[75] Under Chotiner's "interrogation," Buruma shared that he was unconcerned with "the exact nature of [Ghomeshi's] behavior—how much consent was involved." After all, "sexual behavior is a many-faceted business." By September 20, Buruma announced that he felt "forced to resign" from his new job.[76] The #MeToo movement was by 2018 shining its light into the dark corners of the highest reaches of high culture.

We've seen that the movement against sexual abuse and harassment got a major cultural break earlier, in 2016, when fifty-year-old former beauty queen Gretchen Carlson used the first tool of the social movement arsenal, the judiciary, to attack the repulsive septuagenarian Roger Ailes. He had thought she would be good and better if she had sex with him. Even the most deluded observer could not have thought that would be a welcome experience for her. And the editor of the *New York Times* asked his staff what other powerful men might make a good story. It is sad but true that the presence of famous, wealthy, and beautiful mostly white movie actresses in the ensuing flood of accusations finally attracted the attention of the reading and viewing population, in a way the women who accused Bill Cosby could not do for decades. For the two and a half years after Carlson started the most potent action, through the power of narrative and the power of investigative journalism, the movement began to move hearts and minds. In October 2018 the *New York Times* compiled a chart: "#MeToo Brought Down 201 Powerful Men. Nearly Half of Their Replacements Are Women."[77] Women are running Amazon Studios, and cohosting Mark Halperin's political television show *The Circus*, and publishing the *New Republic*. Women are the senior vice president for news and editorial director and executive editor at NPR News, editing DC Comics, hosting the former *Charlie Rose* show (*Amanpour and Company*), covering the White House for the *New York Times*, coanchoring *Today*, editing the *Paris Review*, hosting on WNYC, executive editing *Alternet*, and, of course, sitting on the Senate Judiciary Committee. A woman now sits in the office formally occupied by CBS chief, Les Moonves.

After a pretty good referendum on sex abuse in 2018, the Republicans, and even some liberal pundits,[78] suggested that the Republican takeover of four Democratic Senate seats was the payoff of appointing Brett Kavanaugh. But CNN did the math and figured out that more senators who had opposed Kavanaugh, including one of the endangered red-state Democrats, Jon Tester, had won reelection.[79] Even if the elections had gone the other way, it would seem, there is no unscrambling that cultural omelet. Which is a good thing, because there is much work left to do.

Almost a half century ago, Catharine MacKinnon, then a student at Yale Law School, figured out that sexual harassment and abuse were actually sex discrimination and illegal under the Civil Rights Act of 1964. In 1992, another lawyer, a woman of color named Carol Moseley Braun, realized she stood a chance of taking down the white male senator from Illinois in a political primary, because he had voted to confirm sexual harasser Clarence Thomas to the Supreme Court. In 1980, a gifted Hollywood actor and director, Jane Fonda, decided she could make a really good movie from the harrowing stories of workplace harassment from women who worked 9 to 5. These were origins—legal, political, cultural—of the movement that we have seen catch fire in our very recent lifetimes.

Today, a multimillion-dollar legal defense fund has got the backs of low-wage McDonald's workers in their fight against sexual abuse at work. American citizens are represented in the peoples' House by not one but dozens of women of color and many ethnicities. And Jane Mayer, the woman who wrote the long-ago book about Clarence Thomas, recently coauthored the magazine articles that brought down the attorney general of the State of New York for sexually abusing women.

It is true that women's work is never done. But after an extraordinary fifty-year battle, women have earned and understand their legal, political, and cultural right not to suffer sexual abuse and harassment in the workplace, or in any place.

Acknowledgments

Alyssa Milano, you inspired me to write this book. To David Kuhn, Becky Sweren, and Nate Muscato, of Aevitas Creative, for tireless advocacy. Most of all to Deanne Urmy, extraordinary editor, endlessly patient and an enthusiastic partner in every imaginable circumstance. Thanks to Becky Shavin and Maya Dusenberry and Melissa Dobson, for fact-checking, research, and editing in the trenches!

Notes

Preface

1. Tanya Harrell to author, interview, August 9, 2018.
2. Jodi Kantor and Megan Twohey, "Harvey Weinstein Paid Off Sexual Harassment Accusers for Decades," *New York Times*, October 5, 2017, https://www.nytimes.com/2017/10/05/us/harvey-weinstein-harassment-allegations.html.
3. Nadja Sayej, "Alyssa Milano on the #MeToo Movement: 'We're Not Going to Stand for It Any More,'" *Guardian*, December 1, 2017, https://www.theguardian.com/culture/2017/dec/01/alyssa-milano-mee-too-sexual-harassment-abuse.
4. Riley Griffin, Hannah Recht, and Jeff Green, "#MeToo: One Year Later," *Bloomberg*, October 5, 2018, https://www.bloomberg.com/graphics/2018-me-too-anniversary/.
5. Audrey Carlsen et al., "#MeToo Brought Down 201 Powerful Men. Nearly Half of Their Replacements Are Women," *New York Times*, October 29, 2018, https://www.nytimes.com/interactive/2018/10/23/us/metoo-replacements.html.
6. Linda Hirshman, *Victory: The Triumphant Gay Revolution* (New York: Harper Collins, 2012), 107.
7. Lucia Graves, "Why Hillary Clinton Was Right About White Women — and Their Husbands," *Guardian*, September 25, 2017, https://www.theguardian.com/us-news/2017/sep/25/white-women-husbands-voting.
8. Anemona Hartocollis and Christina Capecchi, "'Willing to Do Everything,' Mothers Defend Sons Accused of Sexual Assault," *New York Times*, October 22, 2017, https://www.nytimes.com/2017/10/22/us/campus-sex-assault-mothers.html.

9. See Fred Strebeigh, *Equal: Women Reshape American Law* (New York: Norton, 2009), 513–14, note 234, on the many versions of MacKinnon's student work that produced the theory.

10. Both were cover stories: "The Marriage Crunch: If You're a Single Woman, Here Are Your Chances of Getting Married," *Newsweek*, June 2, 1986; "Is Feminism Dead?" *Time*, June 29, 1998.

11. Katie Roiphe, *The Morning After: Sex, Fear, and Feminism* (Boston: Back Bay, 1994).

12. Constance Grady, "Shitty Media Men List Creator Moira Donegan on the Year in #MeToo," *Vox*, October 16, 2018, https://www.vox.com/culture/2018/10/16/17955392/moira-donegan-interview-me-too-shitty-media-men-list.

13. Wikipedia "List of Federal Political Sex Scandals in the United States," https://en.wikipedia.org/wiki/List_of_federal_political_sex_scandals_in_the_United_States#1990–1999.

14. David A. Fahrenthold, "Trump Recorded Having Extremely Lewd Conversation About Women in 2005," *Washington Post*, October 8, 2016, https://www.washingtonpost.com/politics/trump-recorded-having-extremely-lewd-conversation-about-women-in-2005/2016/10/07/3b9ce776-8cb4-11e6-bf8a-3d26847eeed4_story.html?utm_term=.8d81d53f319d.

15. Nina Totenberg, "Justice Ruth Bader Ginsburg Reflects on the #MeToo Movement: 'It's About Time,'" *Morning Edition*, NPR, January 22, 2018, https://www.npr.org/2018/01/22/579595727/justice-ginsburg-shares-her-own-metoo-story-and-says-it-s-about-time.

16. Carl Hulse, "'Kavanaugh's Revenge' Fell Short Against Democrats in the Midterms," *New York Times*, November 25, 2018, https://www.nytimes.com/2018/11/25/us/politics/kavanaugh-midterm-elections.html.

17. Lindsey Bever and Emily Guskin, "Democrats Won Women's Vote for Congress by the Largest Margin Seen in Midterm Exit Polls," *Washington Post*, November 7, 2018, https://www.washingtonpost.com/politics/2018/11/07/why-did-democrats-win-house-one-word-women/?utm_term=.4519047cc902.

18. Brian Schaffner to author, Twitter DM, November 10, 2018.

1. Naming It, Claiming It / 1969–80

1. Dan Zak, "What Really Happened at Chappaquiddick?," *Washington Post*, April 4, 2018, https://www.washingtonpost.com/lifestyle/style/what-really-happened-at-chappaquiddick-a-new-movie-explores-the-truth-well-never-know/2018/04/04/c8d6db0e-293b-11e8-874b-d517e912f125_story.html?utm_term=.69aef913fff3.

2. Ibid.

3. Adam Clymer, *Edward M. Kennedy: A Biography* (New York: Harper Collins, 1999), 277.

4. Ibid., 288.

5. Leslie Bennetts, "Women Comparing Carter and Rivals," *New York Times*, No-

vember 11, 1979, https://www.nytimes.com/1979/11/11/archives/women-compar
ing-carter-and-rivals-some-groups-say-president-has-not.html?_r=1.

6. "Kennedy Private Life Questioned: He Is Called 'Known Womanizer,'" *New
York Times*, September 22, 1979, https://www.nytimes.com/1979/09/22/archives/
kennedy-private-life-questioned-he-is-called-known-womanizer.html.

7. Suzannah Lessard, "Kennedy's Woman Problem — Women's Kennedy Problem," *Washington Monthly*, December 1979, pp. 10–14, http://www.unz.org/Pub/
WashingtonMonthly-1979dec-00010.

8. Clymer, *Edward M. Kennedy*, 150.

9. Lin Farley, *Sexual Shakedown: The Sexual Harassment of Women on the Job* (New
York: McGraw-Hill, 1978), 82–84.

10. Enid Nemy, "Women Begin to Speak Out Against Sexual Harassment at Work,"
New York Times, August 19, 1975, https://www.nytimes.com/1975/08/19/archives/
women-begin-to-speak-out-against-sexual-harassment-at-work.html.

11. Victory has a thousand mothers. Farley claims the term originated with her,
and Reva Siegel credits her with it; MacKinnon remembers hearing it from a
Boston group and also Karen Sauvigné: Farley, *Sexual Shakedown*, 48; Reva B.
Siegel, "Introduction: A Short History of Sexual Harassment," in *Directions in
Sexual Harassment Law*, ed. Catharine A. MacKinnon and Reva B. Siegel (New
Haven, CT: Yale University Press, 2003), 8–33.

12. Nemy, "Women Begin to Speak Out."

13. Ibid. Nemy's article was to the issue of sexual harassment what another *New
York Times* article was to HIV/AIDS: Lawrence K. Altman, "Rare Cancer
Seen in 41 Homosexuals," *New York Times*, July 3, 1981, https://www.nytimes.
com/1981/07/03/us/rare-cancer-seen-in-41-homosexuals.html.

14. Enid Nemy to author, interview, January 16, 2018. In 1974 six women at the
Times sued for sex discrimination, claiming to represent a class of some six
hundred employees. "Women Charge the *Times* with Sex Discrimination," *New
York Times*, November 8, 1974, https://www.nytimes.com/1974/11/08/archives/
women-charge-the-times-with-sex-discrimination.html.

15. Enid Nemy, interview with the author.

16. Farley, *Sexual Shakedown*, 95.

17. Ibid., 183.

18. Alyssa Milano to author, interview, April 17, 2018.

19. Farley, *Sexual Shakedown*, 211.

20. Karen Nussbaum to author, interview, February 8, 2018.

21. Alana Newhouse, "A Philistine Prophecy," *Tablet*, December 4, 2017, https://
www.tabletmag.com/scroll/250836/patricia-resnick-9-to-5-movie-sexual-
harassment.

22. Tara Murtha, "'9 to 5' Turns 35, and It's Still Radical Today," *Rolling Stone*, December 18, 2015, https://www.rollingstone.com/music/music-country/9-to-5-turns-
35-and-its-still-radical-today-50499/.

23. Laura McGann, "Exclusive: NYT White House Correspondent Glenn Thrush's

History of Bad Judgment Around Young Women Journalists," *Vox*, November 20, 2017, https://www.vox.com/policy-and-politics/2017/11/20/16678094/glenn-thrush-new-york-times.

24. Karen Nussbaum, interview with the author.

25. Kyle Feldscher, "Lily Tomlin Calls Trump 'a Sexist, Egotistical, Lying, Hypo-critical Bigot,' at Emmys," *Washington Examiner*, September 17, 2017, https://www.washingtonexaminer.com/lily-tomlin-calls-trump-a-sexist-egotistical-lying-hypocritical-bigot-at-emmys.

2. Making the Legal Case for Women / 1975–76

1. Catharine MacKinnon to author, interview, July 14, 2018. The information in this section, "Catharine MacKinnon's Mind Speaks to Her," is from that interview.

2. Strebeigh, *Equal*, 228. Strebeigh interviewed Yale dean emeritus James A. Thomas in 2006.

3. Oyez Project, "Reed v. Reed," https://www.oyez.org/cases/1971/70-4.

4. Geduldig v. Aiello et al., 417 U.S. 484 (1974).

5. Catharine A. MacKinnon, *Sexual Harassment of Working Women* (New Haven, CT: Yale University Press, 1979), 83–99.

6. Rod Boggs to author, interview, October 1, 2018.

7. MacKinnon, *Sexual Harassment of Working Women*, 84 and 262.

8. Kimberlé Crenshaw, "Why Intersectionality Can't Wait," *Washington Post*, September 24, 2015, https://www.washingtonpost.com/news/in-theory/wp/2015/09/24/why-intersectionality-cant-wait/?utm_term=.9a6a9399369c.

9. DeGraffenreid v. General Motors Assembly Div. etc., 412 F.Supp. 142 (1976).

10. Kimberlé W. Crenshaw, "Close Encounters of Three Kinds: On Teaching Dominance Feminism and Intersectionality," *Tulsa Law Review* 46 (Fall 2010), 151. Crenshaw's analysis is subtle and open-ended. She is not to be read as unequivocally endorsing every aspect of MacKinnon's work. But her concept of intersectionality is the main point, and we will see how it explains much of the history presented here.

11. Linda Singer to author, interview, January 9, 2018. Linda Singer was one of the lawyers representing Paulette Barnes.

12. Kimberlé Crenshaw, "Whose Story Is It, Anyway? Feminist and Antiracist Appropriations of Anita Hill," in *Race-ing Justice, En-Gendering Power: Essays on Anita Hill, Clarence Thomas, and the Construction of Social Reality*, ed. Toni Morrison (New York: Pantheon, 1992), 402–40.

13. Strebeigh, *Equal*, 242, note at 514. Strebeigh was unable to confirm MacKinnon's account. Strebeigh to author, interview, 2018. The author also could not confirm it. Susan Low Bloch to author, interview, January 5, 2018.

14. Strebeigh, *Equal*, at 242. MacKinnon told me essentially the same story in our interview; McKinnon, interview with the author.

15. Linda Hirshman, *Sisters in Law: How Sandra Day O'Connor and Ruth Bader*

Ginsburg Went to the Supreme Court and Changed the World (New York: Harper Collins, 2015), 87. In this, the DC Circuit was appropriately following the example of the Supreme Court, which had a record-breaking number of female clerks in the prior term (1974–75) and had produced an unprecedented slew of decisions expanding the constitutional protections against discrimination.

16. Strebeigh, *Equal,* 252–59.
17. Susan Low Bloch, interview with the author.
18. Barnes v. Costle, 561 F.2d 983 (D.C. Cir. 1977).
19. Yla Eason, "When the Boss Wants Sex," http://www.angelfire.com/sc3/ws301/html/eason.html.

3. Redefining Sex / 1979–91

1. MacKinnon, *Sexual Harassment of Working Women,* 89–90. Emphasis added.
2. The story may be apocryphal: Daniel R. Vollaro, "Lincoln, Stowe, and the 'Little Woman/Great War' Story: The Making, and Breaking, of a Great American Anecdote," *Journal of the Abraham Lincoln Association* 30, no. 1 (Winter 2009), https://quod.lib.umich.edu/j/jala/2629860.0030.104/1:1/ — lincoln-stowe-and-the-little-womangreat-war-story-the-making?rgn=div1;view=fulltext.
3. Gabriel Sherman, "The Revenge of Roger's Angels," *Daily Intelligencer, New York Magazine,* September 5, 2016, http://nymag.com/daily/intelligencer/2016/09/how-fox-news-women-took-down-roger-ailes.html; Laurie Penny, "We're Not Done Here: How the MeToo Movement Became a Feminist Sexual Revolution," *Longreads,* January 2018, https://longreads.com/2018/01/18/were-not-done-here/. That's why the #MeToo movement, which actually began with Fox News anchor Gretchen Carlson's lawsuit against Fox CEO Roger Ailes for harassment at work, quickly expanded into an examination of relations of sex everywhere. Bad dates, women feeling pressed to provide sex, all the issues that had been unspeakable were suddenly on the table.
4. Jeff Gluck, "Grab Some Butts? Tony Stewart Gets a Piece Of DeLana Harvick," Nascar, SBNation.com, September 16, 2012, https://www.sbnation.com /2012/9/16/3344996/tony-stewart-delana-harvick-nascar-butt-grab. The clip is on YouTube: https://www.youtube.com/watch?v=dApfKwkgWxQ.
5. Nancy Qualls-Shehata, "Nascar, You Can Do Better Than This," *Muslimah in Progress* (blog), Patheos.com, September 17, 2012, http://www.patheos.com/blogs/muslimahinprogress/2012/09/nascar-you-can-do-better-than-this.html.
6. Thomas Hobbes, *On the Citizen,* https://books.google.com/books?id=O8M-OJJoiGgC&printsec=frontcover&dq=Hobbes+on+the+Citizen&hl=en&sa=X &ved=0ahUKEwil-L2guvXeAhXps1kKHaeFD-gQ6AEIKjAA#v=onepage&q=mushrooms&f=false.
7. Sonia Corrêa and Rosalind Petchesky, "Reproductive and Sexual Rights: A Feminist Perspective," in *Feminist Theory Reader: Local and Global Perspectives,* ed. Carole McCann and Seung-kyung Kim, 3rd ed. (New York: Routledge: 2013), 101, note 2.

8. Ibid, 134–47.
9. Manisha Sinha, *The Slave's Cause: A History of Abolition* (New Haven, CT: Yale University Press, 2016), 178.
10. Harriet Jacobs, *Incidents in the Life of a Slave Girl* (1861; repr., Mineola, NY: Dover: 2001), 48.
11. Catharine A. MacKinnon, "Feminism, Marxism, Method, and the State: An Agenda for Theory," *Signs* 7, no. 3, (Spring 1982), 515–44.
12. Catharine A. MacKinnon, "Feminism, Marxism, Method, and the State: Toward Feminist Jurisprudence," *Signs* 8, no. 4, (Summer 1983), 635.
13. Catharine A. MacKinnon, *Toward a Feminist Theory of the State* (Cambridge, MA: Harvard University Press, 1989), 126–54. Available at https://www.feministes-radicales.org/wp-content/uploads/2010/11/MacKinnon-Sexuality-Method.pdf.
14. MacKinnon, "Feminism, Marxism, Method, and the State: Toward Feminist Jurisprudence," 657.
15. Catharine MacKinnon to author, email, October 28, 2018.
16. Quoted in Fred Strebeigh, "Defining Law on the Feminist Frontier," *New York Times Magazine,* October 6, 1991, http://www.equalwomen.com/nytmagazine1991.html.
17. Of course, MacKinnon used the wealth of existing social science literature from the beginning, especially the extensive empirical studies by Diana E. H. Russell. Catharine MacKinnon, *Feminism Unmodified* (Cambridge, MA: Harvard University Press, 1988), 237.
18. Susan Brownmiller, *Against Our Will: Men, Women, and Rape* (New York: Simon & Schuster, 1975), 9.
19. Your Dictionary, "Susan Brownmiller Facts," http://biography.yourdictionary.com/susan-brownmiller, citing Heller, *Atlantic Monthly.* The issue appears to be November 1975.
20. Angela Y. Davis, *Women, Race and Class* (New York: Random House, 1981), 178.
21. MacKinnon, "Feminism, Marxism, Method, and the State: Toward Feminist Jurisprudence," 646.
22. Chris Gardner, "New Claims Against Harvey Weinstein Go Back to the 1970s," *Hollywood Reporter,* October 30, 2017, https://www.hollywoodreporter.com/news/new-claims-harvey-weinstein-go-back-1970s-1053035.
23. Brownmiller, *Against Our Will,* 390.
24. Dworkin, *Woman Hating* (New York: Dutton, 1974), 53–54, as reproduced at https://www.feministes-radicales.org/wp-content/uploads/2010/11/Andrea-DWORKIN-Woman-Hating-A-Radical-Look-at-Sexuality-1974.pdf.
25. Stuart Jeffries, "Are Women Human?," *Guardian,* April 12, 2006, https://www.theguardian.com/world/2006/apr/12/gender.politicsphilosophyandsociety.
26. Robin Morgan, *Going Too Far: The Personal Chronicle of a Feminist* (New York: Random House, 1977).
27. Linda Lovelace, *Ordeal* (New York: Citadel, 1980).

28. Maki Baker, "'You Disgust Me': Buffalo Woman Tells of 1980 Encounter with Weinstein," *Buffalo News*, October 16, 2017.

29. Kirsten Delegard, "Minneapolis Anti-Pornography Ordinance," MNOPEDIA, July 29, 2015, http://www.mnopedia.org/thing/minneapolis-anti-pornography-ordinance.

30. Margaret Baldwin, "The Sexuality of Inequality: The Minneapolis Pornography Ordinance," *Law & Inequality: A Journal of Theory and Practice* 2, no. 2 (1984), https://scholarship.law.umn.edu/cgi/viewcontent.cgi?article=1296&context=lawineq.

31. American Booksellers Ass'n, Inc. v. Hudnut, 771 F.2d 323 (1985).

32. Catharine A. MacKinnon, "Francis Biddle's Sister: Pornography, Civil Rights, and Speech," in *Applications Of Feminist Legal Theory*, ed. D. Kelly Weisberg (Philadelphia: Temple University Press, 1996), 59–79.

33. Nan D. Hunter and Sylvia A. Law, "Brief Amici Curiae of Feminist Anti-Censorship Taskforce et al. in American Booksellers Association, Inc. v. Hudnut," in *Applications Of Feminist Legal Theory*, ed. D. Kelly Weisberg (Philadelphia: Temple University Press, 1996), 118–30.

34. The FACT brief was joined by the Women's Legal Defense Fund and numerous writers and activists on behalf of women's rights, including Betty Brooks, the director of the Southern California Rape Hotline Alliance and founder of Women Against Sexual Abuse; Susan Estrich, a professor at the University of Southern California Law Center who is an expert on rape law; Betty Friedan, the founding president of the National Organization for Women and a founding member of the National Women's Political Caucus; Joan Howarth, an attorney who helped to establish Women Against Violence Against Women; Kate Millett, author of leading feminist works, including *Sexual Politics* (1980); Adrienne Rich, a widely known lesbian feminist poet; Sue Deller Ross, a professor at Georgetown University Law Center, who coauthored *Sex Discrimination and the Law: Causes and Remedies* (1983); Susan Schechter, a leading author and consultant in the battered-women's movement; Alix Kates Shulman, feminist author; and Wendy Webster Williams, a professor at Georgetown University Law Center who was a founding partner of Equal Rights Advocates.

35. Catherine A. MacKinnon, "Liberalism and the Death of Feminism," *Women's Lives, Men's Laws* (Cambridge, MA: Harvard University Press, 2007), 265.

36. Michael S. Roth, "Freud In America! 100 Years Ago This Month," *Wellness* (blog), *Huffington Post*, November 22, 2009, https://www.huffingtonpost.com/michael-roth/freud-in-america-100-year_b_294855.html.

37. Jeffrey Escoffier, "The Sexual Revolution, 1960–1980," in *glbtq: Online Encyclopedia of Gay, Lesbian, Bisexual, Transgender and Queer Culture*, 2004, http://www.glbtqarchive.com/ssh/sexual_revolution_S.pdf.

38. Louis B. Schwartz, "Morals Offenses and the Moral Penal Code," *Columbia Law Review* 63, no. 4, April 1963, 669–86.

39. Catharine MacKinnon, email to author, July 13, 2018.

40. Nadine Strossen, "Convergence of Feminist and Civil Liberties Principles in the Pornography Debate," Book Review, *NYU Law Review* 62 (April 1987), 201–35, https://digitalcommons.nyls.edu/cgi/viewcontent.cgi?article=1166&context=fac_articles_chapters.

41. Lisa Duggan, Nan D. Hunter, and Carole S. Vance, "False Promises: Feminist Antipornography Legislation," in *Sex Wars: Sexual Dissent and Political Culture*, ed. Lisa Duggan and Nan D. Hunter, 10th Anniversary Edition (New York: Taylor & Francis Group, 2006), 43.

42. Susan Sontag, "The Pornographic Imagination," 233, https://www.remittancegirl.org/wp-content/uploads/2015/07/124506505-The-Pornographic-Imagination-by-Susan-Sontag.pdf.

43. Nadine Strossen, "Convergence of Feminist and Civil Liberties Principles in the Pornography Debate," Book Review, *NYU Law Review* 62 (April 1987), 207; Sara Diamond, "Pornography: Image and Reality," in *Women Against Censorship*, ed. Varda Burstyn (Vancouver: Douglas & McIntyre, 1985), 40.

44. Strossen, "Convergence of Feminist and Civil Liberties Principles in the Pornography Debate," 206 (citing David Richards); Strossen, *Defending Pornography*, (New York: New York University Press, 2000), 151.

4. Mechelle Vinson's Supreme Trial / 1986

1. Strebeigh, *Equal*, 269.

2. Meritor Savings Bank v. Vinson, 477 U.S. 57 (1986). The details of Taylor's sleazy behavior are taken from the opinion by Justice Rehnquist, not a man known for prurient writing.

3. "Mechelle Vinson's Tangled Trials," *Washington Post*, August 11, 1986, https://www.washingtonpost.com/archive/lifestyle/1986/08/11/mechelle-vinsons-tangled-trials/40688848-d73c-4856-8a41-cff3e74277ba/?utm_term=.950f33bd148d.

4. Ibid.; see also DeNeen L. Brown, "She Said Her Boss Raped Her in a Bank Vault. Her Sexual Harassment Case Would Make Legal History," *Washington Post*, October 13, 2017, https://www.washingtonpost.com/news/retropolis/wp/2017/10/13/she-said-her-boss-raped-her-in-a-bank-vault-her-sexual-harassment-case-would-make-legal-history/?utm_term=.0fddecb6e943.

5. Adam Bernstein, "US District Court Judge John Garrett Penn, 75," *Washington Post*, September 12, 2007, http://www.washingtonpost.com/wp-dyn/content/article/2007/09/11/AR2007091102335.html.

6. Vinson v. Taylor, 23 Fair Empl. Prac. Cas. (BNA) 37 (D.D.C. 1980), 42.

7. Strebeigh, *Equal*, 246–48. Vinson had been referred to Patricia Barry, a brilliant if erratic lawyer whose financial resources were never sufficient to do the work she aspired to.

8. Ibid., 270, 523.

9. Bundy v. Jackson, 641 F.2d 934 (D.C. Cir. 1981). The findings of the trial court are included in the opinion of the court of appeals.

10. Bundy v. Jackson, citing lower court finding fact no. 37.

11. J.Y. Smith, "U.S. District Judge George L. Hart Jr. Dies at 78," *Washington Post,* May 22, 1984, https://www.washingtonpost.com/archive/local/1984/05/22/us-district-judge-george-l-hart-jr-dies-at-78/08de1c29-7120-4ce5-a327-faf638d18101/?utm_term=.21b6c9f25270.

12. Henson v. City of Dundee, 682 F.2d 897 (1982).

13. Equal Employment Opportunity Commission, "Commissioners of the EEOC," https://www.eeoc.gov/eeoc/history/35th/history/commissioners.html.

14. Robert Bork, "Dissenting Opinion," Vinson v. Taylor, 760 F. 2d 1330 (1985); Strebeigh, *Equal,* 276–79. I am indebted to Strebeigh for much of the characterization of Bork's opinion. Bork's zeal for conservative lawmaking would cost him a shot at a Supreme Court seat a couple of years later.

15. Strebeigh, *Equal,* 283, note at 525.

16. Supreme Court of the United States, "Meritor Sav. Bank v. Vinson, 1985 U.S. S. Ct. Briefs," No. 84-1979, October term, 1985, December 11, 1985, courtesy of Lexis Nexis.

17. Strebeigh, *Equal,* 286.

18. Justice Lewis F. Powell, Jr. Archives, "Justice Powell's Notes on Meritor Savings Bank v. Vinson," Washington and Lee University School of Law, *Meritor v. Vinson,* 477 U.S. 57 (1986), http://law2.wlu.edu/deptimages/powell%20archives/84-1979_MeritorSavingsVinson.pdf.

19. Ibid. Powell's notes explicitly reflect the fact that the chief justice changed his mind.

20. Joseph Sellers to author, interview, February 17, 2018. Sellers represented Mechelle Vinson on remand.

21. Katz v. Dole 709 F.2d 251 (1983); Henson v. City of Dundee, 682 F.2d 897 (1982). The available information regarding Katz and Henson's race indicates they were white. https://www.ourcampaigns.com/CandidateDetail.html?CandidateID=1017 and https://www.familytreenow.com/records/people/mcpherson/harry/bg2jukvche9wwehcbj6pgg.

22. Luke Mullins, "#HerToo: The Story of the DC Woman Who Helped Make Sexual Harassment Illegal," *Washingtonian,* March 4, 2018, https://www.washingtonian.com/2018/03/04/hertoo-40-years-ago-this-woman-helped-make-sexual-harassment-illegal-sandra-bundy/.

23. K. Sue Jewell, *From Mammy to Miss America and Beyond: Cultural Images and the Shaping of US Social Policy* (New York: Routledge, 1993).

24. Lulu Garcia-Navarro, "When Black Women's Stories of Sexual Abuse Are Excluded from the National Narrative," *Weekend Edition Sunday,* NPR, December 3, 2017, https://www.npr.org/2017/12/03/568133048/women-of-color-and-sexual-harassment.

25. Catharine MacKinnon, interview with the author.

26. Danielle McGuire to author, interview, January 10, 2018. McGuire is the author of *At the Dark End of the Street: Black Women, Rape, and Resistance — A New His-*

tory of the Civil Rights Movement from Rosa Parks to the Rise of Black Power (New York: Vintage 2011).

27. Linda Singer to author, interview, January 9, 2018.

28. Campbell Gibson and Kay Jung, "Historical Census Statistics on Population Totals by Race, 1790 to 1990, and by Hispanic Origin, 1970 to 1990, for the United States, Regions, Divisions, and States" (Population Division, Working Paper No. 56, US Census Bureau, Washington DC, September 2002), https://census.gov/content/dam/Census/library/working-papers/2002/demo/POP-twps0056.pdf.

29. Marya Annette McQuirter, Ph.D. "African American Heritage Trail: Washington, DC," Cultural Tourism DC, 2003, https://www.culturaltourismdc.org/portal/c/document_library/get_file?uuid=e9ded752-0908-42f5-9d30-e4b01555db39&groupId=701982.

30. Charles T. Lester Jr, "The History of the Lawyers' Committee for Civil Rights Under Law 1963–2008," History, Lawyer's Committee, LawyersCommittee.org, https://lawyerscommittee.org/history/.

31. Linda Singer, interview with the author, and Judith Lichtman, interview with the author, January 18, 2018. Lichtman was one of the lawyers for Paulette Barnes.

32. Alice JANSEN, Plaintiff-Appellant, v. PACKAGING CORPORATION OF AMERICA, Defendant-Appellee and Kimberly B. ELLERTH, Plaintiff-Appellant, v. BURLINGTON INDUSTRIES, INC., 123 F.3d 490 (7th Cir. 1997), https://caselaw.findlaw.com/us-7th-circuit/1004965.html. The Supreme Court took review of *Ellerth* and tried to give more guidance; see below.

33. Faragher v. Boca Raton, 524 U.S. 775 (1998); Burlington Industries, Inc. v. Ellerth, 524 U.S. 742 (1998).

34. Joanna L. Grossman, "The Culture of Compliance: The Final Triumph of Form over Substance in Sexual Harassment Law," *Harvard Women's Law Journal* 26 (2003), 3–75.

35. Ibid.

36. Lauren B. Edelman, Howard S. Erlanger, and John Lande, "Internal Dispute Resolution: The Transformation of Civil Rights in the Workplace," *Law & Society Review* 27 (1993), 497–534.

37. "HR Is Not Your Friend," PBS, https://www.pbs.org/video/hr-not-your-friend-xbfehg/.

38. Evangeline W. Swift, *Sexual Harassment in the Federal Workplace: Trends, Progress, Continuing Challenges* (Collingdale, PA: Diane, 1996), 29; Grossman, "The Culture of Compliance," 24.

39. Grossman, "The Culture of Compliance," 3.

40. Louise F. Fitzgerald, Suzanne Swan, and Karla Fischer, "Why Didn't She Just Report Him? The Psychological and Legal Implications of Women's Responses to Sexual Harassment," *Journal of Social Issues* 51, no. 1 (Spring 1995), 117–38.

41. Dylan Scott, "Harvey Weinstein's Victims Release List of 82 Women Who Say They Were Sexually Abused," *Vox*, October 28, 2017, https://www.vox.

com/culture/2017/10/28/16564486/harvey-weinstein-sexual-abuse-list-twit ter; Lisa Ryan and Hunter Harris, "An Exhaustive List of All of the Allega- tions Against Harvey Weinstein," *The Cut,* October 10, 2017, https://www.the cut.com/2017/10/list-harvey-weinstein-sexual-harassment-assault-accusations. html; Kantor and Twohey, "Harvey Weinstein Paid Off Sexual Harassment Ac- cusers for Decades."

42. Sam Reed, "Angie Everhart Says Harvey Weinstein Pleasured Himself in Front of Her," *Hollywood Reporter,* October 13, 2017, https://www.hollywoodreporter. com/news/angie-everhart-says-harvey-weinstein-pleasured-himself-front- her-1048668.

43. Harris v. Forklift Systems, Inc., 510 U.S. 17 (1993).

44. Harris v. Forklift Sys., Inc., No. 3-89-0557, 1991 WL 487444 (M.D. Tenn. Feb. 4, 1991). The Supreme Court opinion modestly reports the inquiry as "promise the guy some sex."

45. Evan D. H. White, "A Hostile Environment: How the 'Severe or Perva- sive' Requirement and the Employer's Affirmative Defense Trap Sexual Ha- rassment Plaintiffs in a Catch-22," *Boston College Law Review* 47, issue 4, no. 4 (2006), 853–90, http://lawdigitalcommons.bc.edu/cgi/viewcontent. cgi?article=2339&context=bclr. This unusually well-researched law student note by one EDH White includes these opinions, among a wealth of other re- ports from the lower courts.

46. Weiss v. Coca-Cola Bottling Company of Chicago, 990 F. 2d 333 (1993).

5. Anita Hill and Clarence Thomas: Confirming Harassment / 1991

1. Jane Mayer and Jill Abramson, *Strange Justice: The Selling of Clarence Thomas* (Boston: Houghton Mifflin Harcourt, 1994), 225.

2. Ibid., 239.

3. Gail Sheehy, "The Road to Bimini," *Vanity Fair,* September 1, 1987, https://www. vanityfair.com/news/1987/09/gary-hart-failed-presidential-campaign.

4. Matt Bai, "How Gary Hart's Downfall Forever Changed American Poli- tics," *New York Times Magazine,* September 18, 2014, https://www.nytimes. com/2014/09/21/magazine/how-gary-harts-downfall-forever-changed-ameri can-politics.html. A later article by James Fallows in *The Atlantic* posits that Re- publican operative Lee Atwater set Hart up. Fallows, "Was Gary Hart Set Up?" *The Atlantic,* November 2018. Bai has not yet conceded; his article recites a long train of adultery. See also Sheehy, "The Road To Bimini."

5. Bai, "How Gary Hart's Downfall Forever Changed American Politics."

6. Mayer and Abramson, *Strange Justice*, 31–61.

7. Ibid., 39.

8. Ibid., 62–81.

9. Anita Hill, *Speaking Truth to Power* (New York: Doubleday, 1997), 29.

10. Mayer and Abramson, *Strange Justice*, 155–62.

11. "Justice Thurgood Marshall: Retirement Press Conference," C-SPAN, June 28, 1991, https://www.c-span.org/video/?c4551573/justice-thurgood-marshall.
12. Mayer and Abramson, *Strange Justice*, 17.
13. Ibid., 215.
14. Ibid., 179.
15. Ibid., 190.
16. "Floyd Brown and Citizens United Justice Thomas," C-SPAN, September 4, 1991, https://www.c-span.org/video/?c4535130/floyd-brown-citizens-united-justice-thomas.
17. Michael Kelly, "Ted Kennedy on the Rocks," *GQ* Archives, February 1990, https://www.gq.com/story/kennedy-ted-senator-profile.
18. Ibid.
19. Mayer and Abramson, *Strange Justice*, 202–43.
20. Joe Biden, *Promises to Keep: On Life and Politics* (New York: Random House, 2007), 85.
21. Annys Shin and Libby Casey, "Anita Hill and Her 1991 Congressional Defenders to Joe Biden: You Were Part of the Problem," *Washington Post,* November 22, 2017, https://www.washingtonpost.com/lifestyle/magazine/anita-hill-and-her-1991-congressional-defenders-to-joe-biden-you-were-part-of-the-problem/2017/11/21/2303ba8a-ce69-11e7-a1a3-0d1e45a6de3d_story.html?utm_term=.a32c693485bc.
22. Ibid.
23. Mayer and Abramson, *Strange Justice*, 214.
24. Biden, *Promises to Keep*, 73.
25. Ibid., 242.
26. Michael Kelly, "Ted Kennedy on the Rocks."
27. Lessard, "Kennedy's Woman Problem," 10–14.
28. Kelly, "Ted Kennedy on the Rocks." Edited to eliminate the names of the women involved.
29. Paul Richter, "5 Panelists Identify with Thomas: Congress: Several on the Senate Committee Have Been Investigated or Had Their Character Questioned. Some Express Empathy with the Nominee," *Los Angeles Times*, October 14, 1991, http://articles.latimes.com/1991-10-14/news/mn-496_1_senate-judiciary-committee.
30. "Thomas Confirmation Hearing Day 2, Part 3," C-SPAN, September 11, 1991, https://www.c-span.org/video/?c4248145/clip-thomas-confirmation-hearing-day-2-part-3.
31. Mayer and Abramson, *Strange Justice,* 218.
32. "Thomas Confirmation Hearing Day 6, Part 3," C-SPAN, September 17, 1991, https://www.c-span.org/video/?21699-1/thomas-confirmation-hearing-day-6-part-3.
33. Nina Totenberg to author, interview, February 21, 2018. Totenberg's wonderful recollection forms the basis of this and the next several paragraphs.

34. John Danforth, *Resurrection: The Confirmation of Clarence Thomas* (New York: Viking 1994), 82–83, is the source for this paragraph.

35. Janet Napolitano, to author, interview, February 9, 2018.

36. Mayer and Abramson, *Strange Justice*, 283–84.

37. Kate Phillips, "Biden and Anita Hill, Revisited," *New York Times*, August 23, 2008, https://thecaucus.blogs.nytimes.com/2008/08/23/biden-and-anita-hill-revisited/.

38. Michael Rosenwald, "Re-watching Joe Biden's Disastrous Anita Hill Hearing," *Washington Post*, September 18, 2018, https://www.washingtonpost.com/news/retropolis/wp/2017/11/24/rewatching-joe-bidens-disastrous-anita-hill-hearing-a-sexual-harassment-inquistion/?utm_term=.da4dcbco5aea.

39. Anita Miller, ed., with preface by Nina Totenberg, *The Complete Transcripts of the Clarence Thomas–Anita Hill Hearings*, 1991 Senate Judiciary Committee, October 11, 12, 13, 1991 (Chicago: Academy Chicago, 1994), 23.

40. Mayer and Abramson, *Strange Justice*, 297.

41. Rich Connell and Louis Sahagun, "Personality in the News," *Los Angeles Times*, October 15, 1991, http://articles.latimes.com/1991-10-15/news/mn-600_1_witness-john-doggett.

42. Julia Jacobs, "Anita Hill's Testimony and Other Key Moments from the Clarence Thomas Hearings," *New York Times*, September 20, 2018, https://www.nytimes.com/2018/09/20/us/politics/anita-hill-testimony-clarence-thomas.html.

43. Janet Napolitano, interview with the author.

44. Ibid.

45. Wendy Sherman to author, interview, February 6, 2018.

46. Catharine MacKinnon, interviewed on *Charlie Rose*, PBS, October 14, 1991, https://charlierose.com/videos/20411.

47. Mayer and Abramson, *Strange Justice*, 321–23.

48. Dennis DeConcini to author, interview, April 2, 2018.

49. Mayer and Abramson, *Strange Justice*, 343–44.

50. Nina Totenberg, interview with the author.

51. James Brudney to author, interview, 2018.

52. Janet Napolitano to author, interview, February 9, 2018.

53. Jill Abramson, interview with the author, June 1, 2018, and Jane Mayer, interview with the author, April 24, 2018.

54. Lena Dunham, "Jill Abramson Is a Pushy Broad," Lenny Letter, March 31, 2017, https://www.lennyletter.com/story/jill-abramson-is-a-pushy-broad; Adam Bernstein, "Sandra Burton Dies at 62," *Washington Post*, March 1, 2004, https://www.washingtonpost.com/archive/local/2004/03/01/sandra-burton-dies-at-62/01aabaca-9541-4999-b82c-c004102926e3/?utm_term=.3f7b90d36a96.

55. *New Yorker*, Contributors, "Connie Bruck," https://www.newyorker.com/contributors/connie-bruck; Association of Magazine Media, "Ellen Pollock," http://www.magazine.org/ellen-pollock; Sydney Ember, "*New York Times* Names Former Businessweek Editor to Head Business Section," *New York Times*, April 18,

2017, https://www.nytimes.com/2017/04/18/business/media/new-york-times-el len-pollock.html; *ABC News,* "Betsy Stark," February 9, 2009, https://abcnews. go.com/WNT/betsy-stark/story?id=127628 and "Betsy Stark Bride of Barney Softness," *New York Times,* April 23, 1979, https://www.nytimes.com/1979/04/23/ archives/betsy-stark-bride-of-barney-softness.html.

56. Jane Mayer to author, interview, April 24, 2018.

57. Jean Marbella, "Who to Believe Three Years After Anita Hill Accused Clarence Thomas of Sexual Harassment, the Nation Is Still Debating..." *Baltimore Sun,* November 2, 1994, http://articles.baltimoresun.com/1994-11-02/fea tures/1994306168_1_clarence-thomas-harassment-justice-thomas.

58. United States Senate, Art and History, "Year of the Woman," November 3, 1992, https://www.senate.gov/artandhistory/history/minute/year_of_the_woman. htm.

59. Helen Dewar, "Democrats Seek to Pull Georgia's Fowler Back from Political Precipice," *Washington Post,* November 18, 1992, https://www.washingtonpost. com/archive/politics/1992/11/18/democrats-seek-to-pull-georgias-fowler-back-from-political-precipice/cdb05486-ffc4-4d9e-a227-31d9e791e4e3/?utm_term=. aeecaf19f44e.

60. Jane Mayer and Jill Abramson, "The Surreal Anita Hill," *New Yorker,* May 24, 1993.

61. Jill Abramson, "Reversal of Fortune: Image of Anita Hill, Brighter in Hindsight, Galvanizes Campaigns — A Year After Hearings, She Inspires Many Women to Challenge Incumbents — More Voters Believe Her Now," *Wall Street Journal,* October 5, 1992, http://online.wsj.com/public/resources/documents/1992anitahill. pdf.

62. Abramson to author, interview, March 20, 2018.

63. Hendrik Hertzberg, "A Cold Case," *News Desk* (blog), *New Yorker,* August 12, 2008, https://www.newyorker.com/news/hendrik-hertzberg/a-cold-case.

6. Bill Clinton, Monica Lewinsky, and Feminism's Swerve / 1992–98

1. David Margolick, "2 Women Take Stage and Stir Bar Meeting," *New York Times,* August 10, 1992, http://www.nytimes.com/1992/08/10/us/2-women-take-stage-and-stir-bar-meeting.html?pagewanted=all.

2. David Maraniss, *First in His Class: The Biography of Bill Clinton* (New York: Simon & Schuster: 1996), 179.

3. Matea Gold, Tom Hamburger, and Anu Narayanswamy, "Two Clintons. 41 Years. $3 Billion," *Washington Post,* November 19, 2015, https://www.washing tonpost.com/graphics/politics/clinton-money/.

4. Jeffrey Schmalz, "Gay Politics Goes Mainstream," *New York Times,* October 11, 1992, https://www.nytimes.com/1992/10/11/magazine/gay-politics-goes-mainstream .html.

5. Julian Zelizer, "Bill Clinton's Nearly Forgotten 1992 Sex Scandal," CNN.com,

April 6, 2016, https://www.cnn.com/2016/04/06/opinions/zelizer-presidential-election-campaign-scandals-bill-clinton/index.html.

6. San Ozan Akdag, "The Shows After the Show: Great Moments in Post-Super Bowl TV," *Rolling Stone,* January 28, 2015, https://www.rollingstone.com/tv/tv-news/the-shows-after-the-show-great-moments-in-post-super-bowl-tv-52388/. The *60 Minutes* episode is ranked as the fourth-most-watched television interview, with forty million viewers, https://en.wikipedia.org/wiki/List_of_most_watched_television_interviews.

7. Steve Kroft, "Special Edition," *60 Minutes,* CBS, January 26, 1992.

8. Janie Velencia, "Americans Didn't Believe Anita Hill," *FiveThirtyEight,* September 17, 2018, https://fivethirtyeight.com/features/americans-didnt-believe-anita-hill-how-will-they-respond-to-kavanaughs-accuser/, citing the October 1992 CNN/USA Today Gallup poll favoring Anita Hill 43 to 39.

9. David Friend, *The Naughty Nineties: The Triumph of the American Libido* (New York: Hachette, 2017); John Williams, "Tell Us 5 Things About Your Book: David Friend on 'The Naughty Nineties,'" *New York Times,* October 3, 2017, https://www.nytimes.com/2017/10/03/books/tell-us-5-things-about-your-book-david-friend-on-the-naughty-nineties.html.

10. Friend, *The Naughty Nineties.* Friend is using the analogy of Moore's law, which, he explains, forecast that "the processing power of . . . integrated circuits [computer chips] would double, even as their cost declined."

11. Jonathan Rauch, "Living with Adultery," *Prospect,* March 20, 1998, https://www.prospectmagazine.co.uk/magazine/livingwithadultery.

12. Friend, *The Naughty Nineties,* note 144, and Jonathan Rauch, "Law and Disorder: Why Too Much Due Process Is a Dangerous Thing," *New Republic,* April 30, 2001, available via Rauch's website, http://www.jonathanrauch.com/jrauch_articles/hidden_law_1_the_legal_assault/index.html.

13. Kenneth W. Starr, *The Starr Report: The Findings of Independent Counsel Kenneth W. Starr on President Clinton and the Lewinsky Affair* (Washington, DC: Public-Affairs, 1998). "During her relationship with the President, Monica Lewinsky spoke contemporaneously to several friends, family members, and counselors about the relationship. Their testimony corroborates many of the details of the sexual activity provided by Ms. Lewinsky to the OIC." Starr's list includes Catherine Allday Davis, a college friend of Monica Lewinsky's; Neysa Erbland, a high school friend of Ms. Lewinsky's; Natalie Rose Ungvari, another high school friend; Ashley Raines, a friend of Ms. Lewinsky who worked in the White House Office of Policy Development Operations; Andrew Bleiler, her high school drama teacher, with whom she had a romantic relationship while in college; Dr. Irene Kassorla, who counseled Ms. Lewinsky from 1992 through 1997; Debra Finerman, Ms. Lewinsky's aunt; Dale Young, a family friend; Kathleen Estep, a counselor for Ms. Lewinsky in November 1996. And of course, Linda Tripp.

14. Ibid.

15. Susan Schmidt, "Tripp's Tapes: How They Got to Starr Is a Complex Tale," *Wash-*

ington Post, October 11, 1998, https://www.washingtonpost.com/archive/poli tics/1998/10/11/tripps-tapes-how-they-got-to-starr-is-a-complex-tale/7be2e8f1-72b9-4bc8-8c21-43f2454f9791/?utm_term=.86bcf785cea2.

16. Quoted in Marjorie Williams, "Clinton and Women," *Vanity Fair,* May 1998, https://www.vanityfair.com/magazine/1998/05/williams199805.

17. Rebecca Kaplan, "Hillary Clinton: Monica Lewinsky a 'Narcissistic Loony Toon,'" CBS News, February 10, 2014, https://www.cbsnews.com/news/hillary-clinton-monica-lewinsky-a-narcissistic-loony-toon/.

18. "President Bill Clinton," transcript, August 17, 1998, *AllPolitics,* CNN, http://www.cnn.com/ALLPOLITICS/1998/08/17/speech/transcript.html.

19. Richard Morin and Claudia Deane, "Poll Finds Approval of Job, Not of Person," *Washington Post,* September 14, 1998, https://www.washingtonpost.com/wp-srv/politics/special/clinton/stories/poll091498.htm.

20. Peter Baker and Helen Dewar, "The Senate Acquits President Clinton," *Washington Post,* February 13, 1999, https://www.washingtonpost.com/wp-srv/poli tics/special/clinton/stories/impeach021399.htm.

21. Gloria Steinem, "Feminists and the Clinton Question," *New York Times,* March 22, 1998, https://www.nytimes.com/1998/03/22/opinion/feminists-and-the-clinton-question.html.

22. Williams, "Clinton and Women."

23. Richard A. Posner, *An Affair of State: The Investigation, Impeachment, and Trial of President Clinton* (Cambridge, MA: Harvard University Press, 1999), 137. *An Affair of State* was listed as one of the *New York Times*'s "Editors' Choice: The 11 Best Books of the Year" in 1999 and a finalist for the *Los Angeles Times* Book Prize in 2000.

24. Ibid.

25. Williams, "Clinton and Women."

26. Andrew Morton, *Monica's Story* (New York: St. Martin's, 1999), 66–67.

27. Neysa Erbland, Grand Jury Testimony, condensed transcript and concordance prepared by Office of the Independent Counsel, February 12, 1998, available at https://www.gpo.gov/fdsys/pkg/GPO-CDOC-106sdoc3/html/GPO-CDOC-106sdoc3-2.htm.

28. Morton, *Monica's Story,* 69.

29. Monica Lewinsky, Grand Jury Testimony, condensed transcript and concordance prepared by: Office of the Independent Counsel, February 12, 1998, available at https://www.gpo.gov/fdsys/pkg/GPO-CDOC-106sdoc3/html/GPO-CDOC-106sdoc3-2.htm.

30. Morton, *Monica's Story,* 82.

31. Erbland, Grand Jury Testimony.

32. Catherine Allday Davis, Grand Jury Testimony, condensed transcript and concordance prepared by Office of the Independent Counsel, March 17, 1998, https://www.gpo.gov/fdsys/pkg/GPO-CDOC-106sdoc3/html/GPO-CDOC-106sdoc3-2.htm.

33. Morton, *Monica's Story*, 76–77.
34. Lewinsky, Grand Jury Testimony.
35. Marcia Lewis, Grand Jury Testimony, condensed transcript and concordance prepared by Office of the Independent Counsel, March 17, 1998, https://www.gpo.gov/fdsys/pkg/CDOC-105hdoc310/html/CDOC-105hdoc310.htm, at note 294.
36. Condensed transcript and concordance prepared by Office of the Independent Counsel, March 17, 1998, https://www.gpo.gov/fdsys/pkg/CDOC-105hdoc310/html/CDOC-105hdoc310.htm, at note 462.
37. Monica Lewinsky, transcript of August 6, 1998, grand jury appearance, available at https://www.abqjournal.com/star_htm/lewinsky0806.html.
38. White House, "The Clinton Presidency: Eight Years of Peace, Progress and Prosperity," Timeline of Major Actions, ClintonWhiteHouse5.archives.gov, https://clintonwhitehouse5.archives.gov/WH/Accomplishments/eightyears-02.html.
39. Williams, "Clinton and Women."

7. Life Among the Ruins of the Feminist Collision with Bill Clinton / 1998–2016

1. Lisa Chase to author, interview, 2018.
2. Francine Prose, "New York Supergals Love That Naughty Prez," *New York Observer,* February 9, 1998, https://observer.com/1998/02/new-york-supergals-love-that-naughty-prez/.
3. Lisa Chase, interview with the author.
4. Prose, "New York Supergals Love That Naughty Prez."
5. Tina Brown, "Fax from Washington," *New Yorker,* February 16, 1998. https://www.newyorker.com/magazine/1998/02/16/fax-from-washington.
6. Jones v. Clinton, 990 F. Supp. 657 (1998). Quotes in this paragraph are from the court transcript. On a motion to dismiss, the court takes the plaintiff's statement as true. The facts in the text are from Paula Jones's statement, as recited in the court's opinion granting the motion to dismiss.
7. Ibid.
8. Catharine MacKinnon, interview with the author. I am indebted to MacKinnon for the insight about *Jones v. Clinton.*
9. Susan Faludi, *Backlash: The Undeclared War Against American Women,* 15th anniversary ed. (New York: Three Rivers Press, 2006).
10. "Is Feminism Dead?," *Time.*
11. "The Marriage Crunch," *Newsweek.*
12. Daniel McGinn, "Marriage by the Numbers," *Newsweek,* June 4, 2006, https://www.newsweek.com/marriage-numbers-110797. The study has since been thoroughly debunked and *Newsweek* retracted the story. Megan Garber, "Marriage By the Numbers," *The Atlantic,* June 2, 2016.
13. *Time,* "Is Feminism Dead?"; Wendy Kaminer, "Feminism's Identity Crisis," *The Atlantic,* October 1993, https://www.theatlantic.com/magazine/archive/1993/10/feminisms-identity-crisis/304921/.

14. Abigail Pogrebin, "How Do You Spell Ms.," *New York*, October 30, 2011, http://nymag.com/news/features/ms-magazine-2011-11/.

15. Deirdre Carmody, "Power to the Readers: Ms. Thrives Without Ads," *New York Times*, July 22, 1991, https://timesmachine.nytimes.com/timesmachine/1991/07/22/594091.html?pageNumber=46.

16. Pogrebin, "How Do You Spell Ms."; Lucinda Franks, "Dissension Among Feminists: The Rift Widens," *New York Times*, August 29, 1975, https://www.nytimes.com/1975/08/29/archives/dissension-among-feminists-the-rift-widens.html. In 1975, contributing editor Ellen Willis, cofounder of the Redstockings, sent in her resignation: "Ms.'s politics [include] a mushy, sentimental idea of sisterhood designed to obscure political conflicts between women . . . I hope that this explanation will be received as the honest feminist criticism it is meant to be."

17. Pogrebin, "How Do You Spell Ms."

18. Jennifer Baumgardner and Amy Richards, *Manifesta: Young Women, Feminism, and the Future,* 10th anniversary ed. (New York: Farrar, Straus, and Giroux, 2010), 116.

19. Pogrebin, "How Do You Spell Ms."

20. Baumgardner and Richards, *Manifesta*, 10th anniversary ed., 116.

21. Ibid., xxi–xxii.

22. Third Wave Foundation, "About Us," ThirdWaveFoundation.org, https://web.archive.org/web/20121007020253/http://www.thirdwavefoundation.org/about-us/history/.

23. Third Wave Fund, "History and Past Initiatives: Third Wave History; Founders of Third Wave Fund," http://thirdwavefund.org/history—past-initiatives.html. The women are Dawn Lundy Martin, Amy Richards, Cat Gund, Rebecca Walker.

24. Nancy Whittier, "From the Second to the Third Wave: Continuity and Change in Grassroots Feminism," in *The US Women's Movement in Global Perspective,* ed. Lee Ann Banaszak (Lanham, MD: Rowman & Littlefield, 2006), 45–67.

25. Baumgardner and Richards, *Manifesta*, 10th anniversary ed., 80.

26. Jennifer Baumgardner, "Is There a Fourth Wave? Does It Matter?" Feminist.com, 2011, https://www.feminist.com/resources/artspeech/genwom/baumgardner2011.html.

27. Baumgardner and Richards, *Manifesta*, 10th anniversary ed., 215.

28. Jennifer Baumgardner and Amelia Richards, "In Defense of Monica," *Nation*, December 21, 1998, https://static1.squarespace.com/static/533b171fe4b0c551757d9ba3/t/5379038fe4b0d45559671234/1400439695119/1998_in-defense-monica.pdf.

29. Baumgardner and Richards, *Manifesta*, 53.

30. "Hillary Clinton Speaks Out on Lewinsky Accusations," *Today*, January 27, 1998, http://www.msnbc.com/today/watch/hillary-clinton-speaks-out-on-lewinsky-accusations-44498499720.

31. Sidney Blumenthal, *The Clinton Wars* (New York: Farrar, Straus and Giroux, 2003), 339–42; Gail Sheehy, *Hillary's Choice* (New York: Random House, 1999),

14–15; Carl Bernstein, *A Woman In Charge: The Life of Hillary Rodham Clinton* (New York: Random House, 2007), 484–36; Jeffrey Toobin, *A Vast Conspiracy: The Real Story of the Sex Scandal That Nearly Brought Down a President* (New York: Random House, 1999), 242–43; Hillary Rodham Clinton, *Living History* (New York: Simon & Schuster, 2003), 441–48.

32. Sheehy, *Hillary's Choice*, 294–25, 404.

33. Adam Nagourney, "Hillary Clinton Begins Pre-Campaign in a New Role for Her," *New York Times,* July 8, 1999, https://www.nytimes.com/1999/07/08/nyre gion/hillary-clinton-begins-pre-campaign-in-a-new-role-for-her.html.

34. Bernstein, *A Woman In Charge.*

35. Telly Davidson, *Culture War: How the '90s Made Us Who We Are Today (Whether We Like It or Not)* (Jefferson, NC: McFarland 2016); Sally Bedell Smith, "White House Civil War," *Vanity Fair,* October 1, 2007, https://www.vanityfair.com/news/2007/11/clinton200711.

36. David W. Moore, "'Clinton Factor' May Be Hurting Gore in Presidential Race," Gallup News Serice, March 16, 2000, https://news.gallup.com/poll/3085/clin ton-factor-may-hurting-gore-presidential-race.aspx.

37. Mark J. Wattier, "The Clinton Factor: The Effects of Clinton's Personal Image in 2000 Presidential Primaries and in the General Election," paper presented at the annual meeting of the American Political Science Association, Boston, August 2002, http://citeseerx.ist.psu.edu/viewdoc/download?doi=10.1.1.514.7882&r ep=rep1&type=pdf.

38. Carter Eskew and Bob Shrum, in *Electing the President, 2000,* ed. Kathleen Hall Jamieson and Paul Waldman (Philadelphia: University of Pennsylvania Press, 2001), 49–78; Gerald M. Pomper, "The 2000 Presidential Election: Why Gore Lost," *Political Science Quarterly,* Vol. 116, Issue 2, Summer 2001, page 201, https://www.uvm.edu/~dguber/POLS125/articles/pomper.htm.

39. Gail Collins and Bret Stephens, "Thirteen Ways of Looking at a Sex Scandal," *New York Times,* November 21, 2017, https://www.nytimes.com/2017/11/21/opin ion/sex-scandal-clinton-moore.html.

40. Morris Fiorina, Samuel Abrams, and Jeremy Pope, "The 2000 US Presidential Election: Can Retrospective Voting Be Saved?" *British Journal of Political Science* 33, no. 2 (April 2003), 163–87, https://web.stanford.edu/~mfiorina/2000%20 BJPS%20Revision2_Paper.pdf.

41. Roger Simon, *Divided We Stand: How Al Gore Beat George Bush and Lost the Presidency* (New York: Crown, 2001), 195.

42. Center for Reproductive Rights, "The Bush Global Gag Rule: Endangering Women's Health, Free Speech and Democracy," July 1, 2003, https://www.re productiverights.org/document/the-bush-global-gag-rule-endangering-wom ens-health-free-speech-and-democracy.

43. Stenberg v. Carhart, 530 U.S. 914 (2000).

44. Gonzales v. Carhart, 550 U.S. 124 (2007).

45. Gabriel Sherman, *The Loudest Voice in the Room: How the Brilliant, Bombastic*

Roger Ailes Built Fox News — and Divided a Country (New York: Random House, 2014), 193–94. Much of the material in the next two paragraphs comes from Sherman's authoritative biography.

46. Ibid., 225.

47. Ibid., 234.

48. John Heilemann and Mark Halperin, *Game Change: Obama and the Clintons, McCain and Palin, and the Race of a Lifetime* (New York: Harper Collins, 2010), 20.

49. Ezra Klein, "The Daschle-Obama Connection," *American Prospect,* December 11, 2008, http://prospect.org/article/daschle-obama-connection.

50. Ibid., 36.

51. University of Virginia Miller Center, Presidential Oral Histories: Bill Clinton Presidency, "Thomas Daschle Oral History, Senator, South Dakota," December 19, 2007, https://millercenter.org/the-presidency/presidential-oral-histories/thomas-daschle-oral-history-senator-south-dakota.

52. Klein, "The Daschle-Obama Connection."

53. Heilemann and Halperin, *Game Change,* 36.

54. David Paul Kuhn, "Iowa Voters Reveal Unexpected Trends," *Politico,* January 4, 2008, https://www.politico.com/story/2008/01/iowa-voters-reveal-unexpected-trends-007706.

55. "2008 Iowa Democratic Caucuses," Wikipedia, https://en.wikipedia.org/wiki/Iowa_Democratic_caucuses,_2008#cite_note-CNN2-10.

56. Associated Press, "Feminists Sharply Divided Between Clinton, Obama," *Politico,* May 12, 2008, https://www.politico.com/story/2008/05/feminists-sharply-divided-between-clinton-obama-010265.

57. Michelle Goldberg, "3 A.M. for Feminism," *New Republic,* June 6, 2008, https://newrepublic.com/article/61960/3-am-feminism.

58. Rebecca Traister, *Big Girls Don't Cry: The Election That Changed Everything for American Women* (New York: Simon & Schuster, 2010), 166–69.

59. Ibid., 169.

60. Jodi Kantor, *The Obamas* (Boston: Little, Brown 2012), acknowledgments.

61. Annie Lowrey, "In Obama's High-Level Appointments, the Scales Still Tip Toward Men," *New York Times,* August 26, 2013, https://www.nytimes.com/2013/08/27/us/politics/under-obama-little-progress-on-high-level-jobs-for-women.html.

8. Feminism Reborn: Online, On Campus / 2003–11

1. Carlene Bauer, "How *Sassy* (Should Have) Changed My Life," *n+1,* July 2007, https://nplusonemag.com/online-only/online-only/how-sassy-should-have-changed-my-life/.

2. Ibid.

3. Jacob Weisberg to author, interview, April 2018.

4. Andi Zeisler to author, interview, April 18, 2018.

5.   Lisa Jervis, "Editors' Letter: Premiere," *Bitch,* Winter 1996, https://www.bitch-media.org/article/introduction.

6.   Heather Wood Rudulph, "Get That Life: How I Co-Founded Bitch Media," *Cosmopolitan,* May 2, 2016, https://www.cosmopolitan.com/career/a57736/andi-zeisler-bitch-media-get-that-life/.

7.   Jessica Valenti to author, interview, May 24, 2018. All quotes from Valenti in this section are from this interview.

8.   Jill Filipovic, Wikipedia, https://en.wikipedia.org/wiki/Jill_Filipovic; https://en.wikipedia.org/wiki/Amanda_Marcotte#cite_note-4.

9.   Hirshman, *Victory,* 295–97.

10. Valenti interview with the author.

11. Rebecca Traister to author, interview, June 5, 2018.

12. Traister, *Big Girls Don't Cry,* 172.

13. Emily Bazelon, Meghan O'Rourke, Hanna Rosin, and Julia Turner, "They Almost Called It Moxie," *Slate,* January 16, 2018, https://slate.com/human-interest/2018/01/a-conversation-with-the-founders-of-doublex.html.

14. Pam Spaulding, "About Pam's House Blend," Pamspaulding.net, July 1, 2013, http://www.pamspaulding.net/p/about-pams-house-blend.html.

15. Much of this section is from Pamela Merritt, interview with the author, September 14, 2018.

16. Pamela Merritt, "Well, Allow Me to Retort . . ." *Angry Black Bitch* (blog), February 19, 2009, http://angryblackbitch.blogspot.com/2009/02/well-allow-me-to-retort.html.

17. Pamela Merritt, "I'm Worried Too, Ms. Steinem . . ." *Angry Black Bitch* (blog), January 8, 2008, http://angryblackbitch.blogspot.com/2008/01/im-worried-too-ms-steinem.html.

18. Anna Holmes to author, interview, April 15, 2018; Jill Filipovic, "Get That Life: How I Founded Jezebel and Became a *New York Times* Columnist," *Cosmopolitan,* May 19, 2014, https://www.cosmopolitan.com/career/advice/a6858/get-that-life-anna-holmes-jezebel/.

19. Anna Holmes and Raghu Manavalan, "My Money Story: Writer Anna Holmes," *Marketplace,* June 27, 2014, https://www.marketplace.org/2014/06/27/your-money/family-money/my-money-story-writer-anna-holmes; Anna Holmes, "Why I've Decided I'm Not Having Kids," *Marie Claire,* March 19, 2015, https://www.marieclaire.com/sex-love/news/a13774/anna-holmes-choice-not-to-have-kids/

20. Moe, "The Annotated Guide to Making Faith Hill 'Hot,'" *Jezebel,* July 16, 2007, https://jezebel.com/278978/the-annotated-guide-to-making-faith-hill-hot; Moe, "Here's Our Winner! 'Redbook' Shatters Our 'Faith' In Well, Not Publishing, But Maybe God," *Jezebel,* July 16, 2007, https://jezebel.com/278919/heres-our-winner-redbook-shatters-our-faith-in-well-not-publishing-but-maybe-god.

21. Jennifer, "Fundamentalist Fashion: Not So Different Than High Design," *Jeze-*

bel, April 22, 2008, https://jezebel.com/382771/fundamentalist-fashion-not-so-different-than-high-design.

22. Andi Zeisler, interview with the author.

23. Moe, "You Know, Models Are In, Like, the Five Percent of People Who Look Like Models," *Jezebel*, February 1, 2008, https://jezebel.com/351740/you-know-models-are-in-like-the-five-percent-of-people-who-look-like-models.

24. Eleanor Morgan, "Unmasked: The Blogging Model Who Rocked the World of Fashion," *Guardian*, July 28, 2009, https://www.theguardian.com/lifeandstyle/2009/jul/29/tatiana-jezebel-jenna-sauers.

25. Jenna Sauers, "Meet Terry Richardson, The World's Most F—ked Up Fashion Photographer," *Jezebel*, March 16, 2010, https://jezebel.com/5494634/meet-terry-richardson-the-worlds-most-fked-up-fashion-photographer.

26. Jenna Sauers, "Exclusive: More Models Come Forward with Allegations Against Fashion Photographer," *Jezebel*, March 18, 2010, https://jezebel.com/5495699/exclusive-more-models-come-forward-with-allegations-against-fashion-photographer.

27. Rebecca Traister, *Good and Mad: The Revolutionary Power of Women's Anger* (New York: Simon and Schuster, 2018).

28. The more neutral phrase "acquaintance rape" is also frequently used and is probably the better descriptor, but date rape appeared first. Not all campus rapes are date or acquaintance rapes, of course.

29. Brownmiller, *Against Our Will*, 16–30.

30. Gary Martin, "The Meaning and Origin of the Expression: Date Rape," Phrase Finder, https://www.phrases.org.uk/meanings/108225.html.

31. Brownmiller, *Against Our Will*, 257.

32. "Rape Is a Crime Often Unpunished," *Anderson (Indiana) Daily Bulletin*, November 15, 1973, https://www.newspapers.com/image/18410100/.

33. Jodi Gold and Susan Villari, eds., *Just Sex: Students Rewrite the Rules on Sex, Violence, Equality and Activism* (Lanham, MD: Rowman and Littlefield, 2000), 6.

34. Alexander v. Yale, 631 F.2d 178 (1980). The procedural history in this case is complicated, but the principle was established.

35. "Date Rape: The Story of an Epidemic and Those Who Deny It," *Ms.* October 1985; The full report appeared in an academic journal, https://www.ncbi.nlm.nih.gov/pubmed/3494755, and in 1988 by Harper and Row under the title *I Never Called It Rape*.

36. Vanessa Grigoriadis, *Blurred Lines: Rethinking Sex, Power, and Consent on Campus* (Boston: Houghton Mifflin Harcourt, 2017), 112–13; Michelle Goldberg, Shining a Light on Campus Rape," *New York Times Book Review*, September 7, 2017, https://www.nytimes.com/2017/09/07/books/review/shining-a-light-on-campus-rape.html.

37. Gebser v. Lago Vista Independent School District, 524 US 274 (1998).

38. Davis v. Monroe County Board of Education, 526 US 629 (1999).

39. Department of Education, Office for Civil Rights, "Dear Colleague Letter: Sexual Violence," April 4, 2011, https://obamawhitehouse.archives.gov/sites/default/files/dear_colleague_sexual_violence.pdf.

40. Andrea Pino and Annie Clark to author, interviews.

41. Stephen Schulhofer to author, interview, May 18, 2018.

42. Katie J.M. Baker "My Weekend In America's So-Called 'Rape Capital,'" *Jezebel*, May 10, 2012, https://jezebel.com/5908472/my-weekend-in-americas-so-called-rape-capital.

43. Richard Pérez-Peña, "College Groups Connect to Fight Sexual Assault," *New York Times*, March 19, 2013, https://www.nytimes.com/2013/03/20/education/activists-at-colleges-network-to-fight-sexual-assault.html.

44. Christopher Robbins, "Spurned By Columbia, Student Says NYPD Mistreated Her While Reporting Rape," *Gothamist*, May 18, 2014, https://web.archive.org/web/20150524012014/http://gothamist.com/2014/05/18/spurned_by_columbia_student_says_ny.php.

45. Jeremy Bauer-Wolf, "Mattress Protest and Its Aftermath," *Inside Higher Ed*, July 24, 2017, https://www.insidehighered.com/news/2017/07/24/media-circus-surrounding-mattress-girl-case-changed-conversation-sexual-assault.

46. Jia Tolentino, "Is There a Smarter Way to Think About Sexual Assault On Campus?," *New Yorker*, February 12 & 19, 2018, https://www.newyorker.com/magazine/2018/02/12/is-there-a-smarter-way-to-think-about-sexual-assault-on-campus. News stories at the time of Sulkowicz's protest cast her as female. The Tolentino piece, written in 2018, notes that Sulkowicz "identifies as non-binary, and uses the gender-neutral pronouns 'they' and 'them.'" When referring to Sulkowicz in the here and now, I will of course defer to their preference. Their importance in this book is mostly situated at a time when the media, which was part of their impact, was identifying Sulkowicz as female.

47. PBS Online, "1987: ACT UP (Aids Coalition to Unleash Power) Is Founded in New York City," Making History 1980–present, Out of the Past, site produced by Candide Media Works, Inc., in association with Out of the Past Film Project, http://www.pbs.org/outofthepast/past/p6/1987.html.

48. Zachary Small, "Queer Identity in the MeToo Movement: A Conversation with Emma Sulkowicz," *Hyperallergic*, August 31, 2018, https://hyperallergic.com/458257/conversation-with-emma-sulkowicz/.

49. Dana Bolger, Alexandra Brodsky, "Sexual Assault Survivor Activists Launch 'Know Your IX' Campaign," *Huffington Post*, April 18, 2013, https://www.huffingtonpost.com/dana-bolger/sexual-assault-survivor-a_b_3104714.html.

50. National Advisory Committee on Violence Against Women, *Final Report* (Washington, DC: Department of Justice, June 2012), https://www.justice.gov/sites/default/files/ovw/legacy/2012/11/30/nac-rpt.pdf.

51. Catherine E. Lhamon, Assistant Secretary, United States Department of Education, Office for Civil Rights, "Questions and Answers on Title IX and Sexual

Violence," April 29, 2014, https://www2.ed.gov/about/offices/list/ocr/docs/qa-201404-title-ix.pdf.

52. Samuel R. Bagenstos, "What Went Wrong With Title IX?" *Washington Monthly*, September/October 2015, https://washingtonmonthly.com/magazine/septoct-2015/what-went-wrong-with-title-ix/.

53. Katha Pollitt, "Why Is 'Yes Means Yes' So Misunderstood?" *Nation*, October 27, 2014, https://www.thenation.com/article/why-yes-means-yes-so-misunderstood/. Cultural sources attribute the doctrine to the Antioch College rules of 1990.

54. Rebecca Beitsch, "#MeToo Movement Has Lawmakers Talking About Consent," PEW Stateline, January 23, 2018, https://www.pewtrusts.org/en/research-and-analysis/blogs/stateline/2018/01/23/metoo-movement-has-lawmakers-talking-about-consent.

55. Christine Helwick, "Affirmative Consent, the New Standard," *Inside Higher Ed*, October 23, 2014, https://www.insidehighered.com/views/2014/10/23/campuses-must-wrestle-affirmative-consent-standard-sexual-assault-essay.

56. Gideon v. Wainwright, 372 U.S. 335, 1963.

57. Elizabeth Bartholet et al., "Rethink Harvard's Sexual Harassment Policy," *Boston Globe*, October 15, 2014, https://www.bostonglobe.com/opinion/2014/10/14/rethink-harvard-sexual-harassment-policy/HFDDiZN7nU2UwuUuWMnqbM/story.html. The twenty-eight faculty members, in addition to Bartholet, were Scott Brewer, Robert Clark, Alan Dershowitz, Christine Desan, Charles Donahue, Einer Elhauge, Allen Ferrell, Martha Field, Jesse Fried, Nancy Gertner, Janet Halley, Bruce Hay, Philip Heymann, David Kennedy, Duncan Kennedy, Robert Mnookin, Charles Nesson, Charles Ogletree, Richard Parker, Mark Ramseyer, David Rosenberg, Lewis Sargentich, David Shapiro, Henry Steiner, Jeannie Suk, Lucie White, and David Wilkins.

58. Peter Jacobs, "Harvard Professor Fears the School's Rape Policy Will Punish Students for Drunk Sex," *Business Insider*, January 7, 2015, https://www.businessinsider.com/elizabeth-bartholet-harvard-students-punished-drunk-sex-2015-1.

59. Andrew M. Duehren, "A Call to Arms," *Harvard Crimson*, May 29, 2015, https://www.thecrimson.com/article/2015/5/28/janet-halley-title-ix/.

60. Janet Halley, *Split Decisions: How and Why to Take a Break from Feminism* (Princeton, NJ: Princeton University Press, 2006); Robyn Wiegman, "Dear Ian," *Duke Journal of Gender Law & Policy*, Vol. 11, Issue 1, Spring 2004, 93, https://scholarship.law.duke.edu/cgi/viewcontent.cgi?referer=https://en.wikipedia.org/&httpsredir=1&article=1084&context=djglp.

61. Emily Shire, "Penn Law Profs Revolt over Sex Assault Rules," *Daily Beast*, February 23, 2015, https://www.thedailybeast.com/penn-law-profs-revolt-over-sex-assault-rules.

62. Jed Rubenfeld, "Mishandling Rape," *New York Times*, November 15, 2014, https://www.nytimes.com/2014/11/16/opinion/sunday/mishandling-rape.html.

63. Jed Rubenfeld, "The Riddle of Rape-By-Deception and the Myth of Sexual Autonomy," *Yale Law Journal* 122, no. 6, (April 2013), https://www.yalelawjournal.org/article/the-riddle-of-rape-by-deception-and-the-myth-of-sexual-autonomy.

64. Nora Caplan-Bricker, "There's a Legal War over the Definition of Rape," *New Republic*, May 6, 2014, https://newrepublic.com/article/117630/jed-rubenfeld-rape-law-feminists-debate-force-versus-non-consent.

65. Tom Dougherty, "No Way Around Consent: A Reply to Rubenfeld on 'Rape-by-Deception,'" *Yale Law Journal* 123, (December 1, 2013), https://www.yalelawjournal.org/forum/no-way-around-consent-a-reply-to-rubenfeld-on-rape-by-deception; Nora Caplan-Bricker, "There's a Legal War Over the Definition of Rape," *The New Republic*, May 6, 2014, https://newrepublic.com/article/117630/jed-rubenfeld-rape-law-feminists-debate-force-versus-non-consent.

66. Dahlia Lithwick and Susan Matthews, "Investigation at Yale Law School," *Slate*, October 5, 2018, https://slate.com/news-and-politics/2018/10/jed-rubenfeld-amy-chua-yale-law-school.html.

67. Anne Ryman, "Faculty Votes to Restrict Teacher-Student Dating," *USA Today*, January 26, 2015, https://www.usatoday.com/story/news/nation/2015/01/26/faculty-votes-to-restrict-teacher-student-dating/22382637/. Stuart Wolpert, "Professor Says University Codes Should Not Restrict Faculty-Student Dating," UCLA Newsroom, University of California Los Angeles, October 11, 2007, http://newsroom.ucla.edu/releases/in-choosing-dating-partners-where-39521. Caroline Forell, "What's Wrong with Faculty-Student Sex? The Law School Context," *Journal of Legal Education* 47, no. 1 (March 1997), 47, https://www.jstor.org/stable/42893469?seq=1#page_scan_tab_contents. For years, universities had been circling around the sensitive subject of student/faculty sexual relations. By 2014, the consensus seemed to be that faculty should stay away from students whom they teach, evaluate, or supervise. Even with this relatively sensible line-drawing, academics, many with a long history of happy marriages to their former teaching assistants, generated some resistance to the restrictions, preferring to categorize all sex as in a realm of special human autonomy. There, again, law schools often led the resistance. There is some obvious overlap between the severity of the rape rules and the rules about what some call "amorous" campus life.

68. Stephanie Kirchgaessner and Jessica Glenza, "'No Accident' Brett Kavanaugh's Female Law Clerks 'Looked Like Models,' Yale Professor Told Students," *Guardian*, September 20, 2018, https://www.theguardian.com/us-news/2018/sep/20/brett-kavanaugh-supreme-court-yale-amy-chua.

69. Craig Silverman, "The Year in Media Errors and Corrections 2014," *MediaWire* (blog), Poynter.org, December 18, 2014, https://web.archive.org/web/20150315015756/http://www.poynter.org/news/mediawire/306801/the-year-in-media-errors-and-corrections-2014/.

70. Stephen Schulhofer, interview with the author.

71. American Law Institute, "About ALI," https://www.ali.org/about-ali/; see also "The A.L.I. at Fifty," *American Bar Association Journal* 59 (July 1973), 761–62.

72. Ronald D. Rotunda, "Increased Controversy over the Future of American Law Institute," *Verdict, Justia,* June 20, 2016, https://verdict.justia.com/2016/06/20/increased-controversy-future-american-law-institute. The description of the elite status of the ALI in this and the next paragraph come from Rotunda's article in *Verdict.*

73. Ibid.

74. Margot Canaday, "We Colonials: Sodomy Laws in America," *Nation,* September 22, 2008, https://www.thenation.com/article/we-colonials-sodomy-laws-america/.

75. Of the plethora of writing on the subject, see especially James J. Tomkovicz, "On Teaching Rape: Reasons, Risks, and Rewards," *Yale Law Journal* 102, no. 2 (1992), https://digitalcommons.law.yale.edu/ylj/vol102/iss2/4.

76. Stephen J. Schulhofer, *Unwanted Sex: The Culture of Intimidation and the Failure of Law* (Cambridge, MA: Harvard University Press, 1998), 283. The proposal is much longer and includes issues like age and inebriation, but this is one of the most difficult and controversial matters.

77. Women's Center Board [Laura Blake, Elizabeth Deutsch, Diana Ofosu, Diana Saverin, Natalia Thompson, Sally Walstrom and Quingan Zhou], "Women's Center Board Members: Responding Maturely to Misogyny," *Yale Daily News,* October 15, 2010, https://yaledailynews.com/blog/2010/10/15/womens-center-board-members-responding-maturely-to-misogyny/.

78. Emily Yoffe, "How *The Hunting Ground* Blurs the Truth," *DoubleX* (blog), *Slate,* June 1, 2015, http://www.slate.com/articles/news_and_politics/doublex/2015/06/the_hunting_ground_a_closer_look_at_the_influential_documentary_reveals.html.

79. Ben Adler, "Heresy on the Right: A Handful of New Web Sites Try to Rewire Conservative Media," *Columbia Journalism Review,* May/June 2009, https://archives.cjr.org/feature/heresy_on_the_right.php.

80. Ashe Schow, "Has the Federal Government Ever Had Sex?" *Washington Examiner,* June 15, 2015, www.washingtonexaminer.com/has-the-federal-government-ever-had-sex/article/2565963

81. Jeannie Suk Gersen, "St. Paul's School and a New Definition Of Rape," *News Desk* (blog), *New Yorker,* November 3, 2015, https://www.newyorker.com/news/news-desk/st-pauls-school-and-a-new-definition-of-rape.

82. Jess Bidgood, "Owen Labrie of St Paul's School Is Found Not Guilty of Main Rape Charge," *New York Times,* August 28, 2015, https://www.nytimes.com/2015/08/29/us/st-pauls-school-rape-trial-owen-labrie.html.

83. Catharine MacKinnon to author, email, October 29, 2018.

84. Meritor Savings Bank v. Vinson, 477 U.S. 57 (1986).

85. Catharine A. MacKinnon, "Rape Redefined," *Harvard Law & Policy Review* 10, no. 2 (2016), 431–77, at 476, http://harvardlpr.com/wp-content/uploads/2016/06/10.2_6_MacKinnon.pdf.

86. Ibid. at 455. MacKinnon, like most sensible scholars, holds ALI reporter Stephen Schulhofer in the highest regard. At the beginning of her article she says, "This article is partly in dialogue with The American Law Institute's ("ALI") process on revision of the Model Penal Code § 213 on Sexual Assault and Related Offenses since 2014. The superb research and illuminating writing by Stephen J. Schulhofer and Erin E. Murphy, Reporters — formulating an expanded, specified, and central role for consent in the law of sexual assault, building on the informed and incisive scholarship of Stephen J. Schulhofer over several decades — provided a rich resource for analysis and enabled streamlined citations, for which I am greatly in debt." I would be remiss if I did not admit that Schulhofer is also a longtime friend of mine.

87. Schulhofer to author, emails, October 27 and 28, 2018.

9. Roger Ailes and Donald Trump: Republicans Corner the Market on Sex Abuse / 2015–16

1. Jennifer Senior, "Review: Megyn Kelly Tells Tales out of Fox News in Her Memoir, 'Settle for More,'" *New York Times,* November 10, 2016, https://www.nytimes.com/2016/11/12/books/review-megyn-kelly-tells-tales-out-of-fox-news-in-her-memoir-settle-for-more.html.

2. Caitlin Flanagan, "Can Megyn Kelly Escape Her Past?" *The Atlantic,* March 2017, https://www.theatlantic.com/magazine/archive/2017/03/can-megyn-kelly-escape-her-past/513842/.

3. "Megyn Kelly and the Question That Changed Her Life Forever," *CBS Sunday Morning,* April 3, 2016, https://www.cbsnews.com/news/megyn-kelly-and-the-question-that-changed-her-life-forever/. All the quotes from the exchange are from this report.

4. Kayla Epstein, "Trump Responds to Megyn Kelly's Questions on Misogyny — with More Misogyny," *Guardian,* August 6, 2015, https://www.theguardian.com/us-news/2015/aug/06/donald-trump-misogyny-republican-debate-megyn-kelly.

5. Tim Marcin, "Megyn Kelly Slams Donald Trump White House For "Hypocrisy" over Anger at Samantha Bee," *Newsweek,* June 1, 2018, http://www.newsweek.com/megyn-kelly-slams-trump-white-house-hypocrisy-samantha-bee-vulgar-joke-954335.

6. Holly Yan, "Donald Trump's 'Blood' Comment About Megyn Kelly Draws Outrage," CNN.com, August 8, 2015, https://www.cnn.com/2015/08/08/politics/donald-trump-cnn-megyn-kelly-comment/index.html.

7. Megyn Kelly, *Settle for More* (New York: Harper Collins, 2016), 262.

8. Ibid., 275.

9. Sherman, "The Revenge of Roger's Angels."

10. Nancy Erika Smith to author, interview, January 22, 2018.

11. Carlson v. Ailes, "Complaint and Jury Demand," Filed with Civil Division of the Superior Court of New Jersey Law Division: Bergen County, July 6, 2016,

https://www.documentcloud.org/documents/2941030-Carlson-Complaint-Filed.html.

12. Gabriel Sherman to author, interview, June 13, 2018.

13. Sherman, "The Revenge of Roger's Angels." Sherman, interview with the author.

14. Brian Flood, "That Time Gretchen Carlson Walked Off 'Fox & Friends' Over Sexism," video, *The Wrap,* July 7, 2016, https://www.thewrap.com/gretchen-carlson-walked-off-fox-and-friends-over-sexism/.

15. Gretchen Carlson, "Sexual Harassment: Not Just a Women's Issue," *Huffington Post,* June 17, 2016, https://www.huffingtonpost.com/gretchen-carlson/sexual-harassment-not-jus_b_7609170.html.

16. Melissa Wylie, "LAW: The Attorney Helping Gretchen Carlson Topple a TV Titan," *Bizwomen, Business Journals,* August 3, 2016, https://www.bizjournals.com/bizwomen/news/profiles-strategies/2016/08/law-the-attorney-helping-gretchen-carlson-topple-a.html?page=all.

17. Nancy Erika Smith, interview with the author.

18. Carlson v. Ailes, "Complaint and Jury Demand," Filed with Civil Division of the Superior Court of New Jersey Law Division: Bergen County, July 6, 2016.

19. Sherman, "The Revenge of Roger's Angels." Much of the information about Carlson and Kelly's roles in taking down Roger Ailes comes from Sherman's outstanding, courageous, and persistent reporting.

20. Gabriel Sherman, "6 More Women Allege That Roger Ailes Sexually Harassed Them," *The Cut, New York Magazine,* July 9, 2016, https://www.thecut.com/2016/07/six-more-women-allege-ailes-sexual-harassment.html.

21. Chris Cillizza, "How Roger Ailes Helped Create Donald Trump," *The Point with Chris Cillizza* (blog), CNN.com, May 18, 2017, https://www.cnn.com/2017/05/18/politics/roger-ailes-donald-trump/index.html.

22. Erik Wemple, "'Fox & Friends' and Trump: An Appreciation of Well-Choreographed Sycophancy," *Washington Post,* November 8, 2016, https://www.washingtonpost.com/blogs/erik-wemple/wp/2016/11/08/fox-friends-and-trump-an-appreciation-of-well-choreographed-sycophancy/?noredirect=on&utm_term=.c1886f1b432f.

23. Sherman, "The Revenge of Roger's Angels."

24. Michael M. Grynbaum and Emily Steel, "With Fox News in Tumult, Another Executive, Bill Shine, Is Ousted," *New York Times,* May 1, 2017, https://www.nytimes.com/2017/05/01/business/media/fox-news-bill-shine.html.

25. Francesca Giuliani-Hoffman, "'Reporting Protects Women': Why the *New York Times'* Jodi Kantor Took On Harvey Weinstein," CNNMoney, *CNN,* October 15, 2017, http://money.cnn.com/2017/10/13/media/jodi-kantor-harvey-weinstein-reliable-sources-podcast/index.html.

26. Paul Farhi, "A Caller Had a Lewd Tape of Donald Trump. Then the Race to Break the Story Was On," *Washington Post,* October 7, 2016, https://www.washingtonpost.com/lifestyle/style/the-caller-had-a-lewd-tape-of-donald-trump-

then-the-race-was-on/2016/10/07/31d74714-8ce5-11e6-875e-2c1bfe943b66_story. html?utm_term=.0840d87ed25c.

27. David A. Fahrenthold, "Trump recorded having extremely lewd conversation about women in 2005," *Washington Post,* October 8, 2016, https://www.washing tonpost.com/politics/trump-recorded-having-extremely-lewd-conversation-about-women-in-2005/2016/10/07/3b9ce776-8cb4-11e6-bf8a-3d26847eeed4_ story.html?utm_term=.a020559fb4fa.

28. Ibid.

29. Brian Steinberg, "NBC News Pushes Back on Latest Allegations on Handling of Ronan Farrow Story," *Variety,* September 4, 2018, https://variety.com/2018/tv/ news/nbc-news-pushes-back-allegations-farrow-1202925888/.

30. Paul Farhi, "*Washington Post*'s David Fahrenthold wins Pulitzer Prize for Dogged Reporting of Trump's Philanthropy," *Washington Post,* April 10, 2017, https://www.washingtonpost.com/lifestyle/style/washington-posts-david-fahrenthold-wins-pulitzer-prize-for-dogged-reporting-of-trumps-philan thropy/2017/04/10/dd535d2e-1dfb-11e7-be2a-3a1fb24d4671_story.html?utm_ term=.96ac75346ba7.

31. Laura Crimaldi and James Pindell, "Kelly Ayotte Withdraws Support of Donald Trump," *Boston Globe,* October 8, 2016, https://www.bostonglobe.com/ metro/2016/10/08/ayotte-withdraws-support-trump-says-she-back-pence-in stead/vNoyeSWKgs1plufUs2XHLN/story.html.

32. Tina Nguyen, "Report: Reince Priebus Urged Trump to Drop Out over *Access Hollywood* Tape," *Vanity Fair,* December 8, 2016, https://www.vanityfair.com/ news/2016/12/reince-priebus-donald-trump-white-house.

33. Kylie McConville, "Mitt Romney Comments on Donald Trump's 'Access Hollywood' Tape Reveal His Disgust," Romper, October 7, 2016, https://www.romper. com/p/mitt-romney-comments-on-donald-trumps-access-hollywood-tape-re veal-his-disgust-20006.

34. Donald J. Trump, "Statement From Donald J. Trump," press release, Donald-JTrump.com, October 7, 2016, https://web.archive.org/web/20170429192721/ https://www.donaldjtrump.com/press-releases/statement-from-donald-j.-trump.

35. Rosie Gray, "Prominent Evangelicals Still Backing Trump After Lewd Video," BuzzFeed.News, October 7, 2016, https://www.buzzfeednews.com/article/ros iegray/prominent-evangelicals-still-backing-trump-after-graphic-vid#.vb-D7oP5qM.

36. Dara Lind, "Poll: Vast Majority of Republican Voters Don't Care Much About the Leaked Trump Tape," *Vox,* October 9, 2016, https://www.vox. com/2016/10/9/13217158/polls-donald-trump-assault-tape.

37. Charlotte Alter, "Donald Trump Highlighted Bill Clinton's Accusers at Debate," *Time,* October 10, 2016, http://time.com/4341892/presidential-debate-donald-trump-bill-clinton/.

38. Ibid.

39. Ron Elving, "What Happened with Merrick Garland in 2016 and Why It Matters Now," *Politics* (blog), NPR.com, June 29, 2018, https://www.npr.org/2018/06/29/624467256/what-happened-with-merrick-garland-in-2016-and-why-it-matters-now.

40. Meghan Keneally, "List of Trump's Accusers and Their Allegations of Sexual Misconduct," ABC News, February 22, 2018, https://abcnews.go.com/Politics/list-trumps-accusers-allegations-sexual-misconduct/story?id=51956410.

41. Megan Twohey and Michael Barbaro, "Two Women Say Donald Trump Touched Them Inappropriately," *New York Times,* October 12, 2016, https://www.nytimes.com/2016/10/13/us/politics/donald-trump-women.html.

42. Karen Tumulty, "Woman Says Trump Reached Under Her Skirt and Groped Her in Early 1990s," *Washington Post,* October 14, 2016, https://www.washingtonpost.com/politics/woman-says-trump-reached-under-her-skirt-and-groped-her-in-early-1990s/2016/10/14/67e8ff5e-917d-11e6-a6a3-d50061aa9fae_story.html?utm_term=.9f03d9427b05.

43. Keneally, "List of Trump's Accusers and Their Allegations of Sexual Misconduct."

44. Chas Danner, "Clinton Maintains Lead in Two New Polls, But Trump Tape Impact Is Mixed," *Daily Intelligencer, New York,* October 16, 2016, http://nymag.com/daily/intelligencer/2016/10/clinton-holds-lead-in-new-polls-but-trump-tape-impact-mixed.html.

45. Ibid.

46. Center for American Women and Politics, "Gender Differences in Voter Turnout, " July 20, 2017, http://cawp.rutgers.edu/sites/default/files/resources/gender-diff.pdf.

47. "Inaugural Address: Trump's full speech," CNN Politics, January 21, 2017, https://www.cnn.com/2017/01/20/politics/trump-inaugural-address/index.html.

10. Pink Pussies at the Women's March / 2017

1. Erica Chenoweth and Jeremy Pressman, "This Is What We Learned by Counting the Women's Marches," *Monkey Cage* (blog), *Washington Post,* February 7, 2017, https://www.washingtonpost.com/news/monkey-cage/wp/2017/02/07/this-is-what-we-learned-by-counting-the-womens-marches/?utm_term=.d8a7fff09c84. The numbers in this paragraph come from the *Post*'s excellent follow-up analysis of the march.

2. Perry Stein, "The Woman Who Started the Women's March with a Facebook Post Reflects: 'It Was Mind-Boggling,'" *Washington Post,* January 31, 2017, https://www.washingtonpost.com/news/local/wp/2017/01/31/the-woman-who-started-the-womens-march-with-a-facebook-post-reflects-it-was-mind-boggling/?utm_term=.a167f2c27191.

3. "Women's March Board," Women's March, WomensMarch.com, https://www.womensmarch.com/team/.

4. Karla Adam, "Worldwide, People Rally in Support of Women's March on

Washington," *Washington Post,* January 21, 2017, https://www.washingtonpost. com/world/worldwide-people-rally-in-support-of-womens-march-on-wash ington/2017/01/21/bc232bd8-de69-11e6-8902-610fe486791c_story.html?utm_ term=.e54cf77cc087.

5. Marcus Gilmer, "How to Watch the Women's March on Washington," Mashable, January 21, 2017, https://mashable.com/2017/01/21/how-to-watch-womens-march-on-washington/#TbfE01j7gOqc.

6. Sage Lazzaro, "The 35 Absolute Best Signs From the Women's March," *Observer,* January 23, 2017, http://observer.com/2017/01/best-signs-from-the-womens-march/#slide18.

7. Brooke Seipel, "Women's March Was Second-Busiest Day in Metro History," *The Hill,* January 22, 2017, https://thehill.com/blogs/blog-briefing-room/ news/315536-dc-metro-womens-march-was-second-busiest-day-in-history.

8. Stephen L. Betts, "Wynonna Responds to Ashley Judd's Women's March Speech," *Country* (blog), *Rolling Stone,* January 23, 2017, https://www.rolling stone.com/country/news/wynonna-responds-to-ashley-judds-womens-march-speech-w462513.

9. *Politico,* "The Women Candidate Tracker," collaboration between the Center for American Women and Politics at Rutgers and the Women in Public Service Project at the Wilson Center, 2018, https://www.politico.com/interactives/2018/ women-rule-candidate-tracker/.

10. Rebecca Nelson, "A Lot of People Are Upset by Trump's Agenda. Women Are Doing Something About It," *Cosmopolitan,* June 12, 2017, https://www.cosmo politan.com/politics/a9968890/women-indivisible-resistance-trump/.

11. The slogan goes back to Tarana Burke's movement for black women and girls in 2006, of course.

12. Eric Johnson, "This Is How the *New York Times* Reports Pulitzer Prize–winning stories," *Recode,* April 26, 2018, https://www.recode.net/2018/4/26/17273564/em ily-steel-new-york-times-michael-schmidt-bill-oreilly-metoo-pulitzer-prize-peter-kafka-podcast.

13. Emily Steel and Michael S. Schmidt, "Bill O'Reilly Thrives at Fox News, Even as Harassment Settlements Add Up," *New York Times,* April 1, 2017, https://www. nytimes.com/2017/04/01/business/media/bill-oreilly-sexual-harassment-fox-news.html.

11. The Press Presses and the Dam Breaks:
Harvey Weinstein / 2017–18

1. Madeline Berg, "After Expulsion from the Academy, Here Are All of Harvey Weinstein's 81 Oscar Wins," *Forbes,* October 13, 2017, https://www.forbes. com/sites/maddieberg/2017/10/13/here-are-all-of-harvey-weinsteins-oscar-wins/#11103f6d946c.

2. Kantor and Twohey, "Harvey Weinstein Paid Off Sexual Harassment Accusers for Decades."

3. Ronan Farrow, "From Aggressive Overtures to Sexual Assault: Harvey Wein-

stein's Accusers Tell Their Stories," *New Yorker,* October 10, 2017, https://www.newyorker.com/news/news-desk/from-aggressive-overtures-to-sexual-assault-harvey-weinsteins-accusers-tell-their-stories.

4. "Weinstein," *Frontline* (season 36, episode 10), PBS, March 2, 2018, produced and directed by Jane McMullen and Leo Telling.

5. Ibid. All allegations in this paragraph are from the *Frontline* "Weinstein" documentary and author interview with David Remnick, May 15, 2018.

6. Bruce Weber and Ashley Southall, "David Carr, Times Critic and Champion of Media, Dies at 58," *New York Times,* February 12, 2015, https://www.nytimes.com/2015/02/13/business/media/david-carr-media-equation-columnist-for-the-times-is-dead-at-58.html. Carr was a media reporter at the *New York Times.* His struggles with and triumph over cocaine and alcohol addiction made him a heroic figure. His reporting is considered unparalleled, and he was a great mentor to young journalists and writers. After his untimely death at fifty-eight, the *Times* created a fellowship for aspiring journalists in his name.

7. Peter Kafka, "The Harvey Weinstein Stories That Got Away," *Recode,* October 11, 2017, https://www.recode.net/2017/10/11/16462632/harvey-weinstein-david-carr-ken-auletta-new-yorker-new-york-magazine.

8. Ken Auletta to author, interview, June 27, 2018. They were consensual affairs, Weinstein insisted.

9. Ken Auletta, "Beauty and the Beast," *New Yorker,* December 16, 2002, http://archives.newyorker.com/?i=2002-12-16#folio=064.

10. Kafka, "The Harvey Weinstein Stories That Got Away."

11. Rebecca Traister, "Why the Harvey Weinstein Sexual-Harassment Allegations Didn't Come Out Until Now," *The Cut, New York Magazine,* October 5, 2017, https://www.thecut.com/2017/10/why-the-weinstein-sexual-harassment-allegations-came-out-now.html.

12. Rocco Parascandola, Tina Moore, and Bill Hutchinson, "Harvey Weinstein Accused of Groping Italian Model, 22, in His Office at Tribeca Film Center: Sources," *New York Daily News,* March 31, 2015, http://www.nydailynews.com/entertainment/gossip/nypd-questions-harvey-weinstein-woman-claims-sex-abuse-article-1.2167098.

13. Ken Auletta, interview with the author.

14. "Weinstein," *Frontline.*

15. Ramin Setoodeh, "Ashley Judd Reveals Sexual Harassment by Studio Mogul (EXCLUSIVE)," *Variety,* October 6, 2015, https://variety.com/2015/film/news/ashley-judd-sexual-harassment-studio-mogul-shower-1201610666/.

16. Richard Morgan, "Harvey Weinstein's Contract Gave Him Outs for Harassment Claims," *New York Post,* June 6, 2018, https://nypost.com/2018/06/06/harvey-weinsteins-contract-gave-him-outs-for-harassment-claims/.

17. The Pulitzer Prizes, "Finalist: Megan Twohey of Reuters," 2014 Pulitzer Prize Finalist in Investigative Reporting, https://www.pulitzer.org/finalists/megan-twohey.

18. Marc Malkin, "The *New York Times* Never Set Out to Take Down Harvey Wein-stein and Bill O'Reilly," *Hollywood Reporter,* October 28, 2017, https://www. hollywoodreporter.com/news/new-york-times-never-set-take-down-har-vey-weinstein-bill-o-reilly-1052732. UNC School of Media and Journalism, "Alumna Emily Steel '06 wins 2018 Pulitzer Prize for Public Service," April 17, 2018, http://mj.unc.edu/news/alumna-emily-steel-'06-wins-2018-pulitzer-prize-public-service.

19. Jacob Weisberg, interview with the author.

20. Jill Abramson, interview with the author.

21. Jodi Kantor, "Harvard Business School Case Study: Gender Equity," *New York Times,* September 7, 2013, https://www.nytimes.com/2013/09/08/education/har-vard-case-study-gender-equity.html.

22. Ken Auletta, "Why Jill Abramson Was Fired," *New Yorker,* May 14, 2014, https:// www.newyorker.com/business/currency/why-jill-abramson-was-fired. In 2014 the *Times* fired Abramson, the first woman executive editor of the paper, af-ter Abramson questioned the fairness of her compensation. Kantor is one of many women in the line from Abramson's tenure. Even Rebecca Corbett, the acclaimed editor of Kantor and Twohey's Weinstein stories, credits Abramson with her role. Abramson had turned both Catherine Rampell, now a star col-umnist at the *Washington Post,* to stories about gender, and directed Alissa Ru-bin, then bureau chief in Kabul, to write about the plight of Afghan women. Ru-bin won a Pulitzer for the work.

23. Ryan Haggerty, "On Location," *Northwestern Magazine,* Winter 2006, https:// www.northwestern.edu/magazine/winter2006/feature/movies.html.

24. Dave Astor, "Tribune Media Services Exec John Twohey to Step Down," *Editor & Publisher,* May 30, 2008, https://www.editorandpublisher.com/news/tribune-media-services-exec-john-twohey-to-step-down/.

25. Callie Grober, "ETHS Alum, Pulitzer Winner Reflects on Career," *Evanstonian,* May 24, 2018, https://www.evanstonian.net/feature/2018/05/24/eths-alum-pu-litzer-winner-reflects-on-career/.

26. Ibid.

27. Megan Twohey, "Buddhist Monks Walk Away from Sex-Abuse Cases," *Chi-cago Tribune,* July 24, 2011, http://articles.chicagotribune.com/2011-07-24/ news/ct-met-monk-sex-cases-20110724_1_thai-monks-buddhist-monks-paul-numrich.

28. Mary Schmich, to author, interview, 2018.

29. Terry Gross, "'*Times*' Reporters Describe How a Paper Trail Helped Break the Weinstein Story," *Fresh Air,* NPR, November 15, 2017, https://www.npr. org/2017/11/15/564310240/times-reporters-describe-how-a-paper-trail-helped-break-the-weinstein-story. This is the most thorough report of their process, pending the publication of their own book.

30. Francesca Giuliani-Hoffman, "'Reporting protects women': Why the *New York Times*' Jodi Kantor took on Harvey Weinstein," CNNMoney, CNN, October 15,

2017, http://money.cnn.com/2017/10/13/media/jodi-kantor-harvey-weinstein-reliable-sources-podcast/index.html.

31. Lauren O'Connor, source: Lauren O'Connor's personal LinkedIn profile.

32. Gross, "'*Times*' Reporters Describe How a Paper Trail Helped Break the Weinstein Story."

33. Isaac Chotiner, "The Weinstein Break," *Slate Magazine*, October 11, 2017, http://www.slate.com/articles/news_and_politics/interrogation/2017/10/jodi_kantor_on_how_she_broke_the_harvey_weinstein_story.html.

34. Terry Gross, "Ronan Farrow: 'I Was Raised with an Extraordinary Sense of Public Service,'" *Fresh Air*, NPR, May 23, 2018, https://www.npr.org/2018/05/23/613495834/ronan-farrow-i-was-raised-with-an-extraordinary-sense-of-public-service.

35. Dylan Byers, "MSNBC Pulls 'Ronan Farrow,' 'Reid Report,'" *On Media* (blog), *Politico*, February 19, 2015, https://www.politico.com/blogs/media/2015/02/msnbc-pulls-ronan-farrow-reid-report-202819.

36. Sopan Deb and Deborah Leiderman, "Woody Allen, Mia Farrow, Soon-Yi Previn, Dylan Farrow: A Timeline," *New York Times*, January 31, 2018, https://www.nytimes.com/2018/01/31/movies/woody-allen-mia-farrow-dylan-farrow-a-timeline.html.

37. Ken Auletta, interview with the author. All material in this paragraph and the next from interview with Auletta.

38. Lachlan Cartwright and Maxwell Tani, "Sources: NBC Threatened Ronan Farrow If He Kept Reporting on Harvey Weinstein," *Daily Beast*, August 30, 2018, https://www.thedailybeast.com/sources-nbc-threatened-ronan-farrow-if-he-kept-reporting-on-harvey-weinstein.

39. Ken Auletta to author, email, October 27, 2018.

40. Alex S. Jones, "Will the Rivalry Between the *Washington Post* and *New York Times* Save Journalism?" *Town & Country*, August 9, 2017, https://www.townandcountrymag.com/society/money-and-power/a10364098/washington-post-new-york-times/.

41. David Remnick, interview with the author.

42. Ken Auletta to author, interview and email.

43. Kantor and Twohey, "Harvey Weinstein Paid Off Sexual Harassment Accusers for Decades." Photo online only.

44. Ibid.

45. Farrow, "From Aggressive Overtures to Sexual Assault."

46. Ibid.

47. Leporello "Catalogue" Aria, Mozart, *Don Giovanni*, Columbia University New York City Opera Project, Spring 2002, http://www.columbia.edu/itc/music/NYCO/DonGiovanniMadamina.html.

48. Ronan Farrow, "Harvey Weinstein's Army of Spies," *New Yorker*, November 6, 2017, https://www.newyorker.com/news/news-desk/harvey-weinsteins-army-of-spies.

49. Alyssa Milano, interview with the author.

50. Hilary Hallett, *Go West, Young Women!: The Rise of Early Hollywood* (Berkeley: University of California Press, 2013).

51. Kelly Faircloth, "The Invention of the 'Casting Couch,'" *Pictorial* (blog), *Jezebel*, October 18, 2017, https://pictorial.jezebel.com/the-invention-of-the-casting-couch-1819613764.

52. Marilyn Monroe, with Ben Hecht, *My Story* (Lanham, MD: Taylor Trade Publishing, 2007), 48. The brilliant screenwriter Ben Hecht is likely responsible for writing the memoir, which is based on the long interview sessions he had with the star. Monroe was forthright about the bargain that she, and pretty much every aspiring movie actress since, was required to make.

53. Kevin Starr, *Inventing the Dream: California Through the Progressive Era* (New York: Oxford University Press, 1985), 294.

54. Robert Gore-Langton, "Harvey Weinstein's Standards Were Par for Hollywood's Golden Years," *Express*, October 19, 2017, https://www.express.co.uk/life-style/life/868302/Harvey-Weinstein-allegations-scandal-hollywood-studio-bosses-harassment.

55. Gerald Clarke, *Get Happy: The Life of Judy Garland* (New York: Random House, 2000), 67.

56. Thelma Adams, "Casting-Couch Tactics Plagued Hollywood Long Before Harvey Weinstein," *Variety*, October 17, 2017, https://variety.com/2017/film/features/casting-couch-hollywood-sexual-harassment-harvey-weinstein-1202589895/.

57. Anthony Summers, *Goddess: The Secret Lives of Marilyn Monroe* (New York: Open Road, 1985), 56.

58. Faircloth, "The Invention of The 'Casting Couch.'"

59. Faragher v. Boca Raton, 524 U.S. 775 (1998); Burlington Industries, Inc. v. Ellerth, 524 U.S. 742 (1998).

60. Nancy Erika Smith, interview with the author.

61. Farrow, "From Aggressive Overtures to Sexual Assault."

62. Ibid.

63. Sara Salinas, "Intel's Brian Krzanich Is Forced Out as CEO After 'Consensual Relationship' with Employee," CNBC, June 21, 2018, https://www.cnbc.com/2018/06/21/intel-ceo-brian-krzanich-to-step-down-bob-swan-to-step-in-as-interim-ceo.html.

64. Karen Robinson-Jacobs and Melissa Repko, "Texas Instruments' Swift Action Part of Broader Crackdown on Misbehaving CEOs," *Dallas News*, July 20, 2018, https://www.dallasnews.com/business/technology/2018/07/20/texas-instruments-swift-action-part-broader-crackdown-misbehaving-ceos.

65. Ronan Farrow, "Les Moonves and CBS Face Allegations of Sexual Misconduct," *New Yorker*, August 6 & 13, 2018, https://www.newyorker.com/magazine/2018/08/06/les-moonves-and-cbs-face-allegations-of-sexual-misconduct.

66. Ronan Farrow, "As Leslie Moonves Negotiates His Exit from CBS, Six Women Raise New Assault and Harassment Claims," *New Yorker*, September 9, 2018,

https://www.newyorker.com/news/news-desk/as-leslie-moonves-negotiates-his-exit-from-cbs-women-raise-new-assault-and-harassment-claims.

67. Ashley Cullins, "Brett Ratner Defends Defamation Lawsuit Against Accuser," *Hollywood Reporter,* January 22, 2018, https://www.hollywoodreporter.com/thr-esq/brett-ratner-defends-defamation-lawsuit-accuser-1077169.

68. Gus Garcia-Roberts, "Director Bryan Singer Faces Lawsuit over Alleged Rape of Teen in 2003," *Los Angeles Times,* December 7, 2017, http://www.latimes.com/business/hollywood/la-fi-ct-bryan-singer-assault-lawsuit20171207-story.html. The Kohler case has since settled: Ashley Cullins, "Brett Ratner Defamation Settlement Signals End of First Major Time's Up Legal Battle," *Hollywood Reporter,* October 2, 2018, https://www.hollywoodreporter.com/thr-esq/brett-ratner-defamation-settlement-signals-end-first-major-times-up-legal-battle-1148735.

69. Farrow, "From Aggressive Overtures to Sexual Assault."

12. #MeToo / 2017–18

1. Alyssa Milano, interview with the author.

2. @Alyssa Milano, Twitter, October 15, 2017, https://twitter.com/alyssa_milano/status/919659438700670976?lang=en.

3. Sayej, "Alyssa Milano on the #MeToo Movement."

4. Alyssa Milano, interview with the author.

5. Guobin Yang, "Narrative Agency in Hashtag Activism: The Case of #BlackLivesMatter," *Media and Communication,* 4, no. 4 (2016), 13–17, https://www.cogitatiopress.com/mediaandcommunication/article/viewFile/692/692.

6. Evgeny Morozov, "Foreign Policy: Brave New World Of Slacktivism," *Opinion* (blog), NPR, May 19, 2009, https://www.npr.org/templates/story/story.php?storyId=104302141.

7. Hannah Chubb, "Hashtag Activism: A Timeline," *Marie Claire,* May 24, 2018, https://www.marieclaire.com/culture/a20886254/hashtag-activism/.

8. Megan Leonhardt, "The Lasting Effects of Occupy Wall Street, Five Years Later," *Money,* September 16, 2016, http://time.com/money/4495707/occupy-wall-street-anniversary-effects/.

9. Craig Kanalley, "Occupy Wall Street: Social Media's Role in Social Change," *Huffington Post,* October 6, 2011, https://www.huffingtonpost.com/2011/10/06/occupy-wall-street-social-media_n_999178.html.

10. Serena Lei et al., "Nine Charts About Wealth Inequality in America (Updated)," *Features,* Urban.org, Urban Institute, October 5, 2017, https://apps.urban.org/features/wealth-inequality-charts/.

11. Yang, "Narrative Agency in Hashtag Activism."

12. Yarimar Bonilla and Jonathan Rosa, "#Ferguson: Digital Protest, Hashtag Ethnography, and the Racial Politics of Social Media in the United States," *American Ethnologist* 42, no. 1 (February 2015), 4–17, https://anthrosource.on

linelibrary.wiley.com/doi/abs/10.1111/amet.12112; Yang, "Narrative Agency in Hashtag Activism," 16.

13. Irin Carmon, "Elliot Rodger's War on Women," MSNBC.com, May 26, 2014, http://www.msnbc.com/msnbc/elliot-rodger-war-women-yesallwomen-hashtag.

14. Karlyn Kohrs Campbell, "Agency: Promiscuous and Protean," *Communication and Critical/Cultural Studies*. 2, no. 1 (2005), 1–9, https://www.tandfonline.com/doi/abs/10.1080/1479142042000332134; Yang, "Narrative Agency in Hashtag Activism," 15.

15. Melena Ryzik, Cara Buckley, and Jodi Kantor, "Louis C.K. Is Accused by 5 Women of Sexual Misconduct," *New York Times*, November 9, 2017, https://www.nytimes.com/2017/11/09/arts/television/louis-ck-sexual-misconduct.html?smid=tw-nytimesarts&smtyp=cur&_r=0.

16. David Remnick, interview with the author.

17. Sarah Almukhtar, Michael Gold, and Larry Buchanan, "After Weinstein: 71 Men Accused of Sexual Misconduct and Their Fall from Power," *New York Times*, February 8, 2018, https://www.nytimes.com/interactive/2017/11/10/us/men-accused-sexual-misconduct-weinstein.html.

18. Ibid. The names appeared in the *New York Times* on February 28, 2018, as part of a list of almost a hundred accused abusers as of February.

19. Stephen Schulhofer, email to author, June 25, 2018.

20. Jeff Green, "#MeToo Snares More Than 400 High-Profile People," *Bloomberg*, June 25, 2018, https://www.bloomberg.com/news/articles/2018-06-25/-metoo-snares-more-than-400-high-profile-people-as-firings-rise.

21. Laura McGann, "The Still-Raging Controversy over Al Franken's Resignation, Explained," *Vox*, May 21, 2018, https://www.vox.com/2018/5/21/17352230/al-franken-accusations-resignation-democrats-leann-tweeden-kirsten-gillibrand.

22. AP, "A timeline of the sexual misconduct allegations against Al Franken," December 7, 2017, https://www.twincities.com/2017/12/07/al-franken-sexual-misconduct-allegations-timeline-senator-minnesota/.

23. Steven Lemongello, "Al Franken Will Not Appear at Bill Nelson Fundraiser," *Orlando Sentinel*, November 16, 2017, http://www.orlandosentinel.com/news/politics/political-pulse/os-franken-nelson-fundraiser-20171116-story.html.

24. Michael Tomasky, "Senator Al Franken's Resignation Is Deeply Unfair," *Daily Beast*, January 2, 2018, https://www.thedailybeast.com/senator-al-frankens-resignation-is-deeply-unfair (citing polls).

25. Susan Davis, "Democratic Congressman Acknowledges Settlement, But Denies Sexual Harassment Claim," NPR, November 21, 2017, https://www.npr.org/2017/11/21/565681045/rep-john-conyers-acknowledges-settlement-but-denies-sexual-harassment-claim.

26. Kimberly Kindy, "Conyers's Accusers Described Sexual Advances and Inappropriate Remarks," *Washington Post*, December 5, 2017, https://www.washing

tonpost.com/politics/conyerss-accusers-described-sexual-advances-and-inap
propriate-remarks/2017/12/05/2b4a49a0-d4a6-11e7-a986-d0a9770d9a3e_story.
html?utm_term=.d31388a10c19.

27. Stephanie McCrummen, Beth Reinhard, and Alice Crites, "Woman Says Roy
Moore Initiated Sexual Encounter When She Was 14, He Was 32," *Washington Post,* November 9, 2017, https://www.washingtonpost.com/investigations/
woman-says-roy-moore-initiated-sexual-encounter-when-she-was-14-he-
was-32/2017/11/09/1f495878-c293-11e7-afe9-4f60b5a6c4a0_story.html?utm_
term=.09ca211f4f50.

28. Philip Bump, "Timeline: The Accusations Against Roy Moore," *Washington Post,* November 16, 2017, https://www.washingtonpost.com/news/politics
/wp/2017/11/16/timeline-the-accusations-against-roy-moore/?utm_term=
.45d1b9cc8548.

29. Samantha Cooney, "All the Women Who Have Accused Sen. Al Franken of
Sexual Misconduct," *Time,* November 30, 2017, http://time.com/5042931/al-
franken-accusers/.

30. Marina Fang, "Kirsten Gillibrand Only Regrets Not Calling for Al Franken to Quit Sooner," *Huffington Post,* February 12, 2018, https://www.huff
ingtonpost.com/entry/kirsten-gillibrand-al-franken-sexual-misconduct_
us_5a81b24de4b08dfc93065fc3.

31. Tina Dupuy, "I Believe Franken's Accusers Because He Groped Me, Too," *Atlantic,* December 6, 2017, https://www.theatlantic.com/politics/archive/2017/12/i-
believe-frankens-accusers-because-he-groped-me-too/547691/.

32. Michael Tomasky, "Here's Why Democrats Forced Al Franken to Do the Right
Thing — And Why They May Come to Regret It," *Daily Beast,* December 7,
2017, https://www.thedailybeast.com/heres-why-democrats-forced-al-franken-
to-do-the-right-thing-and-why-they-may-come-to-regret-it; Margaret Carlson, "Did Democrats Just Fall Into Roger Stone's Trap?" *Daily Beast,* December
8, 2017, https://www.thedailybeast.com/did-democrats-just-fall-into-roger-
stones-trap.

33. Heather Caygle, "Another Woman Says Franken Tried to Forcibly Kiss Her,"
Politico, December 6, 2017, https://www.politico.com/story/2017/12/06/al-fran
ken-accusation-sexual-harassment-2006-281049.

34. Greg Sargent, "Al Franken Is Gone. Roy Moore Will Likely Remain. Why?" *The
Plum Line* (blog), *Washington Post,* December 8, 2017, https://www.washington
post.com/blogs/plum-line/wp/2017/12/08/al-franken-is-gone-roy-moore-will-
likely-remain-why/?utm_term=.f18a6654e9b9.

35. Scott Clement, Emily Guskin, and Darla Cameron, "Exit Poll Results: How Different Groups Voted in Alabama," *Washington Post,* December 13, 2017, https://
www.washingtonpost.com/graphics/2017/politics/alabama-exit-polls/?utm_
term=.006027c34d8e.

36. Laura McGann, "The Still-Raging Controversy over Al Franken's Resignation, Explained," *Vox,* May 21, 2018, https://www.vox.com/2018/5/21/17352230/

al-franken-accusations-resignation-democrats-leann-tweeden-kirsten-gillibrand.

37. Michael Tomasky, "Senator Al Franken's Resignation Is Deeply Unfair," *Daily Beast,* January 2, 2018, https://www.thedailybeast.com/senator-al-frankens-resignation-is-deeply-unfair.

38. McGann, "The Still-Raging Controversy over Al Franken's Resignation."

39. Craig Melvin, "Bill Clinton Wouldn't Do 'Anything Differently' with Lewinsky Affair Amid #MeToo Movement," *Today,* NBC News, June 4, 2018, https://www.nbcnews.com/nightly-news/video/bill-clinton-wouldn-t-do-anything-differently-with-lewinsky-affair-amid-metoo-movement-1248091203538.

40. Chris Ariens, "Bill Clinton to Craig Melvin: 'Someone Should Be Asking You These Questions,'" *TVNewser* (blog), *Adweek,* June 4, 2018, https://www.ad-week.com/tvnewser/bill-clinton-to-craig-melvin-someone-should-be-asking-you-these-questions/366282.

41. Callum Borchers, "Bill Clinton's Lame Excuses for Bad Answers," *The Fix* (blog), *Washington Post,* June 6, 2018, https://www.washingtonpost.com/news/the-fix/wp/2018/06/06/bill-clintons-lame-excuses-for-bad-answers/?utm_term=.0c84acbdb5fd.

42. Travis Gettys, "Morning Joe Panel Writes Epitaph for Bill Clinton's Political Career After Disastrous Today Interview," *RawStory,* June 4, 2018, https://www.rawstory.com/2018/06/morning-joe-panel-writes-epitaph-bill-clintons-political-career-disastrous-today-interview/.

43. Bruce Haring, "Time's Up Empowerment Group Starts Legal Defense Fund for Sex Harassments," *Deadline Hollywood,* January 1, 2018, https://deadline.com/2018/01/times-up-empowerment-group-starts-legal-defense-fund-for-sex-harassment-cases-1202234089/.

44. Desiree Murphy, "Time's Up: How Reese Witherspoon Spearheaded the Movement Ahead of 2018 Golden Globes," *ET Online,* January 5, 2018, https://www.etonline.com/times-how-reese-witherspoon-spearheaded-movement-ahead-2018-golden-globes-93598.

45. Christina Cauterucci, "Hollywood's Official Response to #MeToo Is Off to a Rocky Start," *The XX Factor* (blog), *Slate,* January 2, 2018, http://www.slate.com/blogs/xx_factor/2018/01/02/time_s_up_hollywood_s_response_to_metoo_is_off_to_a_rocky_start.html.

46. Haring, "Time's Up Empowerment Group Starts Legal Defense Fund."

47. Stephanie Eckardt, "What's Next for Time's Up According to Tina Tchen, the Powerhouse Lawyer Behind the Famous Faces," *W,* January 8, 2018, https://www.wmagazine.com/story/times-up-legal-defense-fund-tina-tchen-interview. Tchen told her story to *W* magazine. This paragraph is drawn from that report. Despite multiple requests, she would not speak to me.

48. Robbie Kaplan to author, interview, May 10, 2018, and email October 27, 2018.

49. Lyle Denniston, "Opinion Analysis: Wal-Mart's Two Messages," *SCOTUS*

blog, June 20, 2011, http://www.scotusblog.com/2011/06/opinion-analysis-wal -marts-two-messages/.

50. Dominic Rushe, "McDonald's Workers Walk Out in 10 US Cities over 'Sexual Harassment Epidemic,'" *Guardian,* September 18, 2018, https://www.theguard ian.com/business/2018/sep/18/mcdonalds-walkout-workers-protest-sexual-ha rassment-epidemic.

51. Ibid.; Tanya Harrell, interview with the author, for this paragraph and the next.

52. National Women's Law Center, "TIME'S UP Legal Defense Fund Provides Financial Support for Low-Wage Women Workers Filing Sexual Harassment Charges Against McDonald's," press release, May 22, 2018, https://nwlc.org/ press-releases/times-up-legal-defense-fund-provides-financial-support-for-low-wage-women-workers-filing-sexual-harassment-charges-against-mcdon alds/.

53. National Partnership for Women and Families, "Survey Shows Two in Five Women in Fast-Food Industry Face Sexual Harassment on the Job," press release, October 5, 2016, http://www.nationalpartnership.org/news-room/press-releases/women-in-fast-food-industry-face-sexual-harassment.html.

54. Ibid.

55. Ben Rooney, "McDonald's: Union attack on the brand," CNNMoney, June 9, 2015, https://money.cnn.com/2015/05/21/news/mcdonalds-fast-food-protest/in dex.html.

56. "'Fight for $15' Workers Join Guild," The NewsGuild, November 30, 2017, http:// www.newsguild.org/mediaguild3/fight-for-15-workers-join-guild/.

57. Dave Jamieson, "Labor Critic Claims Union Behind The 'Fight for $15' Cut Funding for Fast-Food Campaigns," *Huffington Post,* March 31, 2018.https://www.huff ingtonpost.com/entry/union-behind-the-fight-for-15-cuts-funding-for-fast-food-campaign_us_5abfe925e4b055e50ace1a2d.

58. Dave Jamieson and Michael McLaughlin, "Fast Food Strikes Hit Cities Throughout the Country," *Huffington Post,* November 10, 2015, https://www.huffington post.com/entry/fast-food-strikes-protests_us_5641e226e4b0b24aee4bb262.

59. Emily Jane Fox, "McDonald's workers sue for wage theft," CNN Business, March 14, 2014, https://money.cnn.com/2014/03/13/news/companies/mcdon alds-wage-theft-class-action/index.html.

60. Cora Lewis and Ema O'Connor, "McDonald's Staff Complain of Rampant Sexual Harassment," BuzzFeed.News, October 5, 2016, https://www.buzzfeednews. com/article/coralewis/mcdonalds-staff-complain-of-rampant-sexual-harass ment#.txNx7nbmW.

61. Cervantes and Chisholm to author, interview, July 11, 2018.

62. Chantal Da Silva, "McDonald's is facing sexual harassment claims from workers backed by Time's Up," *Newsweek,* May 22, 2018. https://www.newsweek. com/mcdonalds-workers-sexual-harassment-claims-timesup-939380.

63. Interview Cervantes and Chisholm. Ibid.

64. Tanya Harrell, interview with the author, for this and next five paragraphs.

65. Ronan Farrow and Deirdre Foley-Mendelssohn, "Ronan Farrow Talks with Deirdre Foley-Mendelssohn at the New Yorker Festival," New Yorker Festival, New York City, October 5, 2018, https://festival.newyorker.com/event/ronan-farrow-talks-with-deirdre-foley-mendelssohn/; Margaret Sullivan [*Washington Post* columnist and former public editor, *New York Times*] to author, interview, October 6, 2018.

66. Interview Margaret Sullivan to author, interview, October 6, 2018, and email, October 27, 2018.

67. "The *New York Times*'s Lawyer Responds to Donald Trump," *New York Times*, October 13, 2016, https://www.nytimes.com/interactive/2016/10/13/us/politics/david-mccraw-trump-letter.html.

13. The Year of Reckoning: 2018

1. The order of the initiatives may be different, of course. The contemporary conservative revival started with the culture, as the Fox News section of chapter 7 reflects.

2. And the Heritage Foundation, a conservative think tank. Shane Goldmacher, Eliana Johnson, and Josh Gerstein, "How Trump Got to Yes on Gorsuch," *Politico*, January 31, 2017, https://www.politico.com/story/2017/01/trump-supreme-court-gorsuch-234474.

3. Kavanaugh was a late addition to the original list. "Supreme Court Nominee Brett Kavanaugh Was Included on the List the Heritage Foundation Helped Compile," Heritage Foundation, August 31, 2018, https://www.heritage.org/impact/supreme-court-nominee-brett-kavanaugh-was-included-the-list-the-heritage-foundation-helped.

4. Amanda Hollis-Brusky, *Ideas with Consequences: The Federalist Society and the Conservative Counterrevolution*, (New York: Oxford University Press, 2015), 213.

5. Richard Wolf and Christal Hayes, "Supreme Court Justice Brett Kavanaugh: The Plot Twists and Moments That Got Us Here," *USA Today*, October 6, 2018, https://www.usatoday.com/story/news/politics/2018/10/06/brett-kavanaugh-moments-supreme-court-confirmation/1539791002/. For this paragraph and the next two.

6. Ryan Grim, "Dianne Feinstein Withholding Brett Kavanaugh Document from Fellow Judiciary Committee Democrats," *Intercept*, September 12, 2018, https://theintercept.com/2018/09/12/brett-kavanaugh-confirmation-dianne-feinstein/.

7. Nicholas Fandos and Catie Edmondson, "Dianne Feinstein Refers a Kavanaugh Matter to Federal Investigators," *New York Times*, September 13, 2018, https://www.nytimes.com/2018/09/13/us/politics/brett-kavanaugh-dianne-feinstein.html.

8. Emma Brown, "California Professor, Writer of Confidential Brett Kavanaugh Letter, Speaks Out About Her Allegation of Sexual Assault," *New York Times*,

September 16, 2018, https://www.washingtonpost.com/investigations/cali fornia-professor-writer-of-confidential-brett-kavanaugh-letter-speaks-out-about-her-allegation-of-sexual-assault/2018/09/16/46982194-b846-11e8-94eb-3b-d52dfe917b_story.html?noredirect=on&utm_term=.267338d6c367.

9. Ronan Farrow and Jane Mayer, "Senate Democrats Investigate a New Allega-tion of Sexual Misconduct, from Brett Kavanaugh's College Years," *New Yorker,* September 23, 2018, https://www.newyorker.com/news/news-desk/senate-dem ocrats-investigate-a-new-allegation-of-sexual-misconduct-from-the-supreme-court-nominee-brett-kavanaughs-college-years-deborah-ramirez.

10. C-SPAN, "Supreme Court Nominee Brett Kavanaugh Sexual Assault Hearing, Professor Blasey Ford Testimony," Senate Judiciary Committee, September 27, 2018, https://www.c-span.org/video/?451895-1/professor-blasey-ford-testifies-sexual-assault-allegations-part-1&playEvent.

11. Rebecca Traister, "Fury Is a Political Weapon. And Women Need to Wield It," *New York Times,* September 29, 2018, https://www.nytimes.com/2018/09/29/ opinion/sunday/fury-is-a-political-weapon-and-women-need-to-wield-it.html.

12. "Updates from the Riveting Testimonies of Christine Blasey Ford and Brett Kavanaugh," *New York Times,* September 27, 2018, https://www.nytimes. com/2018/09/27/us/politics/kavanaugh-hearings-dr-ford.html, for this and the following paragraphs about the testimony.

13. Peter Baker and Nicholas Fandos, "Show How You Feel, Kavanaugh Was Told, and a Nomination Was Saved," *New York Times,* October 6, 2018, https://www. nytimes.com/2018/10/06/us/politics/kavanaugh-vote-confirmation-process. html.

14. Specifically, as I recalled, watching the hearings, the aria "Sangue" from Verdi's *Otello,* where an increasingly unhinged military hero calls for the blood of his wife, Desdemona, believing her to be lying about sex. Giuseppe Verdi, *Otello,* Act II, https://www.metopera.org/discover/synopses/otello/; http://www.mu rashev.com/opera/Otello_libretto_English_Italian.

15. "Updates From the Riveting Testimonies of Christine Blasey Ford and Brett Kava-naugh," *New York Times.*

16. Jonathan Allen, "Trump Mocks Kavanaugh Accuser Christine Blasey Ford at Campaign Rally," NBC News, October 2, 2018, https://www.nbcnews.com/poli tics/politics-news/trump-mocks-christine-blasey-ford-mississippi-campaign-rally-n916061.

17. Jared Gilmour, "Senators Behind Collins Steal the Show as She Explains Kava-naugh Vote in Long Speech," *Miami Herald,* October 5, 2018, https://www.miami-herald.com/news/nation-world/national/article219570050.html#storylink=cpy.

18. Murkowski voted present, as one of her GOP colleagues had to be at his daugh-ter's wedding that day.

19. "Beers and Cheers as Trump, Republicans Celebrate Kavanaugh's Rise to Su-preme Court," SBS News, October 7, 2018, https://www.sbs.com.au/news/beers-

and-cheers-as-trump-republicans-celebrate-kavanaugh-s-rise-to-supreme-court.

20. Jeremy W. Peters, "Kavanaugh Uproar in Senate Fuels G.O.P. Races for Governor and House," *New York Times,* October 9, 2018, https://www.nytimes.com/2018/10/09/us/politics/kavanaugh-republican-midterm-races.html.

21. Gregg Re, "Kavanaugh Slugfest Could Boost GOP in Midterms, As Polls Show Voter Interest Rising," Fox News, October 4, 2018, https://www.foxnews.com/politics/kavanaugh-slugfest-could-boost-gop-in-midterms-as-polls-show-voter-interest-rising.

22. Peters, "Kavanaugh Uproar in Senate Fuels G.O.P. Races."

23. Cas Mudde, "Brett Kavanaugh Confirmation May Be the Midterm Boost Republicans Need," *Guardian,* October 8, 2018, https://www.theguardian.com/commentisfree/2018/oct/08/brett-kavanaugh-confirmation-may-be-the-midterm-boost-republicans-need.

24. Jennifer Agiesta, "CNN Poll: Majority Oppose Kavanaugh, but His Popularity Grows with GOP," CNN Politics, October 11, 2018, https://www.cnn.com/2018/10/08/politics/cnn-poll-kavanaugh-confirmation/index.html; Lawrence O'Donnell, "Poll: Democrats Gain After Kavanaugh Fight," *The Last Word,* MSNBC, October 9, 2018, https://www.msnbc.com/the-last-word/watch/poll-democrats-gain-after-kavanaugh-fight-1340553283844?v=raila&.

25. Janie Velencia, "Americans Didn't Believe Anita Hill. How Will They Respond to Kavanaugh's Accuser?" *FiveThirtyEight,* September 17, 2018, https://fivethirtyeight.com/features/americans-didnt-believe-anita-hill-how-will-they-respond-to-kavanaughs-accuser/.

26. Kathy Reakes, "More Americans Believe Christine Blasey Ford, Marist Poll Finds," *Southwest Dutchess Daily Voice,* October 5, 2018, https://southwest-dutchess.dailyvoice.com/politics/more-americans-believe-christine-blasey-ford-marist-poll-finds/742879/.

27. Dylan Matthews, "Impeaching a Supreme Court Justice, Explained," *Vox,* October 5, 2018, https://www.vox.com/2018/9/27/17910524/supreme-court-impeach-impeachment-brett-kavanaugh.

28. Dylan Matthews, "Court-Packing, Democrats' Nuclear Option for the Supreme Court, Explained," *Vox,* October 5, 2018, https://www.vox.com/2018/7/2/17513520/court-packing-explained-fdr-roosevelt-new-deal-democrats-supreme-court.

29. Gregory A. Caldeira, "Public Opinion and The U.S. Supreme Court: FDR's Court-Packing Plan," *American Political Science Review* 81, no. 4 (December 1987), 1139–53, https://www.jstor.org/stable/1962582?read-now=1&loggedin=true&seq=1#page_scan_tab_contents. See also Michele Landis Dauber, *The Sympathetic State: Disaster Relief and the Origins of the American Welfare State* (Chicago: University of Chicago Press, 2012). The relevance of the court-packing plan and its history is covered extensively in Dauber's book.

30. "California Primary Election Results," *New York Times,* June 11, 2018, https://

www.nytimes.com/interactive/2018/06/05/us/elections/results-california-pri
mary-elections.html?module=inline.

31. Augie Martin, Holly Yan, and Dan Merica, "Voters Oust Judge Who Gave
Brock Turner 6 Months for Sex Assault," CNN, June 6, 2018, https://www-m.
cnn.com/2018/06/06/us/judge-aaron-persky-recall-results-brock-turner/index.
html?r=https%3A%2F%2Fwww.google.com%2F; Tracey Kaplan, "Recall Aftermath: Will the Removal of Judge Aaron Persky Prompt a New Legal Battle?"
Mercury News, June 6, 2018, https://www.mercurynews.com/2018/06/06/judge-
persky/.

32. Ballotpedia, "Aaron Persky Recall, Santa Clara County, California (2018),"
https://ballotpedia.org/Aaron_Persky_recall,_Santa_Clara_County,_Califor
nia_(2018). Ballotpedia does a thorough and objective job of reciting the facts
of the recall.

33. Katie J. M. Baker, "Here's the Powerful Letter the Stanford Victim Read to
Her Attacker," Buzzfeed.News, June 3, 2016, https://www.buzzfeednews.com/
article/katiejmbaker/heres-the-powerful-letter-the-stanford-victim-read-to-
her-ra.

34. Catharine MacKinnon, interview with the author.

35. Maggie Mallon, "Stanford Sexual Assault Case Survivor Emily Doe Speaks Out
at Glamour's Women of the Year Awards," *Glamour,* November 15, 2016, https://
www.glamour.com/story/stanford-sexual-assault-case-survivor-emily-doe-
speaks-out-at-glamours-women-of-the-year-awards.

36. Michele Dauber to author, interview, July 12, 2018, and email, November 11,
2018.

37. Administration, "SCCBA Statement on Judicial Independence," blogs, SC-
CBA, June 14, 2016, https://sccba.site-ym.com/blogpost/1133925/249782/SC-
CBA-Statement-on-Judicial-Independence?hhSearchTerms=%22Persky%22&t
erms=. The 2003 resolution provides that the SCCBA should speak out against
"statements and actions which exceed the bounds of proper criticism and
threaten judicial independence."

38. Commission on Judicial Performance, "Commission on Judicial Performance
Closes Investigation of Judge Aaron Persky," press release, December 19, 2016,
https://cjp.ca.gov/wp-content/uploads/sites/40/2016/08/Persky_Explanatory_
Statement_12-19-16.pdf.

39. Jose A. Del Real, "Activists Try to Recall Judge in Stanford Sex Attack Case.
Some Say They've Gone Too Far." *New York Times,* February 2, 2018, https://
www.nytimes.com/2018/02/02/us/brock-turner-judge-recall-stanford.html.

40. Tracey Kaplan, "Brock Turner: Leading law school professors issue letter opposing judge's recall," *East Bay Times,* July 27, 2016, https://www.eastbaytimes.
com/2016/07/27/brock-turner-leading-law-school-professors-issue-letter-op
posing-judges-recall/.

41. Robert W. Gordon "Law and Ideology," *Tikkun* 3, no. 1 (January/February 1988),
14–18; 83–87, https://www.tikkun.org/nextgen/wp-content/uploads/2011/12/
Law-and-Ideology.pdf.

42. Robert Gordon to author, interview, August 6, 2018.

43. Ibid.

44. Ballotpedia, "Aaron Persky recall, Santa Clara County, California (2018)," https://ballotpedia.org/Aaron_Persky_recall,_Santa_Clara_County,_Califor nia_(2018).

45. International Museum of Women, "The Year of the Woman," Global Fund for Women, http://exhibitions.globalfundforwomen.org/exhibitions/women-power-and-politics/elections/year-woman.

46. Karen Tumulty, "Twenty Years On, 'Year of the Woman' Fades," *Washington Post,* March 24, 2012, https://www.washingtonpost.com/politics/twenty-years-on-year-of-the-woman-fades/2012/03/21/gIQA41UUYS_story.html?utm_term=.e88a5d9a03b2.

47. "Full list: 2018 Midterm Election Seats That Flipped" Axios, November 20, 2018, https://www.axios.com/full-list-2018-midterm-election-seats-flipped-34d 99826-0929-41c6-a1f0-e4d02861c835.html.

48. Carmin Chappell, "In Historic Election for Female Candidates, Republican Women Lose Ground in the House," CNBC, November 21, 2018, https://www. cnbc.com/2018/11/21/democratic-women-make-big-gains-in-house-as-gop-women-lose-ground-in-historic-election.html.

49. "Republican Candidates Are Being Punished for Trump's Sexism," WTHH, November 8, 2018, https://wthh.dataforprogress.org/blog/2018/11/8/republican-candidates-are-being-punished-for-trumps-sexism.

50. "Exit Polls," CNN Politics, 2018, https://www.cnn.com/election/2018/exit-polls.

51. Enough Is Enough Voter Project, https://enoughisenoughvoter.org/candi-date/matt-rinaldi/, and https://enoughisenoughvoter.org/candidate/matt-manweller/.

52. Matt Wynn, John Fritze, and Brad Heath, "Wealthy Suburban Voters, Women: How Democrats Captured the House in the 2018 Midterms," *USA Today,* November 7, 2018, https://www.usatoday.com/story/news/politics/elec tions/2018/11/07/elections-results-2018-wealthy-voters-women-democrats-won-house/1918202002/.

53. The presence of a woman on the ballot unequivocally made things better for Democrats.

54. "Exit Polls," CNN Politics, 2018.

55. Pew Research Center, "An Examination of the 2016 Electorate, Based on Val-idated Voters," August 9, 2018, http://www.people-press.org/2018/08/09/an-ex amination-of-the-2016-electorate-based-on-validated-voters/.

56. William H. Frey, "2018 Exit Polls Show Greater White Support for Democrats," *The Avenue* (blog), The Brookings Institution, November 8, 2018, Table A, https://www.brookings.edu/blog/the-avenue/2018/11/08/2018-exit-polls-show-greater-white-support-for-democrats/.

57. Schaffner to author, Twitter DM, November 10, 2018.

58. Quoted in Christina Pazzanese and Colleen Walsh, "The Women's Revolt: Why Now, and Where To," *Harvard Gazette,* December 21, 2017, https://news.har

vard.edu/gazette/story/2017/12/metoo-surge-could-change-society-in-pivotal-ways-harvard-analysts-say/.

59. Crystal N. Feimster, "When Black Women Reclaimed Their Bodies," *Slate*, February 2, 2018, https://slate.com/human-interest/2018/02/how-formerly-en slaved-black-women-fought-for-human-dignity-and-sexual-justice.html.

60. Marama Whyte, "The Media's #MeToo Problems Will Continue Until Its Culture Changes," *Washington Post*, September 14, 2018, https://www.washington post.com/outlook/2018/09/14/medias-metoo-problems-will-continue-until-its-culture-changes/?utm_term=.67ac7dfcfce2.

61. Minyvonne Burke and Diana Dasrath, "Paz de la Huerta Files Lawsuit Against Harvey Weinstein Alleging Sexual Assault," NBCNews, November 13, 2018, https://www.nbcnews.com/news/us-news/paz-de-la-huerta-files-lawsuit-against-harvey-weinstein-alleging-n935806.

62. John Koblin, "Ronan Farrow's Ex-Producer Says NBC Impeded Weinstein Reporting," *New York Times*, August 30, 2018, https://www.nytimes.com/2018/08/30/business/media/ronan-farrow-weinstein-producer.html.

63. Yashar Ali and Lydia Polgreen, "How Top NBC Executives Quashed The Bombshell Harvey Weinstein Story," *Huffington Post*, October 11, 2017, https://www.huff ingtonpost.com/entry/nbc-harvey-weinstein_us_59de5688e4b0eb18af059685.

64. Farrow, "Les Moonves and CBS Face Allegations of Sexual Misconduct."

65. Dade Hayes, "Mirror Awards Go to Probes of Charlie Rose, Harvey Weinstein; Honoree Confronts 'The System in This Room,'" *Deadline Hollywood*, June 14, 2018, https://deadline.com/2018/06/mirror-awards-honor-probes-charlie-rose-harvey-weinstein-1202410669/.

66. James B. Stewart, "Threats and Deception: Why CBS's Board Turned Against Leslie Moonves," *New York Times*, September 12, 2018, https://www.nytimes.com/2018/09/12/business/cbs-les-moonves-board.html.

67. Farrow, "As Leslie Moonves Negotiates His Exit From CBS, Six Women Raise New Assault and Harassment Claims."

68. Linda Bloodworth Thomason, "'Designing Women' Creator Goes Public with Les Moonves War: Not All Harassment Is Sexual," guest column, *Hollywood Reporter*, September 12, 2018, https://www.hollywoodreporter.com/news/design ing-women-creator-les-moonves-not-all-harassment-is-sexual-1142448.

69. Rebecca Traister, "Our National Narratives Are Still Being Shaped by Lecherous, Powerful Men," *The Cut, New York Magazine*, October 27, 2017, https://www.thecut.com/2017/10/halperin-wieseltier-weinstein-powerful-lecherous-men.html.

70. Margaret Sullivan, "Abusive Media Moguls Harmed More Than Just Individual Women. They Shaped a Misogynistic Culture," *Washington Post*, September 13, 2018, https://www.washingtonpost.com/lifestyle/style/abusive-media-mo guls-harmed-more-than-just-individual-women-they-shaped-a-misogynis tic-culture/2018/09/13/a3712638-b74a-11e8-a2c5-3187f427e253_story.html?utm_ term=.3c48ba00574f.

71. The *NYRB* was dead last in the count of gender parity at literary magazines in 2017 according to Women in Literary Arts, "'NYRB' Plummets, 'Paris Review' Creeps Upward On 2017 VIDA Count," *Publishers Weekly,* June 18, 2018, https:// www.publishersweekly.com/pw/by-topic/industry-news/publisher-news/ article/77287-nyrb-plummets-paris-review-creeps-upward-on-2017-vida-count.html.

72. Anne Kingston, "Jian Ghomeshi: How he got away with it," *MacLean's,* November 6, 2014, https://www.macleans.ca/news/canada/jian-ghomeshi-how-he-got-away-with-it/.

73. Jian Ghomeshi, "Reflections from a Hashtag," *New York Review of Books,* October 11, 2018, https://www.nybooks.com/articles/2018/10/11/reflections-hashtag.

74. Aja Romano, *"New York Review of Books* defends gender bias with snarky form letter," *Daily Dot,* August 23, 2013, https://www.dailydot.com/irl/new-york-re view-books-gender-publishing-vida-count/.

75. Isaac Chotiner, "Why Did the *New York Review of Books* Publish That Jian Ghomeshi Essay?" *Slate* Interrogation, September 14, 2018, https://slate.com/news-and-politics/2018/09/jian-ghomeshi-new-york-review-of-books-essay.html.

76. Gabriella Paiella, "Ian Buruma Out at the *New York Review of Books," The Cut, New York Magazine,* September 25, 2018, https://www.thecut.com/2018/09/ian-buruma-out-new-york-review-of-books.html (updated).

77. Audrey Carlsen et al., "#MeToo Brought Down 201 Powerful Men. Nearly Half of Their Replacements are Women," *New York Times,* October 29, 2018, https://www.nytimes.com/interactive/2018/10/23/us/metoo-replacements. html.

78. Joan Vennochi, "How the GOP Stole the 'Kavanaugh Effect' from the Democrats," *Boston Globe,* November 7, 2018, https://www.bostonglobe. com/opinion/2018/11/07/how-gop-stole-kavanaugh-effect-from-democrats/7d7Y4XQqOpj2ncXPxeGbZI/story.html.

79. Z. Byron Wolf, "Republicans' Midterms Secret Weapon? Brett Kavanaugh," *The Point with Chris Cillizza,* CNN Politics, https://edition.cnn.com/2018/11/07/poli tics/brett-kavanaugh-midterms/.

Index

sexual harassment cases (*cont.*)
corporate response to, 51–52, 56–58, 224–25
Harris, 58–59
Hill/Thomas hearings, xv, 80–85
litigation of, 55–58, 99, 220–21
Vinson, xiii, 27, 42–44, 45–52, 54–55, 99
Wal-Mart v. Dukes, 220–21, 225
See also employer liability in sexual harassment cases
Sexual Harassment of Working Women (MacKinnon), 23, 24
sexuality
MacKinnon's theory on, 28–30
scientific study of, 37
Valenti on, 138–39
sexual revolution, 37–40, 249
Sexual Shakedown (Farley), 6
Sherman, Gabriel, 175–76, 177
Sherman, Wendy, 84
She Should Run, 187
"Shitty Media Men" list, xv
Shulman, Alix Kates, 263n34
Siegel, Reva, 259n11
Signore, Andy, 212
Silberman, Rosalie Gaull, 47
Simon, Paul, 61, 78, 79
Simon, Roger, 126
Simpson, Alan, 79, 86
Singer, Bryan, 207
Singer, Marty, 220
60 Minutes, 95–96, 98, 250
Skelly, J., 45
slactivism, 210
See also hashtag activism
Slate, 141, 148, 165, 196
slavery, 25, 26–27, 53, 249
Smart Girls, 154–55
Smith, Nancy Erika, 56, 173–74, 205
Smith, William Kennedy, 69
social media and campus sexual assault, 152–53
social movements, x, xi–xii, xviii, 231
See also specific movements
Sontag, Susan, 39
Sorvino, Mira, 202–3
Souter, David, 63

Sowell, Thomas, 65
Spacey, Kevin, 213
Spaulding, Pam, 141
Specter, Arlen, 82, 83
Starr, Kenneth, 46, 99, 102, 233
Starr Report, the, 99–100, 104
State v. Rusk, 162
Steel, Emily, 188–89, 196
Steele, Lockhart, 212
Steinem, Gloria
on Bill Clinton, xiv, 105–6, 108
endowment of, 202
on Hillary Clinton, 133, 143
Ms. magazine and Ms. Foundation for Women, 119–20
on pornography, 33
reputation of, 12
at Women's March, 186
Stevens, John Paul, 50
Stewart, Maria W., 249
Stewart, Tony, 24–25
Stonewall riots (1969), x, 173
Story of O (Réage), 33
storytelling and hashtag activism, 210–12
Strange Justice (Abramson and Mayer), 91–92
Strossen, Nadine, 39
suffrage movement, xii, 133, 248
Suk Gersen, Jeannie, 165
Sulkowicz, Emma, 153–54, 279n46
Sullivan, Margaret, 227–29, 252–53

Take Back the Night, 32, 144, 150
See also campus sexual assault
Taylor, Sidney, 41–42, 51, 264n2
See also *Meritor Savings Bank v. Vinson*
Tchen, Tina, 220
"Ted Kennedy on the Rocks" (Kelly), 74–75
Temin & Co., 213
Tester, Jon, 254
Texas Instruments, 206
third-wave feminism, xv, 121–24, 140
Third Wave Foundation (formerly Third Wave Direct Action Corporation), 121
Thomas, Clarence
book about, 86–92
confirmation of, xv, 61, 254